The Girl Who Wanted to Belong

# The Girl Who Wanted to Belong

## The True Story of a Devastated Little Girl and the Foster Carer Who Healed her Broken Heart

ANGELA HART

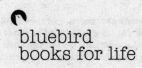

bluebird
books for life

First published 2018 by Bluebird
an imprint of Pan Macmillan
20 New Wharf Road, London N1 9RR
Associated companies throughout the world
www.panmacmillan.com

ISBN 978-1-5098-7394-4

3 5 7 9 8 6 4

A CIP catalogue record for this book is available from the British Library.

Typeset by Palimpsest Book Production Ltd, Falkirk, Stirlingshire
Printed and bound by CPI Group (UK) Ltd, Croydon, CR0 4YY

Visit **www.panmacmillan.com** to read more about all our books
and to buy them. You will also find features, author interviews and
news of any author events, and you can sign up for e-newsletters
so that you're always first to hear about our new releases.

# The Girl Who Wanted to Belong

# 1

## *'So many questions!'*

'That's wonderful!' Jess exclaimed. 'I'll let the social worker know right away. Thanks *so* much. This is great news for Lucy. Please thank Jonathan from me. What would I do without you two? I shudder to think!'

Jess had been our support social worker for some time and we'd got to know each other well. She was a good ten years younger than my husband Jonathan and me – we were in our forties now – yet Jess always seemed wise beyond her years. She was extremely efficient at her job and had a way of always saying the right thing, even when she was completely snowed under with work.

'Thanks, Jess. We look forward to meeting Lucy. It'll be nice to have another little girl in the house.'

'Lucy's very fortunate,' Jess replied, sounding relieved. 'I think you are the ideal foster carers for her. Let me make the arrangements and I'll call you back as soon as I can. Hopefully we'll get her to you tomorrow. Is that OK?'

'Perfect.'

When I put the phone down I felt supported and appreciated, just as I always did after talking to Jess. I was also excited, apprehensive and slightly nervous about meeting our new arrival. To this day those emotions still collide whenever a new child is due to start a placement. I love the sense of anticipation, wondering what the child will be like, how we will get along and how we will be able to help. I immediately start thinking about how to make him or her welcome when they turn up at our door; I want them to feel comfortable from the moment they arrive, although that's not always possible. No child comes to us without issues and I always have underlying worries about what state they will be in, what problems we may need to deal with and whether or not we really will be the right foster carers for the job.

Lucy had recently turned eight years old and Jess had explained to me on the phone that she was described by family members as being 'disruptive', 'aggressive', 'belligerent' and 'totally impossible to live with'. She had support in the classroom, which suggested she had some special educational needs, but there were no further details. Her mum was off the scene – Jess didn't know the details – and Lucy was left with her father, two brothers and her little sister. Problems started when her dad moved his new partner and her young daughter into the family home. Lucy clashed with her 'stepmother' so badly she was sent to live with two different aunties, miles out of town. They either didn't want her or couldn't cope and so Lucy was packed off to stay with her elderly grandmother who lived even further away, in a different county. Lucy had missed a lot of school during this period and it was her struggling gran who had reluctantly called Social Services, asking for help after finding herself unable to cope.

Jess also told me that Lucy's placement would be short term. The little girl missed her daddy and siblings and desperately wanted to go home, despite the issues she had with her new stepmother. It would be our job to help integrate Lucy back into the family unit. Her father and stepmother and possibly some of the children would be given support in the form of family counselling, to help pave the way for Lucy's return. Lucy would see a psychologist and also take part in group family therapy. It was expected the whole process would take two or three months, although understandably nothing was set in stone.

Jonathan and I are well used to taking in children at short notice and not knowing how long they will be staying. We'd been fostering for more than a decade at this point in time. We'd looked after dozens of kids and many had come to us as emergency cases, at even shorter notice than Lucy. I was delighted we could offer Lucy a home, and as soon as I'd finished talking to Jess I went to sort out a bedroom for her, to make sure she would feel as welcome as possible.

The following day Lucy arrived with a social worker called Brian. I was standing on the pavement in front of our flower shop, helping to take in the last of the displays, when they pulled up in a bright red Mini. To my amusement Brian looked exactly like Rowan Atkinson; the likeness was uncanny. As he got out of the car and shook my hand I thought to myself, *I'm glad his car's not green or I'd have thought Mr Bean had arrived!*

'May I present Lucy,' Brian said very brightly as the small and very slender little girl climbed out of the back of the car.

I was struck by Brian's energy. He had collected Lucy from her grandmother's house, which I'd been alarmed to discover was more than a hundred miles away. He must have been driving for hours and it was a Friday too and so the traffic can't have been great, especially in the afternoon rush. Nevertheless, Brian was all smiles and looked as fresh as a daisy. Lucy appeared remarkably bright in the circumstances too. She gave me a broad grin and said hello enthusiastically, which I was very pleased about. As she smiled I noticed she'd lost her two front teeth; her adult teeth were just starting to push through the top gum. Lucy looked very young for her age and she could have passed for a child of seven or maybe even six. She was very pretty, with bright blue eyes, a sprinkling of pale freckles on her nose and beautiful honey-blonde hair that framed her little face and bounced on her shoulders. I grinned back at her, thinking how appealing she looked and how friendly she seemed. It was almost as if she'd come for a social visit, rather than arriving for a foster care placement, which was very heartening to see.

'I'm Angela. It's lovely to meet you Lucy. Come and meet my husband Jonathan, he's in the shop.'

'Is this your shop?'

'Yes. It's a family business. We've been running it for a very long time. My mum ran it before us. You'll meet her soon enough, I'm sure.'

'I thought you were just foster carers. Wow! Do you own all these flowers? What's your mum's name? Where does she live? Does she live with you as well?'

Lucy was standing in the middle of the shop now, taking everything in, her eyes darting everywhere.

'So many questions!' my husband said cheerfully, stepping from behind the counter. 'Hello Lucy, I'm Jonathan. Very pleased to meet you.'

She said hello politely and I introduced Jonathan to Brian. 'Decent journey?' Jonathan asked.

Before Brian could answer, Lucy was off again. 'What do you do with all the flowers you don't sell? Where do you grow them all? You must have a big garden. Who does the gardening? I like gardening. Have you got flowers in your house? Do you have to water them all? Does it take ages? It must take ages. What's this stuff for?'

'We try not to have too many flowers we don't sell, but if we do have any going past their sell-by date we often put them in the house, so we can enjoy them. Jonathan goes to collect them from the wholesalers, we do have a garden, but we don't grow any of the flowers for the shop. Yes, they all need watering, and that green foamy stuff is for making flower arrangements. It's called oasis and it helps the flowers stand up and stay in place. You push the stalks into it, to keep them upright. Does that answer your questions?'

'Er . . . I think so.'

'My mum's called Thelma, by the way,' I said. 'She lives nearby and she loves to meet all the children who stay with us. She babysits for us sometimes.'

'Oh! Do you have a baby?'

'No, I mean she looks after the children we foster for us sometimes.'

Lucy nodded and seemed to approve. 'I like the smell in here. Can I help you? I'd love to work in a shop!'

'Indeed you can, but not right now,' Jonathan said. 'We're about to shut up for the evening and you must be tired after all that travelling. Let's go through to the house.'

We left our assistant Barbara to finish closing the shop. She'd been working with us for many years and was well used to seeing different children coming and going.

'I'll see you again soon, by the sound of it,' Barbara said kindly, and Lucy gave her a smile.

Jonathan and I led Lucy and Brian through the store-room at the back and into our adjoining town house. Her eyes were everywhere still and she continued to ask lots of questions. I glanced at Brian, thinking, *I wonder if he's had this for hours on end in the car? That man deserves a medal!*

'Do you have children?' Lucy asked, looking me directly in the eye. 'Who else lives here? Do I have to share a room?'

I told her we had another girl living with us called Maria, who was just a little bit older than Lucy. Maria was upstairs in her bedroom and no, Lucy would not have to share a room.

'We have three floors and your bedroom is on the top

floor of the house, next to Maria's. I've got it all ready for you but I haven't put the duvet cover or pillow cases on yet as I thought you might like to choose which colour set you want.'

'OK. Thanks. Have your own children left home?'

'No, we don't have children of our own.'

'Oh.' She narrowed her eyes. 'Is Maria adopted?'

'No, we are fostering her too, just like you.'

'Oh. Do you like fostering then?'

We went into the kitchen, and as Lucy and I continued to chat – or, should I say, Lucy continued to interview me – Jonathan fetched everyone a glass of water. It was an unusually warm, sunny day in early spring and Brian said he needed a cold drink after driving for so long in the heat.

'Thirsty work, wasn't it Lucy?' he said jovially, which made Lucy burst out laughing. There was obviously an in-joke going on here, but they didn't elaborate.

Lucy carried on quizzing me and Brian tactfully took the opportunity to run through the routine paperwork with Jonathan, talking quietly on the other side of the kitchen. By now Lucy had moved on to ask me lots of questions about our garden and what was in the shed she could see from our kitchen window. I was happy to keep chatting while Brian went through the formalities, handing over all the usual forms with contact numbers on, emergency Social Services numbers and so on. Sometimes kids sit in silence during this initial handover, which is never ideal and always makes me feel uncomfortable.

Brian didn't have a great deal of background information on Lucy. This is not uncommon on the first day of a placement, and Lucy had never been in care before so there were no old records on file. In any case, Brian was not Lucy's actual social worker and had simply been drafted in to transport her to our house as he was based in the county where her grandmother lived. She would be assigned a social worker from the area her parents lived in as soon as possible.

As they filled in the paperwork Brian told Jonathan that he had stopped for a cup of tea with Lucy's grandmother. 'She seems like a lovely, sweet old lady,' he said. 'She told me she's very sorry she's had to get Social Services involved and wishes she could care for Lucy herself, but she's too old and frail. I felt sorry for her, to tell the truth. I told her she'd done the right thing.' Brian was aware of the fact that Lucy's schooling had been disrupted with all the moves she'd made between relatives' houses.

'Do you happen to know how much school she's missed?' Jonathan asked.

'All in all I reckon she's missed about half a term from what she's said, but don't quote me on that.'

'I see. I don't suppose you know if she's statemented? Our support social worker mentioned she had help in the classroom. Was anything said to you along those lines?'

'Nothing official, but Lucy told me she always had a lady helping her in her old school, so I guess she must be.'

'OK. That's good to hear. Hopefully it won't be too difficult to find her a school place here.'

If a child has special needs and is statemented it generally makes it easier for us to secure them a school place, particularly at short notice. This is because schools receive extra funding for statemented children, from the local education authority (LEA), which makes it easier for the head teachers to provide the extra support the child will need. I reckoned it would take over an hour to get Lucy to her old school, near her family home. It wasn't feasible for her to return there while she was living with us and so we'd have to get her a local place. We'd make this a priority, as we always do.

After Brian had completed his handover he said he'd pop back out to his car to fetch Lucy's bags from the boot. She'd carried one small rucksack in herself and I had assumed that was all she had with her, as a lot of kids arrive with very few belongings.

'Oh, I forgot about my bags,' she said. 'I'll come and help you.'

'There's no need, Lucy. You stay here. Won't take me a minute.'

'But you know I like to *help*!'

The two of them started to laugh again. Brian then explained that Lucy had insisted on 'helping' when they stopped at a service station and bought cold drinks earlier in the day. Lucy had offered to hold Brian's drink but then decided to stand the cup on the bonnet of the Mini while she fastened up the Velcro on her trainers. Brian didn't notice what she'd done and then Lucy got distracted and forgot all about the drink. The upshot was that Brian began to drive away with the full cup still on the bonnet of the car. Luckily he spotted the drink before it toppled over and they had evidently both had a good laugh about it.

'I don't need any more *help*,' Brian teased, which made me realise why his 'thirsty work' comment had made Lucy laugh so much a few minutes earlier. 'Leave the bags to me,' he said jovially. 'I can manage perfectly well on my own, thank you very much!'

It was great to see that Lucy had a sense of humour and seemed so at ease. I thought Brian had done a fabulous job in delivering her to us in this frame of mind. So many children arrive at our door looking miserable, nervous or even angry and hostile. Often it takes days to raise the faintest smile, let alone a laugh like this. Lucy was as relaxed as I think a child could be in a situation like this.

Brian fetched two sports holdalls from the car and then stayed and made chit-chat for a few more minutes, telling a very funny story about how he once drove for miles through France with his sunglasses on the roof of his car. When he left Lucy wanted to go outside and wave him off, and she asked if she would ever see him again. Unfortunately she wouldn't, I explained, telling her that she would be assigned her own social worker, from the county she came from.

'Oh well,' she said. 'I liked Brian. If I have to have a social worker I hope mine is as nice as him. Why do I have to have a social worker?'

I explained in simple terms why she needed a social worker while we watched the Mini disappear around the corner, Brian's head millimetres from the roof. Lucy laughed. 'He's funnier than Mr Bean!'

Now it was my turn to laugh, and I told Lucy I thought she was spot on about that.

Jonathan carried the holdalls upstairs and Lucy and I followed. I explained the layout of our house as we climbed the two flights of stairs and I told her about a few house rules.

'OK,' she said thoughtfully before launching into another round of questioning. 'But why can't you have food in the bedroom? Why do people take their shoes off in the hall? Why do I need to ask before I help myself to food from the kitchen? Why . . .' She went on and on, wanting to get to the bottom of every single rule I had in place. I explained how the rules were simply designed to keep the house clean, safe and tidy, and the people in it healthy and as well cared for as possible.

'Oh, I thought you'd just made them up to show who's boss,' Lucy said seriously.

'No, I wouldn't do that. I want everyone to be happy and comfortable and safe. That's the point of the rules. It's not about showing who's boss.'

'*Some* people would do that.'

'Some people would?'

'Some people would just make up rules to wind other people up and be bossy! That's all I'm saying. *Some* people are nasty like that.' Lucy buttoned her lips and said no more and I didn't press her. Usually children take many weeks, if not months and sometimes even years to get things off their chest. There was no way of telling when Lucy might make any disclosures that might help us to understand what had gone wrong at home. We'd just have to wait and see, and let her take things at her pace. I hoped her openness and willingness to communicate boded well, however. I had a feeling she was going to be very talkative about her family and her past when she was good and ready, if not with me then with the specialists who were going to provide family therapy and counselling.

The ultimate aim was to iron out whatever difficulties Lucy had experienced at home and move her back in with her family. It was what she desperately wanted, and I wanted to help her in any way I could.

# 2

### *'I miss you, Daddy. When can I come home?'*

Lucy looked very pleased with her large room and began explaining that at home she had to share a bunk bed with her stepsister, who had a habit of rattling the frame to annoy her. 'I'm on the top bunk and she kicks my mattress from below. She's such a wind-up merchant. My little sister sleeps on the fold-up bed in the same room. It's not a big room like this. It's tiny. You can't see the carpet when my sister's bed is pulled out. Then my brothers share the smallest room and then Daddy—'

Lucy suddenly stopped talking.

'Daddy?'

'Daddy has the other room, with *her*.'

I let this statement hang in the air for a moment so as not to rush or pressure Lucy into talking about anything she might find difficult to discuss. She didn't elaborate and so I casually asked how old her brothers and sisters were.

'My brothers are both nine. Josh and Liam. I've only got one sister, Milly. She's seven.'

I guessed the boys must be twins but I'd let Lucy tell me that, as perhaps one was a half-brother, who knows? You can never be too careful. Kids can be very sensitive about such matters and clearly Lucy's family dynamics had already caused her a lot of trouble.

'Did you say I could pick my duvet cover?'

'Yes,' I said, showing her a selection in the ottoman on the landing, where I stored the large collection of linen and towels I'd accumulated over the years. Lucy didn't mention her stepsister again and so I had no idea how old she was, or what her name was. It would be interesting to find out more about what had gone on at home, and I was very curious to know why Lucy was the only one of the five children not to have adjusted to the new family unit. All the other children were still living at home, so what had gone wrong with Lucy?

So far Lucy's behaviour certainly didn't match the very negative description Social Services had been provided with. What had Jess said to me? 'Disruptive,' 'aggressive,' 'belligerent' and 'totally impossible to live with.' I didn't know which family member or members had described Lucy this way but from my first impressions I really couldn't imagine her being so bad. Mind you, it wasn't just her own family who struggled to deal with her, was it? Two separate aunties had failed to cope with her under their roof, and things must have been pretty bad for Lucy to be pulled out of school and sent a hundred miles away to live with her elderly grandmother.

Nevertheless the whole scenario seemed extreme to me. It was very difficult to imagine this angelic-looking young girl being so difficult, but I reminded myself that I'd been caught out in the past by the so-called 'honeymoon period' of fostering. It's natural for kids to want to please you when they first arrive, though every child is different. Experience told me only time would tell what Lucy's behaviour was truly like. My job for now was to settle her in and provide a loving and safe environment, to help her recalibrate and hopefully move forward in a positive way with her family.

'The blue stripes,' Lucy said triumphantly, pulling out a duvet cover and two pillowcases from the ottoman. Then she wrinkled her nose, looking at a bright pink set with fairies all over. 'Urgh! I don't like pink or any of those sparkly kind of things.'

I smiled. Normally little girls went for the pink or lilac sets of bedding but despite her sweet little face I could see Lucy was not someone you might describe as a typical 'girly' girl. She was wearing jeans and a bottle-green football shirt for a start, and when she began to unpack her bags I could see that most of her clothes were in dark colours and styles more typically chosen by boys. Lucy had combat trousers, T-shirts with robots and dragons on and her pyjamas had Ninja Turtles emblazoned across the chest. They were very popular characters at the time, in the nineties, but usually it was boys who liked Ninja Turtles more than girls.

Some of Lucy's clothes looked a little worn out and shabby although I was pleased to see they were clean and neatly folded, and she had a toilet bag with a toothbrush and hairbrush in it. I imagined that was the work of Lucy's grandmother. The old lady must have found it very tough indeed to call Social Services, I thought. If what I'd heard so far was true, she'd been put in a very unfortunate position, and I really felt for her.

I introduced Lucy to Maria, who looked the younger child up and down with an air of suspicion even though I'd told her the previous day another girl would be moving in. Maria had been with us on and off for a few years. We'd also had two teenage boys staying with us for some time too, but they'd left now. I think Maria was quite enjoying being the only child living with us long term, although of course we'd had other children for respite and short-term stays, as we always do when we have the space.

Even though Maria was used to being introduced to new arrivals you could never be sure how she might react, as she had behavioural difficulties of her own and a history of falling out with girls the same age as herself. I hoped that with Lucy being a year younger, Maria might try to be kind to her, and that the two would get on.

'Hello,' Lucy said. 'What are you doing?'

'Just stuff, in my room.'

'Can I see your room?'

'NO, not now. I'm busy.'

'OK then.'

Maria retreated into her room, shutting the door too loudly.

'Bye!' Lucy called through the door.

I called after Maria too, telling her to try not to slam the door next time. I didn't want to let her get away with rude behaviour like that and I wanted to show Lucy it was unacceptable to slam doors. Then I explained to Lucy that Maria was probably doing some homework, to get it out of the way for the weekend. The last thing I wanted was for Lucy's mood to be upset by Maria's very lukewarm welcome.

'It's OK. It's not like I'm going to be *living* here. I don't mind. It's only for a bit . . .'

I wondered what Lucy's expectations were, exactly, about the length of her stay. It was possible nobody had given her any indication of what Social Services was planning. A sudden thought hit me, *Is this why she's taking everything in her stride and doesn't seem anxious or concerned about being in foster care?*

'I know you're only here for a short stay,' I said. 'I expect it'll be for the next two or three months, over the summer. Like you say, it's only for a bit, but I hope you and Maria are going to get along.'

Lucy's face was deadpan and I had no idea if this was disappointing news or something she already knew. 'Will I have to go to school here?'

'Yes, of course. We'll need to sort that out next week.'

'Can I go back to my old school?'

'No, sweetheart. You'll need to go to one near us. Your old school is too far away.'

There was an added complication here, though I didn't mention this to Lucy. Not only was her old school an hour away, it was in another county and under a completely separate local authority to ours. Social Services in Lucy's home town hadn't been able to find a foster carer close to the family home and had asked the authorities in our county to help them out. This would inevitably have created a lot of red tape – we'd been through this in the past on more than one occasion – and it would most likely lead to arguments over which county was responsible for funding the statement at the school.

I was going to try to sort out Lucy's schooling first thing on Monday. Social workers can and do contact schools and the LEA to help make the arrangements, but from experience I knew that if I got the ball rolling myself things usually moved a lot quicker. Social workers are so busy and have a large number of children to deal with, so I'm always happy to take on the task. Having children at home, and sometimes under my feet, when they should be at school is no good for anyone.

Jonathan went out and bought fish and chips for us all that evening. I hadn't had time to cook and we thought it would be nice for the girls to have a takeaway, which was something we often did for a treat on a Friday in any case. Maria gobbled her food down in record time, which wasn't unusual, while Lucy was suddenly quieter than she had been since she arrived and she picked at her food like a little bird. I didn't say anything about this and thankfully she'd eaten enough by the end of the meal to ensure she wouldn't go hungry.

Most children take a while to settle into a routine, and I

understand that eating food around the dinner table with strangers is not the easiest thing for a young child to do. Some children have never eaten at a table before, having eaten all their meals on their lap, in front of the television. We've found that sitting together as a family gives us a chance to talk, and so we always make it a rule to sit and eat with the children, either in the dining room or around the kitchen table.

Jonathan and I did most of the talking. I asked the girls if they fancied going swimming the following day, as soon as we could get away from the shop. They both readily agreed. I'd noticed Lucy had brought a swimming costume with her, but she told me it didn't fit any more and she needed a new one.

'My *stepmother* said it would do me, but it's way too small. I kept telling her.'

She sounded uncomfortable when she used the term stepmother and almost spat the word out, curling her lip.

'Don't worry,' I said. 'We can get you a new costume tomorrow. We can call in to the retail park. There are a couple of sports shops there and if they're no good there's a little shop by the reception at the leisure centre. They usually have a good selection in there. I'm sure we'll be able to get one you like.'

After we'd eaten Maria carried her plate to the kitchen sink and went straight back up to her room to listen to music. Lucy asked if she could phone her granny and her daddy. I'd been provided with their numbers and there were no restrictions on her calling them.

'Of course you can. Let me just clear the table and I'll show you how to use the phone.'

Lucy helped me clear up and as she did so she suddenly perked up and began talking in my ear, non-stop. 'Where does this go? What do you use this for? Do you always have fish and chips on Friday? Do you like curry? My daddy loves curry. Does Jonathan go fishing? Daddy's brilliant at fishing. He caught a fish that was two-foot long once but he threw it back in the water.'

We'd eaten in the dining room instead of the kitchen that night, simply because Maria had chosen to set the table in there and we used either room. Lucy followed me back and forth to the dining table, walking so close behind me she caught my heels a few times and made me lose one of my slippers.

'Careful!' I said. 'Can you just give me a bit of space, sweetheart?'

'Oops I didn't mean to do that. It was an accident. Did I hurt you?'

'No, not at all. Just don't walk so close to me, as you're going to stand on my heels again if you do.'

Lucy looked a bit bemused – or was she cross? And she continued to get under my feet at every turn as I tidied the kitchen. I felt I could hardly move for fear I'd bash into her.

'Lucy, sweetheart, it's lovely that you're helping me but please just be careful where you're standing. I nearly caught you with the door of the dishwasher.'

'Sorry I'm such a *nuisance*! I was only trying to help. I

like helping. You don't mind if I help do you? How come Maria isn't helping?'

'You're not being a nuisance and I was only trying to explain that I don't want to trip over you or for you to get knocked by something because you're standing in the way. I don't want you to get hurt. Now come on, let's sort your phone calls out. Do you want to call your daddy first, or Granny?'

'Daddy first, then Granny.'

Lucy was being calm and polite again now and flashed me a great big friendly smile, but I was in no doubt I'd had my first little glimpse of her being a bit disruptive and aggravating.

I showed Lucy how to use the phone in the lounge and explained that I would have a quick word with her father first, to introduce myself and pass on our phone number to him, in case he didn't have it. Social Services hadn't asked me to keep our number private, or to listen in on the conversations as they occasionally did. I told Lucy I'd leave her to it once the introductions were done, and to come and find me when she was ready to call her granny.

I dialled Lucy's home number and a very polite and unassuming man answered. He spoke quietly and gently, telling me his name was Dean.

'I'm ever so grateful to you, Mrs Hart,' he said. 'I don't know what we would have done if you hadn't been able to take Lucy in. I'm glad she's safe and sound with you.'

'I'm pleased we can help. And please call me Angela. My husband is called Jonathan.'

'Thank you very much, Angela. Is Lucy there? Can I have a word?'

'Yes, of course. No doubt we'll speak again soon. Bye for now.' I passed our number on to him.

Lucy's blue eyes were shining when she took the handset off me.

'Daddy!' she gasped breathlessly. 'I miss you, Daddy. When can I come home?'

I slipped out of the room, leaving Lucy to talk privately.

She appeared in the kitchen about twenty minutes later.

'Can we call Granny now?'

'Yes, of course. Everything OK?'

'Yes. I wish I could have spoken to Daddy for longer though.'

I looked at the clock. 'I thought you had quite a long conversation?'

'I had to talk to everyone who was in, but I only wanted to talk to Daddy.'

'I see. So you talked to everyone?'

'I had to talk to *her*. I don't know why I have to talk to *her*. And Gemma.'

'Gemma?'

'Gemma's *her* daughter, my *stepsister*. I don't think Gemma wanted to talk to me either, but *she* put her on the phone.'

Lucy had a curled lip again and clearly didn't like using the word stepsister any more than she liked the term stepmother.

She told me her stepmum's name was Wendy. 'It's not a very nice name, is it? Can we phone Granny now?'

'OK, let's go.'

The phone rang out for a long time.

'Granny can't move fast,' Lucy said. 'She has bad hips. You have to let it ring.'

Sure enough, Lucy's gran eventually got to the phone. She was quietly spoken, polite and gentle-sounding, and extremely grateful.

'Please call me Ivy, Mrs Hart,' she said.

'And please call me Angela. My husband is Jonathan.'

Ivy told me that she had the utmost respect for foster carers.

'I fostered once myself, very briefly, in my younger days. I think it's a marvellous service. I'm heartbroken I can't take care of Lucy myself but it's not the right thing for either of us. I'm just too old I'm afraid, and Lucy's a handful, in a lovely way, of course, most of the time. She's far better off with youngsters like you and your husband!'

I laughed and told Ivy we were in our forties and had been fostering for nearly a decade but she insisted we were still youngsters compared to her, and far better equipped to care for a lively and challenging eight-year-old.

I warmed to Ivy instantly. She sounded genuinely sorry she couldn't take her granddaughter on full time and once again my heart went out to her. She had been put in an awful situation, and she clearly cared for Lucy very much. She told me Lucy had been with her for just a few days before she realised it was going to be impossible to care for

23

her. The fact Lucy had no school place didn't help, and Ivy confirmed that Lucy had missed approximately half a term of school since things went wrong at home. The two aunties she had stayed with both lived some distance from her primary school and hadn't taken her in, and of course Ivy lived a hundred miles away.

'Don't know what anyone was thinking,' she said. 'How was it going to work? I know she's my Noreen's girl, but even so. It was never a good plan.'

I would have loved to find out more about Lucy's mother but I couldn't pry. Lucy was standing close by, looking at me in eager anticipation. I didn't want to keep her waiting any longer, although I was intrigued about how the two aunties had failed to send Lucy to school, and why Lucy's birth mother was apparently out of the picture.

'I think Lucy was bored stiff when she came to me,' Ivy continued. 'She likes to be busy. I imagine you've probably already seen that for yourself. She's a good girl, I'm sure of that. I wish you the very best of luck.'

'Thanks. I'm pleased to have spoken to you and I have a young lady here who is itching to talk to you. I'll hand her over.'

Before I did so I gave Ivy our phone number.

'Granny! Guess what? I've just spoken to Daddy!'

I walked out of the room and just as I went to close the door behind me I heard Lucy excitedly telling her granny, 'He said I'll be able to go home soon!'

I hoped Lucy's father hadn't given her any false hopes. Nothing was decided yet about the length of her stay with us, but there was clearly work to be done to heal the rift in the family unit. Whatever happened it would be at least a couple of months before she went home, and that's a long time to a young girl.

I wondered if Lucy would talk to me about the phone call with her daddy. Most children in her position wouldn't, but somehow I felt Lucy might. However, she'd had an extremely busy day and said she was very tired, so I reminded her to clean her teeth before going to bed and I let her make her own way to her room. As she climbed the stairs I said, 'Night night, sweetheart.'

'Night night Angela. I like it here. It's a nice house and you're kind. I can't wait to go home. My house is nice too. Very nice. I miss Daddy.'

I think she must have fallen asleep almost immediately.

# 3

## *'She wanted to hurt me'*

Lucy knocked on our bedroom door at just after four o'clock the next morning. I woke with a start, got up immediately and went to see what was wrong.

'Nothing's wrong. What time does the shop open? Can I come and help?'

I had to explain to her that it was too early to get up. I told her Barbara was opening up the shop that day and Jonathan was going out on the morning deliveries. We didn't need to get up for several hours yet.

'Oh,' Lucy said, crossing her arms and fixing me with a stare. 'But I'm wide awake. I want something to do.'

She pushed her hair out of her face, rubbed her eyes and gave a little frown, wrinkling up her freckled nose as she did so. Then she stuck the tip of her tongue out and wriggled it around under her two newly emerging front teeth, as if trying to work out if they'd grown while she'd been asleep. I was feeling quite groggy after being so rudely awakened, but I couldn't be cross. Lucy looked adorable, standing there in her Ninja Turtle pyjamas, impatiently wanting to get on with her day.

'Lucy, I'm afraid it really is far too early and you do need to go back to bed for a few hours. Come on, sweetheart, I'll walk back to your room with you.'

Jonathan pretended to be fast asleep although I knew he wasn't really: after so many years of fostering we had both become light sleepers, always alert to the goings-on in the house.

'Do I have to go back to bed?'

'Yes, you do. Look, Jonathan and Maria are still fast asleep. Don't wake them up. There are lots of things we can do later today, but you need your rest first. Did you remember we're going swimming with Maria?'

'Yes.'

'Well then, you need to get some more sleep or you'll be too tired to go to the leisure centre and do all the other things I have planned.'

'What are all the other things?'

'OK, well first I was going to make some pancakes for breakfast and I thought you might like to help me. Then I was going to show you where all the toys and books are. We've got a computer too, with some games you can play, and then if you wanted to, you could come into the shop when I give Barbara a break, and I can teach you the names of some of the flowers. Then we'll go for a swim after the shop's shut. Oh, and we need to buy you a swimming costume, don't we?'

By the time I'd finished spinning out all the 'plans' I had, which were mostly ideas that came to mind in the spur of the moment, we'd reached Lucy's room and she was climbing into bed.

'Can I do something good in the shop, like serving customers? I don't just want to learn flower names. I'm not very good at remembering things. I'd rather pack the boxes. Can I do the deliveries with John?'

'With Jonathan?'

'Yes, that's what I meant. Jo-na-than. See I *told* you I had a bad memory.'

'I'm sure you can help Jonathan. We'll talk about it again at breakfast time.'

I showed Lucy the clock and checked she could tell the time. 'If you wake up before 7.30, please try to go back to sleep or do something quietly in your room, like reading a book.'

'Have you got any Lego?'

'Yes.'

'Can I do that? Can I build something?'

'Yes. It's in the top of the cupboard, hang on a minute.'

I fetched the Lego bricks and Lucy grinned. 'What about Meccano?'

'We did have some of that but it hasn't been played with for years. I think it's in the loft now. I'll ask Jonathan later. Now you try to get back to sleep.'

Lucy appeared at our door at 7.30 on the dot.

'Can we make pancakes now?'

28

Luckily I was already awake and I didn't mind getting straight up.

'Yes,' I said. 'Just give me a minute. You go down to the kitchen and wait quietly for me. Don't start without me, please just wait.'

I put on my dressing gown and slippers and went to the kitchen, where Lucy was already searching the cupboards.

'Do you know what we need to make pancakes?'

'A mixer.'

'Yes, but I meant the ingredients.'

'No. I want to see what kind of mixer you have. My granny has got a really good one. A super-duper mega-big fast one, with lots of spinny things you can nail on.'

I imagined she meant different blades and tools you could attach. I smiled, and found myself rummaging in a cupboard, hoping my little hand-held mixer wouldn't be too disappointing. I'd had it since I got married so it was at least twenty years old and had seen better days, but Lucy looked approvingly at it. 'My auntie has got one of these. My stepmum had one too. I *hated* her.' Lucy twisted the two whisks in her hands as she spoke, admiring how shiny they were and snapping them into place.

'You hated your stepmum?'

'Yes. She told my daddy lies. Lots of lies and fibs. Big fat liar! She put salt in my tea and pins in my bed. She wanted to hurt me.'

'She wanted to hurt you?'

'Yes. But she said I did it all myself, to get her in trouble. She said I wanted to get rid of her. I *did* want to get rid of her. I was frightened of her, I was. I thought she was going to kill me and my brothers and sister.'

'You did? You thought that did you, Lucy?

'Yes. She wanted Daddy all to herself. Big fat hairy liar she was! I hated her. That's why I hated her. Can we have sugar on the pancakes? Have you got syrup? Daddy likes lemon and sugar but I like just sugar or syrup. Or chocolate spread.'

Lucy stared at me, her face expressionless.

'Yes, I've got sugar and syrup but not chocolate spread. So, you said you were frightened of your stepmum, and you wanted to get rid of her?'

'Yes, I was. She hated me. She was so horrible to me. Anyway, that's that! Can I press the button and do the mixing? Whizz-whizz. I like things that go whizz-whizz and make a noise.'

'Yes, you can but I'll show you exactly how it works first. There's a knack, so the mixture doesn't fly everywhere. Let's get all the ingredients out first. Do you want a cup of tea or would you like milk or orange, or water?'

'Tea please. Can I make it?'

'I tell you what, how about if I boil the kettle and pour the water in the teapot and you can do the milk and sugar and pour the tea when it's brewed?'

'Yes. You wouldn't put salt in my tea, would you? I think you're nice, not like her. She put dog dirt in my hair and told Daddy I did it myself, on purpose. But you're nice. You wouldn't do that. What time does Maria get up?'

'Oh, she'll be a bit later. She'd not an early bird like you.

Mind you, perhaps the smell of the pancakes will get her up. She loves pancakes.'

'I can see that, she's round, isn't she? She's got a big, round belly!'

'Lucy, it's not polite to talk about the size or shape of another person. I don't think Maria would like that.'

'Oh, sorry. I didn't know that. I was only *saying*.'

The breakfast went down well, even if it was quite stressful for me supervising Lucy with the kettle and the mixer. She wanted to do everything herself but of course I had to make sure she was safe and supervise her every step of the way. I don't think she was used to that, and she got a bit irritated. I had sugar and lemon on my pancake and I looked at my plate and thought it was rather apt: Lucy was sweet as sugar one minute and as sour as lemon the next.

She went to have a shower, clean her teeth and get dressed. I showed her where everything was and left her to it, and while she was upstairs I took the opportunity to quickly make a note in my diary of the things she had said about her stepmother. I had no idea if any of it was true. All I could do was make notes to pass on to Social Services, as I do routinely with any potentially important information.

As I wrote I found myself desperately hoping that what Lucy had told me was untrue, yet at the same time I also wondered how and why a little girl of eight years old might make up such awful accusations about her stepmother, if that was what Lucy had done? Even if Lucy's tales were grossly exaggerated or a complete invention, it was very concerning that Lucy had come out with them, because what did that say about herself and her relationship with her stepmother?

Whatever the truth, Lucy clearly disliked her step-mother intensely. By contrast, it was clear Lucy adored her dad. She had been absolutely thrilled to talk to him on the phone and she obviously couldn't wait to see him again. From what Lucy had said about her stepmother wanting her daddy 'all to herself' it seemed to me that she resented Wendy for coming into the family and taking some of her daddy's attention away. Was she jealous of her stepmother and was that at the root of the trouble at home? It was an obvious question to consider, but of course that was all I could do at this stage. I didn't note down any of my per-sonal thoughts or worries. Social Services only want facts, not opinion. Nevertheless I would keep a close eye on what-ever Lucy said on this subject. Getting her integrated back into the family – if that was the safe and proper thing to do – was key.

Jonathan came back from his deliveries just before lunch and Lucy and I went into the shop to give Barbara her break. I felt quite mentally drained by that time. Maria had gone off to visit her grandmother as soon as she was up so I was alone with Lucy for several hours, during which time she talked and talked and asked hundreds of questions, practically non-stop. She'd shadowed me a lot too, standing on my heels several times because she got so close, as she had done the night before.

I was starting to see that keeping Lucy occupied was no small task. She'd already built countless Lego cars and houses and got stuck into the Meccano with terrific enthusiasm. I'd had to get the ladders out and fetch it from the loft myself as she was very impatient and couldn't wait for Jonathan to get back and fetch it, as I'd suggested.

'Can you teach me how this works?' she asked, peering at everything along the shop counter before fixing her gaze on the till.

I was serving a customer and Lucy watched me like a hawk.

'I think we'd better leave the till. You need to be sixteen before you can work the till really, but I'll show you how some other things work.'

'OK. What can I do then? Is there anything that needs doing? What can you show me?'

Lucy's eyes were everywhere and my customer made a remark about what a willing little helper I had.

'I know. Aren't I lucky?' I smiled at Lucy and asked her to get the door for my customer, as she'd bought a display in a wide basket. Lucy jumped to it and held the door open like she'd done it all her life.

'Thank you! Goodbye! Come back soon!'

'Thanks, Lucy. Now how about moving those carnations into the space by the window? The last of the gypsophila can fit in the corner over there.'

'Gypsy what?'

'Ah, you see, I thought you might need to learn the names. Let me give you a little tour and teach you what's what. You don't need to remember them all but I'll teach you the important ones.'

I walked Lucy around the displays and all the buckets of flowers on the ground and she hung on my every word. As soon as I'd finished my mini tour she immediately started rearranging the window display and moving the carnations, exactly as I'd suggested.

'These gladiators could go in together now,' she said thoughtfully, as she busied herself with placing the half a dozen bunches of gladioli we had left neatly into one bucket.

'Good idea. They're gladioli, not gladiators. You were nearly right, well done.'

'Oh, I thought that was a weird name. Gladioli. I'll try to remember that.'

We were in the shop for about half an hour and Lucy busied herself the whole time, not stopping for a second. She was a chatty ball of energy and I enjoyed having her with me. She tidied the area underneath the counter, re-arranged some boxes in the storeroom and swept the floor in the back, even though none of the jobs really needed doing. She only seemed to be happy when she was busy and I figured this was no bad thing, although I must admit that when Jonathan returned I whispered to him, 'Just as well we're going swimming later. I think we'll need to wear her out – it might be the only way to get her to stop!'

I took Lucy shopping in the afternoon, to buy her a new swimsuit. She chose one she liked very quickly, in a large sports shop at the retail park, and I also picked up a couple of pairs of jogging pants for her and two sweatshirts, as the ones she had brought with her were a bit small and worn out.

'It's nice to have my own stuff,' she commented.

'I remember you said the swimming costume you brought with you belonged to your little sister.'

'Mmm, yes,' she said absent-mindedly. 'And did you know, the jogging pants are my brothers' old ones? I bet Wendy won't like my new stuff. She hates me having any-thing new. What's the swimming pool like? Can you do diving? Are there slides? Is Maria a good swimmer? Can you and Jonathan swim?'

I described the pool and explained that all three of us enjoyed swimming and tried to go at least once a week.

'There's only one diving board and no slides but it's a decent-sized pool. I think you'll like it. We all enjoy going.'

'I'm looking forward to it, but I want to see my daddy. When am I going to see him? I want to give him a great big cuddle.'

'I don't know yet, but you'll have plenty to tell him, won't you? You can tell him all about the shop, for one thing.'

She nodded. 'When?'

'I honestly don't know, sweetheart.'

I explained that there would be a meeting arranged as soon as possible, when Lucy would meet her new social worker. Her dad and stepmother would be invited to the meeting and our support social worker Jess would also be there, as would Jonathan and myself. Jess had told me she was hoping to get this arranged within the week, but nothing was confirmed so I didn't want to go into too much detail.

'Normally what happens is that everybody sits down together and has a chat about the plans, but we'll hopefully know more on Monday, when I talk to Jess. Does that sound OK?'

'Yes. So I'll see Daddy soon?'

'I don't want to make any promises, but I know Social Services will certainly try to arrange the meeting as soon as they can.'

'Does *she* have to come?'

'She?'

'Wendy.'

'Your stepmother will be invited but I can't say for sure if she'll come.'

'Why is she even invited? I don't want to see her. I only want to see Daddy.'

Lucy paused for breath and then stared at me, looking very serious. 'You don't know what she's like. She's just as bad as Val.'

'Val?'

Lucy sighed as if she was irritated with me. 'Val was my *old* stepmother. I've already *told* you about her. She was the *stepmonster*!'

Lucy growled and put her hands up like two clawed paws, as if she were an angry bear. I knew there'd been a film out a few years earlier called *Stepmonster* so it wasn't the first time I'd heard this word. I assumed that's where Lucy had picked it up from, but I couldn't let her talk like that about her former stepmother.

'Lucy, it's not kind to use that word. Please say step-mother, or Val, or Wendy. So you were saying, "She's just as bad as Val"?'

'I *told* you, didn't I, what Val was like? I thought she was going to kill me. She hated us. I think she wanted us all DEAD! My brothers and my sister. She wanted Daddy all to herself, just like Wendy does now. Do you know what? She made me wear frilly dresses whenever we went out. She put big bows in my hair and painted my nails with glittery nail varnish. She was such a *weirdo*. She got me shoes with heels for my birthday and one of the heels broke off. She told Daddy she saw me snap it off on purpose but I never did it. She lied all the time. Big fat liar! I know it was her who put pins in my bed and salt in my tea.'

The penny dropped. Understandably, when Lucy first spoke about how horrible her 'stepmother' was I had imagined she was talking about Wendy. I didn't know there had been a previous stepmother. Now I thought to myself, *If Lucy's telling the truth about all these horrible things Val did, at least this woman is off the scene now. At least she is not the stepmother Lucy needs to get along with. Thank God for that.*

'So you say you know it was Val who did things like put pins in your bed and salt in your tea?' I repeated back. I remembered that Lucy had said this stepmother put dog dirt in her hair – how could I forget? – but I didn't mention it because Lucy didn't bring it up again.

'She did so many horrible things. Urgh, Val! Hate, hate, hated her. What time are we going swimming? I haven't been swimming for ages. Can you do front crawl or do you do breast stroke? Is there a snack machine? Can we get hot chocolate and crisps?'

After collecting Maria from her grandmother's house we set off to the leisure centre. Jonathan drove, I sat in the passenger seat and the two girls were buckled in the back of the old Volvo estate we had at the time.

'Do you say Granny or Nanny?' Lucy asked Maria as we set off.

'Nanny,' Maria said suspiciously. She clearly wasn't yet sure what to make of the new girl who was suddenly in her face again.

'I say Granny. My granny lives a long way away. You're lucky your granny lives close by.'

'Nanny.'

'What?'

'I call her Nanny, not Granny.'

'I know. You told me. So why are you living with them?'

'What?'

'Them.'

It was clear she was talking about Jonathan and me.

'Why don't you live at home?'

'None of your business.'

'I was only wondering if you had a mummy and a daddy? So have you?'

'I'm not telling you, nosy parker!'

Jonathan and I swapped glances and I quickly turned round. It's unusual for children in foster care to ask one another about their background and Maria wasn't used to being quizzed like this. It wasn't Lucy's fault that she was chatty and inquisitive and didn't understand the boundaries, but I had to put a stop to this. Maria looked very uncomfortable, and I didn't want the girls to fall out.

'Lucy, that's enough now. Please don't ask Maria any more questions.'

'Why? What's the problem? I only asked if she had a mummy and a daddy. Owwww!'

'Maria! Please let go of Lucy's hair, right now.'

Jonathan indicated and pulled over as soon as he could. Maria had her fist balled around a section of Lucy's hair and she had a steely glint in her eyes, one I'd seen before when Maria was very angry.

'I said, please let go of Lucy's hair.'

Maria slowly let go, folded her arms across her chest and scowled at me.

'I'll do it again if she doesn't shut up!'

'Now girls,' Jonathan said, raising his voice a little, to assert his authority. 'We want you both to get along and in order for that to happen you need to be kind and polite to each other. Lucy, I don't want you to ask Maria any more personal questions. If she wants to tell you about her family that is up to her, but please don't ask again. Maria, if you are unhappy with anything that happens between you and Lucy please tell us straight away. Angela and I will deal with it. Under no circumstances are you to pull Lucy's hair or fight with her in any way whatsoever. Is that clear?'

'Yes,' Maria muttered.

'Yes,' Lucy muttered. 'How long does it take to get to the leisure centre? What are we having to eat tonight?'

'Ten minutes and there'll be spaghetti Bolognese and salad waiting for us when we get back.'

'Urgh, I hate salad,' Lucy said.

Maria hated salad too and she laughed, and by the time we pulled up at the leisure centre the tension between the girls had eased off. Happily, once we were inside the argument seemed to be forgotten. The girls were looking forward to the swim and Maria was enjoying being the one in charge, showing Lucy the lockers and the changing area and telling her all about the wave machine and sprinklers that came on in the pool. Lucy was thrilled by this and got changed first and waited patiently for the rest of us by the poolside.

'Come on Maria!' she said when the two of us arrived at the same time. 'Let's do some lengths. Shall we have a race?'

'I'll thrash you!' Maria joked.

Jonathan joined me and we watched the girls jump in the water together and start to do lengths.

'Now that's the kind of "thrashing" we can cope with,' he smiled.

'I'm not so sure,' I said. 'I think we're going to have to watch these two like hawks.'

At that moment the siren sounded all around the pool, warning swimmers the waves were about to start up. 'I think you're right,' Jonathan shouted over the siren. 'And I also think both Lucy and Maria are quite capable of making waves all by themselves!'

# 4

## *'The sooner she starts school again the better'*

On the Monday morning I called Jess to discuss Lucy's schooling.

'How's it going so far?' she asked.

'Not bad,' I said, filling her in. 'I'm finding that when Lucy's occupied she's generally no trouble.'

I told Jess that the previous day Lucy had aggravated Maria by staring at her, following her around and invading her personal space. We'd had my mum over for Sunday lunch as we often did, and thankfully this diffused the tetchy atmosphere. Lucy was interested to meet Mum and embroiled her in countless board games, which my mother thoroughly enjoyed. Maria joined in a few but when my mum went home and the two girls tried to play a game together it ended in an argument. 'I think the sooner we get Lucy into school the better,' I said. 'Is there any news?'

'Actually there is. I've just put the phone down to the head of St Bede's. I've arranged a meeting for this afternoon. I hope that's not too short notice?'

'Absolutely not. I'm delighted. As Lucy's social worker hasn't been assigned yet, I was going to offer to phone round the local schools myself this morning, but I'm very glad you've beaten me to it, Jess!'

'Good. The only thing is I've no news on whether Lucy's statemented. I'm still waiting on that but I thought we'd take the appointment anyhow. You never know, I might hear back later this morning, if we're lucky.'

I took down the details and told Lucy we'd be going along to see what would potentially be her new school while she was living with us. I also reminded her that Jonathan and I had a support social worker called Jess, who she'd meet at the appointment with the school.

'Will I have a helper?' Lucy asked, narrowing her eyes. 'I had a helper before. I don't like school really. I don't want to go to school without a helper.'

'This is something we need to talk about at school. Did you always have a helper then, every day?'

'Yes, every day. I like her. She's called Miss Jenner. She helped with my reading mostly, and maths.'

I knew the head of St Bede's, Mr Morris-Butler, but this was not necessarily a good thing. Unfortunately we'd had a very difficult child staying with us some years earlier, who was extremely disruptive in the classroom. As a result I was called up to the school on many occasions. I always found Mr Morris-Butler to be a rather cold and foreboding character for a primary school head teacher and I can't say we gelled very well. He was a real stickler for rules and red tape, and I found myself thinking, *We'll have no chance of getting Lucy in there if she isn't statemented.*

I kept Lucy occupied that morning by setting her up on the laptop with some spelling and maths CD-ROMS. I intended to do some housework and catch up with a few phone calls I had to make, but I didn't get a thing done.

'Angela, can you help me with this?'

'Yes, of course, sweetheart. Let's see where you are up to.'

'I've done this page and now I'm on the next one. It's a number puzzle. I'm not doing the spelling one. It's too hard.'

'OK. How can I help you?'

'Can you do it with me?'

'Are you stuck?'

'No, I just want you to help me.'

'Why don't you make a start and I will give you some clues if you can't do it on your own?'

'OK.'

I needed to make appointments at the dentist, doctor and optician for Lucy, as we need to do for every new child we take in. This is a Social Services requirement, and I like to get it done as quickly as possible after a child moves in so that any problems are picked up and dealt with sooner rather than later.

I called the doctor's first and was put on hold. Lucy was working on the dining-room table and I was just next door, in the kitchen.

'ANGELA!' she called at the top of her voice.

'I'm just on hold on the phone,' I said, hovering in the doorway with the phone to my ear. 'What is it?'

'I need help. Can you help me?'

Muzak was plinking away down the line so I put the call on speakerphone and went to see what Lucy was stuck on.

'What's a dozen?'

'A dozen is twelve.'

'Is it?'

'Yes. Oh, hang on a moment.'

The doctor's receptionist was on the line now, but Lucy didn't seem to register that I needed to take the call and she continued to talk non-stop.

'ANGELA? Which number is wrong? Can you help me? I can't move on to the next clue, can I, if this one is wrong?'

I pointed to the phone and stepped out of the room so I could concentrate and book the appointment. I was still on the line when Lucy once again bellowed, 'ANGELA, can you help me? Is this right? Angela?'

I walked to the far end of the kitchen to finish my call and then returned to the dining room, where I explained to Lucy that I couldn't have two conversations at the same time and she needed to be patient while I was on the phone.

'OK. But why is it called a dozen? Why can't it just be twelve? Are there names for other numbers? What are they?'

I started to tell her that some other numbers had names too, like score for twenty. The phone rang again. This time it was the optician calling me back as I'd left a message earlier. I went to take the call in the kitchen and Lucy followed me, standing on the back of my heels and tugging at the back of my shirt as she did so.

'Yes, that's fine. Three o'clock. Ideal. Thank you.'

'What's happening at three o'clock?'

'Yes, I know you've moved premises. I know how to find you. Car parking now at the back. Got it, thank you.'

'What are premises?'

I put my finger to my lips to indicate to Lucy that she needed to be quiet while I completed the call, and when I hung up I repeated what I'd just said about not being able to hold two conversations at once.

'Sorry. Can you help me now? I think I've got stuck.'

It didn't matter how much I encouraged Lucy to work independently and how many times I explained I needed to get on with a couple of jobs around the house, she nagged me over and over again and seemed to have a very short attention span. By the time we set off to meet Jess at the school I was really hoping the meeting would go well, and I was wishing that Lucy could start school that week, if not the next day! I knew this was ambitious, given the various processes and paperwork we'd have to go through with the LEA and Social Services, but I had my fingers crossed nonetheless.

Jess met us in the car park and I introduced her to Lucy. Under normal circumstances Jess would have met Lucy at our house when she first arrived, but on that particular afternoon Jess had been called out to the police station, to deal with another child on her list who had got himself into trouble.

'How's it going, Lucy?'

'Good.'

'What have you been up to today?'

'Had breakfast. Did stuff on the computer. Had a tuna sandwich for lunch. Helped Angela empty the dishwasher.'

'Great. Are you looking forward to starting back at school?'

'Yes, because I'm bored. At home Daddy lets me do loads of jobs. I like helping him do the garden and all that. I want to go home. When can I go home?'

Jonathan was standing next to me and Jess glanced at both of us, as if to say, 'Oh dear.'

'Well, I was about to tell you there's a meeting on Friday to discuss how long you'll be staying with Angela and Jonathan, and then we'll be able to tell you more.'

'Good. I miss Daddy.'

'I'm sure you do. Now, shall we go and sort your school place out? That will keep you busy in the meantime.'

Lucy nodded and Jonathan walked on ahead with her, leading the way to reception. Unfortunately Jess still didn't know if Lucy was statemented or not, which wasn't ideal.

'Let's hope that doesn't cause too much of a holdup,' she said. 'Lucy certainly likes to be a busy bee, doesn't she? The sooner she starts school again the better.'

'I couldn't agree more. She's a lovely girl and I'm already very fond of her, but I can see how things might unravel if she isn't occupied or stimulated enough.'

The meeting didn't get off to a great start. Despite Lucy sitting right next to me, listening to everything, Mr Morris-Butler immediately brought up the fact that the last child in our care who attended his school was extremely disruptive and caused no end of trouble. It was clear the head teacher had his reservations about taking in another 'cared for' child, as he put it, but Jess handled the situation diplomatically and explained that Lucy was of course a *different* child and was very willing to learn.

'Lucy has just told me she's bored and wants to get back to school as quickly as possible,' Jess said, giving Lucy an encouraging smile.

Mr Morris-Butler gave a curt nod of the head.

'Did you have a support worker with you in your last school?' he asked Lucy.

'Yes. Miss Jenner always helped me in my old school. I like her.'

The head seemed pleased with this response but then asked a series of questions none of us knew the answers to, such as what Lucy's specific needs were, when she was statemented and so on. He then told us that before any decision could be made as to whether Lucy would be granted a place at St Bede's he would need to see all the relevant paperwork from her previous school and LEA.

Mr Morris-Butler dismissed us; it wouldn't have surprised me if he'd rung a bell and told us to walk on the left-hand side of the corridor on our way out.

Lucy fired another round of questions at us after we said goodbye to Jess and walked back to our car.

'When can I start? What's it's like? What class will I be in? Do you think I will make friends? Do they let you play football at lunchtime?'

I didn't want to make any promises I couldn't keep, and so I told Lucy we would just have to be patient and wait to hear from the head teacher.

'So you like football?' Jonathan asked.

I smiled to myself thinking, *Typical Jonathan: the master of distraction.*

'Yes. I LOVE football.'

'So do I. We could have a kick around when we get back to our house if you like?'

'Wicked! Daddy's good at football. Are you any good?'

'I'll let you be the judge of that,' Jonathan said. 'Come on. Let's go!'

# 5

**'I'm happy, very happy. I love you!'**

'Tell her to stop staring at me, will you?' Maria snapped.

Maria had given Lucy another lukewarm reception when she got in from school. She had fallen out with a friend in her class and was tired and impatient. I think the staring was Lucy's way of trying to show she wasn't very happy about the way Maria was treating her. It started at the dinner table. Lucy had enjoyed playing football with Jonathan that afternoon and seemed in a good mood, but when the four of us sat down to eat Lucy gave Maria a long, cold stare across the table. She did this on and off throughout the meal and I had to ask her several times to stop before she finally gave up.

'What are you staring at?' Maria barked at Lucy.

'Nothing!'

'Well look at something else!'

'They're my eyes, I can do what I want with them.'

Though she was clearly rattled by Lucy's staring Maria wasn't put off her food. She tucked in and ate a large meal while once again Lucy only picked at her food. Her green salad was untouched, but that didn't surprise me. Maria herself had asked me more than once why I 'spoiled' perfectly good meals with salad! I encouraged Lucy to eat a bit more of her quiche and potatoes, but she objected to the onions in the quiche, which she picked out before eating it, and said she had never had new potatoes with skins on before and thought they were 'weird'. She wouldn't even entertain the coleslaw on her plate: again the onion put her off, and she said it smelled 'funny'.

I made a mental note to seat both girls side by side instead of opposite each other at the dinner table in future, to reduce the chances of Lucy staring at Maria. I could see I'd need to keep a very close eye on Lucy's diet. She was quite happy to eat breakfast and snacks and she did OK with things like sandwiches or crackers for lunch, but evening meals seemed to faze her. It was true she was very slight and therefore didn't need to eat a huge amount, but I wanted to make sure she was eating enough of the right foods and not filling up on snacks too much during the day. I told myself that she was still settling in, of course, and nerves might be hampering her appetite. This wasn't uncommon, and I'd just have to monitor the situation and nudge her in the right direction, without making an issue of it.

The following day Lucy was up early and the first thing she asked was, 'How many days until I see Daddy?'

'We'll see him on Friday, at the meeting.'

'Good. That's . . . Tuesday, Wednesday, Thursday – only three sleeps!'

'That's right. Not long at all.'

'What are we going to do until then?'

The goalpost Jonathan had assembled the afternoon before was still set up in the garden. I suggested to Lucy that she could do a fun science CD-ROM programme I had on the laptop and then she could go and kick the ball around before lunch, as it was warm and dry and the sun was shining. In the afternoon Lucy had a dental appointment. I'd managed to get a cancellation, and I told her that as it was such a nice day we could walk to the surgery across town and do a bit of food shopping on the way back, as I needed some ingredients for dinner as well as a few basics.

She happily agreed. 'Can I help you make it?'

'Yes, if you want to. I'd be glad of the help. We're having lasagne and garlic bread. I need to buy some fresh fruit and veg too.'

'Daddy grows fruit and veg. He likes gardening. Once he grew two carrots that were stuck together and we said they were twins like Josh and Liam!'

I told Lucy my mum had a vegetable patch and that we'd go to her house one day so she could see it, and maybe even do a bit of gardening ourselves. She seemed thrilled at the idea.

'Does she grow carrots? I like horses, you know. Once I was allowed to help my cousin's friend with her horse and we fed him carrots. Do you know anyone with a horse?

'As a matter of fact I do. There's a lady in the neighbourhood who has several horses. I could ask her if you can visit some time, if you like? She's called Diane and she's a good friend.'

'OK, but can it be soon? Can it be tomorrow? Or the next day? Because I'm going home with Daddy on Friday . . . probably.'

Her voice trailed off at the end of the sentence. I gently explained to Lucy that even though she was seeing her daddy and stepmother at the end of the week, it was only going to be during the meeting to decide how long she was staying with us. I told her, gently, that she would not be going home with them on that day.

'Do you remember we talked about you staying with us for a bit? Perhaps two or three months? Well, the meeting is going to decide what the best length of time will be. You'll be staying with us for a little while – probably until the summer holidays – and that's why we're setting up a school place for you, for the summer term. It's also why we've found you a dentist here, and things like that.'

'Oh, yes. I just forgot.'

I was starting to feel quite anxious about the meeting. I wanted it to run smoothly and for Lucy to have the reassurances she craved from her family, about being able to go home when everything had settled down. I knew that these meetings didn't always run to plan, however. It would be a big day for Lucy, and I found myself thinking about it a lot, and hoping it would go well and not upset or disrupt Lucy too much at this early stage in her placement.

As planned, after breakfast Lucy sat at my laptop and had a go at the science CD-ROM. It kept her attention for a short time and she said she liked the challenges. There wasn't a great deal of reading to be done on level one – it was an educational game that mostly involved dragging different ingredients into jugs and effectively playing matching pairs. When she reached level two and had to read sets of instructions on the screen she lost interest and said it was boring. I suspected she was struggling with the text and asked if she needed any help.

'No. I know what to do but I don't want to play any more.'

She abandoned the laptop and built a large model of a robot out of Lego before going outside to do some target practice with a football in the garden. She was a good shooter and she also turned out to be very adept at 'keepy-uppys', explaining that she had won a sponsored challenge at school the year before for doing the highest number of keepy-uppys in her class.

'Watch me! Look at this! Can you keep count for me?'

'Well done. Yes, go on. One, two, three, four . . . Never mind. Start again. You're doing brilliantly! I'll be back out in a few minutes. I'm just going to fetch the washing to hang on the line. I can see you from the kitchen window.'

'Can't you watch out here? Can you count again? Look! Watch me!'

Despite the fact she was happy and occupied doing the

keepy-uppys Lucy still wanted me to stay close, cheering her on.

'Am I good? Do you want a competition? Can you do this? Watch me score a goal! Do you reckon I will get this one in from here?'

When Jonathan took his mid-morning tea break from the shop the two of us flopped on the garden bench and watched Lucy practise her skills. We clapped when she scored a goal and called 'well done!' and 'brilliant!' every time she hit the targets she set herself with her keepy-uppys.

She asked if she could have a look in our garage and her eyes immediately fell on the collection of bikes we kept there. We'd acquired several over the years and they were in varying states of repair.

'Which is your bike, Jonathan? Why has it got a flat tyre? Why don't you repair it? I could repair it. Do you want me to repair it? Do you go biking when your bike is working? Which one is Maria's? Why doesn't she go to her granny's on it? Why doesn't she live with her granny? Was her bike new or second hand? Why is that one so dirty? Do you ride through mud? Where do you go?'

Jonathan did his best to provide the answers, and before changing the subject Lucy ruefully told him she would love to have a bike of her own but her stepmother wouldn't let her have one. She claimed Wendy said she didn't deserve a bike because she was 'too naughty'. 'I *wasn't* naughty,' she insisted. 'Wendy was just being mean to me.'

'So you like riding bikes?' Jonathan asked.

'Yes! I'm a good bike rider. I love bike riding. Can I ride one of these?'

'Yes, when I've got time we'll see which one suits you best and get it cleaned up and ready for you. Maria loves cycling in the country park, we all do. We must do that together. It'll be fun, and you're right, all the bikes could do with a spruce up, especially now the weather is so nice. I'll sort it out. You've inspired me, Lucy!'

She beamed.

The snooker table was the next item in the garage to capture Lucy's attention. 'Who does that belong to? Why is it standing up against the wall? Why don't you play with it? How long have you lived here? Can you teach me how to play? My daddy plays pool in the pub.'

At lunchtime Lucy ran over to me in the kitchen as I was making sandwiches and gave me a big hug.

'I'm happy, very happy,' she said. 'I love you!'

I was taken aback. It's unusual for a child to say this after just a few days and I wasn't expecting it at all.

'I care for you very much too, Lucy,' I replied. 'You're such a nice girl. I'm so pleased you're staying with us.'

In the afternoon we walked to the dentist, as I'd explained we would. Lucy chatted the whole way there, asking questions about everything and anything we encountered on our route, and about her appointment.

'Who lives there? Why is there a traffic triangle thingy here? What's the dentist like? Will I have to have my teeth pulled out?'

Lucy could not remember the last time she had a dental appointment, and the dentist was not impressed with her teeth. He advised her to brush twice a day and to cut down on sweets. She already had four fillings and was told that she needed to be extra careful about her teeth now all her adult teeth were nearly through.

Afterwards she told me, 'Wendy took Gemma to the dentist but she never took me. She bought Gemma a toothbrush with a battery and a flashing light on it. I wanted one but she said no. Granny buys me toothbrushes sometimes, nice ones, not big, horrible scratchy ones.'

When we went shopping on the way home I asked Lucy if she'd like to choose a new toothbrush in the chemist, as the one she had with her looked quite old and probably needed replacing. She loved this and picked one that had a spaceman on the handle and beeped when you'd cleaned your teeth for two full minutes. It was a pleasure shopping with her. She was interested in everything and was polite to the cashier when she made conversation about the fact that 'in her day' they never had such fun toothbrushes.

We picked up the food shopping before heading home, and Lucy helped me prepare the lasagne I was making for dinner, as I'd mentioned to her first thing that morning. I was doing a simple recipe I'd made a hundred times and so it didn't take long.

'Can we make pudding?'

'I was going to do ice cream and fruit. You can chop the fruit and make a fruit salad if you like? Here, I've got a few kitchen gadgets I think you might like. I'll show you how to use them.'

I dug out a melon-baller, and a lemon zester and I even found one of those pineapple-corers in the back of the cupboard. I hadn't used it for years and I never normally bothered with any of those things when I made fruit salad, but I had a good idea Lucy would like them. I was right, and with my supervision she had great fun preparing the fruit salad. I even had a small can of glacé cherries, and I opened it and suggested she could pop a few on top, to finish off her creation.

'I can't wait for Jonathan and Maria to see *this*,' she said.

Despite all the preparations and Lucy's interest in helping to make the meal, she still didn't eat a great deal.

'I'm sure you'd like some fruit salad, after all the hard work you put into making it.'

'No thanks, just ice cream.'

Jonathan and I swapped glances and Maria grinned.

'Why would you want to spoil a perfectly good bowl of ice cream with fruit?' Maria asked cheekily.

The two girls giggled and I didn't mind joining in. It was good to see them connecting like this, even if the very large bowl of fruit salad sitting on the table hardly had a dent in it.

In the evening I phoned my neighbour who kept horses. I'd known Diane for years, first as a customer in our shop and then through fostering, as she'd become a foster carer a few years earlier. We often went to training sessions together and were good friends now. Diane was a naturally helpful and positive person and she always had a tip to share or an article she'd read that she wanted to show the group, in case it might be helpful.

I explained that we had Lucy staying with us and asked if I could pop round with her to see the horses. Diane was more than happy to help and reassured me that she had had all the necessary health and safety certificates she was required to obtain before letting any children interact with the horses, adding that all her dogs had been checked as well: she loved animals and also had three Border collies. The horses had been 'risk-assessed' by Social Services, which allowed her foster children to be able to assist with cleaning out stables and grooming the horses. They could ride only if they had permission from their legal guardian. Lucy was on a voluntary care order, otherwise known as a Section 20 order, meaning she'd been taken into care by agreement rather than by court order and Dean therefore maintained his parental rights. This meant that if Lucy wanted to ride one of the horses, I'd need to check with her social worker and we'd have to ask permission from her father. I thanked Diane and told her that for the time being I was sure Lucy would be happy just to visit and perhaps give the horses some carrots, if they were allowed them. We arranged to go over the following afternoon, and this turned out to be a really good move.

Lucy's face lit up like a Christmas tree when she saw the horses. Diane – a lifelong Abba fan – had three beautiful animals called Frida, Benny and Agnetha.

'How old are they? What do they like to eat? Can I give them some food? Do they wear horseshoes?'

Lucy's eyes were absolutely everywhere. Diane enthusiastically gave Lucy a tour of the stables, showing her where the hay and water were kept and explaining the routine the horses had and what needed to be done each day to keep them healthy, clean and well exercised.

'Can I come and help you? Can I ride them? Do they do jumping or racing?'

Diane explained that Frida, a beautiful dapple-grey mare, was the best horse for young children to ride, as she was the smallest and had a very calm and laid-back temperament. Diane's teenage daughter Clare took part in gymkhanas regularly on her horse Agnetha, and the family had a horsebox and often travelled all over the country for competitions.

'I'd LOVE to do that. Angela, can I? Am I behaving myself well enough? Am I being good enough?' Her eyes were shining with excitement and expectation.

Diane gave me an understanding smile when Lucy asked those questions. Most children would not ask questions in that way, but as a foster carer you are constantly surprised by the things the kids come out with. Diane was well used to this and, like me, she probably imagined that other adults in Lucy's life had told her she needed to behave well, and better, if she wanted things to go her way.

'I think you're behaving very well,' I told Lucy. 'But let's take it one step at a time, shall we? What do you say, Diane?'

'I agree. Why don't you help me walk Frida around the yard? I'm sure she'd like to stretch her legs.'

It was a perfect visit and Lucy didn't want to leave. I spoke to Diane about asking Social Services and Dean for permission for her to ride some time, and she was all for it.

'Happy to help,' she said. 'By the way, can I ask you a favour in return?'

'Of course.'

'I have a teenager staying with me who needs to do some work experience. Matty's interested in retail. Any chance he could help out in the shop?'

I agreed, of course. That's often how it goes with foster carers. We always help each other out if we can, because ultimately we're helping the children, which is what it's all about.

The following day we finally had a visit from Lucy's new social worker. She was a newly qualified young woman called Bella, who spoke with a strong Scottish accent.

Lucy stared at her when she spoke, but Bella was not fazed.

'Some people find my accent a wee bit hard to follow,' she smiled. 'I won't be offended if you have to ask me to say things twice.'

'What's your name?'

'Bella. It's very good to meet you, Lucy.'

Lucy stared and I wondered if she was going to ask Bella to repeat her answer, but she didn't. 'Billa,' Lucy said, as if trying to commit the name to memory.

'Yes, that's right. It sounds like "Billa" in my accent I suppose, but you spell it B, e, l, l, a. It's short for Isabella.'

Lucy looked confused and said she wasn't good at spelling.

'Will you be at the meeting with my daddy? I want to go home. I miss him. Can you tell him that? Can you tell him two times, or three times or four times!'

Bella took this in her stride and patiently explained what would happen at what she called the 'core meeting'.

'We'll all get together. That's me, you, Angela, Jonathan, their support social worker, Jess, plus your daddy and step-mother, Wendy. We'll all have a chat about what's going to happen over the next few months, so we can work together to help you move back home.'

'Does it have to be months? That's a long time. I think it's all fine now. I think I can go home quicker than that. How quick can it be?'

'This is what we're going to work out. How are things going here, with Angela?'

I slipped out of the living room so they could talk privately, as social workers normally prefer this, and as I walked away I heard Lucy telling Bella, 'I love Angela. Jonathan's nice. But I still want to go home because I miss Daddy.'

I returned with a tray of drinks to find Bella smiling broadly.

'I can't believe how much you've packed in since Lucy arrived. I've heard all about the swimming with Maria, the football with Jonathan, the shopping and cooking, the science game and the Lego and, of course, horses!'

I had a good feeling about Bella. There was a great atmosphere in the room and Lucy looked animated.

'I've told Bella I can ride Frida if she'll let me.'

'I see. Yes. I was going to talk to Bella about that but you've beaten me to it, Lucy!'

'Where there's a will there's a way,' Bella grinned.

'What does that mean?' Lucy asked.

'It means that when someone really wants something they will find a way to make it happen,' the social worker said. 'And I think you are someone who knows what they want, which is no bad thing.'

Lucy smiled. 'I am,' she said. 'I want to go home.'

I hoped very strongly that she'd get her wish sooner rather than later, and I was now feeling more optimistic about the core meeting and looking forward to hearing what strategies would be put in place to help reunite the family.

'Lucy's not a bad girl at all,' I said to Jonathan that evening. 'I can't imagine how things have gone so wrong at home. It'll be interesting to meet Wendy and Dean, and find out more.'

# 6

## *'She frightened me to death'*

On Friday morning, as we all got ready to attend the core meeting, Lucy was very chirpy and excited. She had spoken to her daddy on the phone the night before and told him she couldn't wait to see him.

'I want to give you a big hug!' she squealed.

I guessed her dad had told Lucy he was going to put her stepmother Wendy on the phone next, because I then heard her say, 'It's OK, I'll see Wendy, I mean Mum, tomorrow. No, it's fine. I don't need to talk to her now. Oh, OK then.' The tone of Lucy's voice had quickly changed from animated to what could only be described as wary.

'Hello, er, Mum,' she said flatly. 'Yes I've been good. I've been busy and Angela is really nice. So is Jonathan. They've got a flower shop, you know. I still want to come home. I don't want to stay here. I miss Daddy, and, well, everyone. See you tomorrow. Bye.'

Buckled in the back of the car on the way to the Social Services office in town, Lucy seemed to only be thinking about her daddy. She started to tell us all kinds of things about him.

'I can't wait for you to meet him. My daddy is tall and thin with curly brown hair. He's got blue eyes and always has a suntan. He planted trees at the mayor's house once, and by the big new centre. His hands are big and he's always trying to scrub the mud out from under his nails, but he never can!'

I imagined she meant the town hall, as she went on to tell us her dad worked as a gardener for the local town council and had met the mayor 'loads of times'.

'I bet your garden at home is lovely,' I said. 'It sounds like your dad has very green fingers.'

'No. The mud is always brown.'

Jonathan chuckled and explained what it meant to be green-fingered.

'Oh! Wendy would have taken the mickey if she heard me say that. I'm glad I didn't say *that* in front of *her*.'

Lucy stared out of the window for a minute or two.

'Are we nearly there yet?'

'Yes! That's the building there.'

The second the car was stationary Lucy unplugged her seat belt and tried to get out, but the child lock was on her door and she couldn't open it.

'There's my dad's van!' she said, pulling the handle of the car repeatedly. 'Can we go in? He's in there already. Can you unlock the door? Quick! Can you do it now? I want to get out!'

Her little face was shining in anticipation and she practically launched herself out of the car the second we unlocked her door.

The three of us walked into reception.

'Daddy! Daddy! Daddy!'

'Lucy-lu, how are you?'

Her father scooped her into his chest and gave her a giant hug while Lucy giggled with delight.

'I want to come home! I've missed you. How is everyone?'

'Well, Mum is right there.'

Lucy's dad nodded to his right, where Wendy stood looking slightly frosty and aloof. Nevertheless she pulled on a smile as she spoke to Lucy.

'Hello Lucy,' she said. 'You been behaving yourself for these nice people?'

Lucy glanced at Jonathan and me and took a step closer to us. It looked quite obvious to me that she wanted to avoid having to give her stepmother a hug.

'Hi. Yes. Er . . .'

Lucy shyly turned to me and I took my cue and introduced myself and Jonathan to Wendy and Dean. They were both polite and friendly as we said our hellos, though Dean was noticeably warmer than Wendy. He thanked us for having Lucy, and for bringing her to the meeting.

'I'm very grateful indeed. I'm very glad she's with you, safe and sound. It's the right thing, for the time being. Thank you for having her at short notice.'

'It's our pleasure,' I said. 'We're enjoying having her to stay.'

Dean gave an appreciative smile. He looked exactly as I imagined he would from Lucy's description. I guessed he was in his late thirties, and he had the air of being a humble, unassuming man. He'd put on smart clothes for the occasion, as had Wendy. She looked a bit older than Dean – early forties perhaps – and was tall and well built and seemed very self-assured.

'Yes, we do appreciate it,' she said curtly. 'You are *so* good to take Lucy in the way you have. It can't be easy, being foster carers. I know I couldn't do it, not for all the tea in China.'

Wendy smiled broadly but at the same time she raised her chin an inch or two, which made me feel like she was looking down on me. She gave Jonathan the same impression and we both felt slightly intimidated by her. Wendy had steel-grey eyes and hair so black it had a cobalt-blue sheen to it under the harsh lighting of the modern council office block. She looked like a force to be reckoned with, and it didn't come as a surprise that Lucy was keeping her distance.

Bella appeared and took Lucy to one side to have a chat, which is the norm before such a meeting. I knew the social worker would be explaining the purpose of the meeting again and making sure Lucy felt comfortable to sit in the meeting with the adults and hear what everyone had to say. Bella would also be asking Lucy again how things were going at our house, just in case there was anything new to report, and she'd be telling her that she might be asked questions in the meeting, and she should answer them as honestly as she could.

When we finally all sat around the large oval table in the council office I felt extremely nervous on Lucy's behalf. Lucy was seated next to her dad, who had Wendy on the other side of him. Jonathan and I were opposite the family, next to Bella, and there was a Social Services manager present, at the far end of the table. Jess's mobile phone vibrated just as she was about to sit down opposite her manager.

'Sorry, I should take this,' she said urgently. 'Can you excuse me for a moment?'

Her manager nodded and began to examine some paperwork. The room fell silent for a moment and then Wendy turned to Lucy, looking her up and down.

'New clothes?'

Lucy was wearing the new joggers and tracksuit top I'd bought her at the retail park.

Lucy nodded shyly.

'What was wrong with your own stuff? Did you take everything with you?'

'Nothing's wrong with my stuff. Yes. I didn't leave anything at Granny's.'

Wendy turned to me. 'I have to tell you, Angela, I don't like kids of her age wearing branded clothing.'

I said it was pure chance that the clothes were Nike and explained that we chose them because they fitted Lucy well and were practical. I added that we purchased them at the very reasonably priced discounted sports store at the retail park, to make the point that we hadn't been extravagant or paid over the odds simply to have a well-known brand. I also said Lucy's old joggers were a little on the small side. 'Kids grow out of things before you can blink,' Jonathan said wisely, as the last thing we wanted to do was imply that Wendy was at fault in any way.

'Yes, it's not your fault. But she knows how I feel about labels, don't you Lucy?'

She nodded guiltily, lowering her eyes and pulling two handfuls of her hair from the sides of her face cross her cheeks, as if to hide herself as much as possible.

Jess reappeared, made her apologies for having to take the call and sat down. I glanced at Lucy, who was now looking sideways at her father. She had a loving expression on her face but her father was looking the other way, in Wendy's direction. No doubt he was concerned about her mood: Wendy did not look pleased at all, and she sat with her arms crossed tightly in front of her chest and with her face set in a stony grimace.

After the manager welcomed everyone Bella spoke first, discussing how she had arranged for both Lucy and her father and stepmother to attend regular sessions at what she called the 'Child and Family' counselling group, in the county where the family lived. As the name implied, Lucy, Wendy and Dean would all attend sessions together, and Lucy's siblings and stepsister Gemma might also be invited along, once progress was being made. Lucy would also see a child psychologist separately, for some one-to-one therapy.

I'd never heard of the Child and Family group before but

it was explained to Jonathan and me that it was similar to CAMHS (Child and Adolescent Mental Health Services), with which we were very familiar.

Jonathan and I were asked if we could take Lucy there once a fortnight and I said that yes we could, as long as the sessions were early enough in the day so that we could be back in time to be home for Maria after school.

'Yes, I can fix them up for mid-morning, and if you ever have any problems we can always send a car for Lucy, with a support worker to accompany her.'

'Thanks, but we can take her,' I said, as I thought it might be stressful for Lucy to go in a taxi with a stranger. There was no mention of Wendy and Dean helping with lifts, although it would have been a long run for them to collect her from our house, go to the meetings and drop her back to us before returning home.

Bella moved on. 'I'm pleased to report that Lucy has settled in very well with Angela and Jonathan. She is happy living with them, although she would like to return home as soon as possible.' Looking at Dean, she added, 'It would be helpful if you could tell me a little bit about what was going on at home, when Lucy was living with you.'

Wendy snorted. 'What was going on was that she was a manipulative little madam. Isn't that right Dean?'

Lucy's dad suddenly appeared to be incredibly interested in his fingernails. He stared at them and began scratching at his cuticles nervously.

'Well, I think that's putting it a bit—'

'It's the truth. The problem was that Lucy played me up

something rotten. Good as gold when her dad was around, but when it was me and her? Forget it! She turned.'

'Turned?' Jess enquired, keeping an even and professional tone in her voice.

'Yes, turned. Told lies, bullied my daughter, stole her toys, demanded food, caused no end of trouble, I'm telling you. It was like she had a switch. When her dad came home from work she was as good as gold. Sweetness and light. Little angel, oh yes . . .'

I looked at Lucy and saw she was pink in the cheeks. Thankfully, Jess cut in and stopped Wendy sharing any more of her forthright opinions. I'm glad she did or I think I would have stepped in myself, because Wendy's manner seemed inappropriately harsh in front of the little girl. *You should be focusing on improving matters, not making a meal of criticising and embarrassing an eight-year-old*, I thought.

'Mr Harrison, can I ask your view? How did you see things?'

Dean looked flustered and Wendy shot him a look as if to say, 'Don't you dare dispute what I've said.'

'Well, like Wendy says, when I was there Lucy was good.'

He flicked an encouraging glance at Lucy and I could almost see her relax a little. Unfortunately, Wendy then piped up again.

'She frightened me to death. That's the reason we had to move her out of the house – because I never knew what she might do next.'

'She frightened you?'

It was Jess who asked this question. No doubt she was thinking about Lucy's placement with Jonathan and myself, and assessing whether there were truly any risks involved in having Lucy living with us.

'Yes. I'm afraid of her. Like I say, she can turn at the flick of a switch. She tells so many lies. My daughter was in tears all the time. Lucy ripped Gemma's clothes and pretended my daughter did it herself. She stole her toys and hid them in the garden, in the dirt. I don't know why she's the way she is. There's something wrong with her. I can't live with her, and it's not just me. Her aunties couldn't cope with the lies and all the aggro either, and nor could her grand-mother.'

I was becoming increasingly upset and angry about the way Wendy spoke about Lucy, but she didn't seem at all concerned that she might hurt the child's feelings or make matters worse. In fact, Wendy bossily asked for her comments to be recorded in the minutes of the meeting.

Bella changed the subject to the issue of schools. She explained that she had contacted Lucy's old primary school and established that she'd missed seven weeks of her education.

'We've also requested details of Lucy's statement,' Jess said.

Wendy looked confused. 'What do you mean?'

'She has help in the classroom, doesn't she?'

'Yes,' Dean interjected. 'She has help with her reading. She's done really well since she's had a helper.'

Jess explained that we'd applied for Lucy to take up a

place at St Bede's and that we should be hearing any day from the head.

'We're hoping she can start next week,' Jess said.

'I'll bet you are!' Wendy chided, but nobody responded.

It was my turn to speak and I talked about what Lucy had been doing and how well she had settled in. The social workers agreed that we should aim to have Lucy returned home by the end of August, to reduce the disruption to her education. Lucy smiled when she heard this: I could almost see her mind ticking over, working out that this was roughly three months, as we'd expected.

Contact visits with the family were next on the agenda. There were no legal restrictions or orders in place preventing Lucy from having contact or overnight stays with any of her relatives, but at this early stage it was decided it was best if Lucy didn't stay overnight in the family home. This arrangement would be reviewed fortnightly as the Child and Family sessions progressed, and it was hoped she'd soon start to stay one night, then build up to two and so on. There was some talk of Lucy being able to spend time in the school summer holidays with her grandmother; apparently this was something Lucy had discussed with Bella, and this would be looked at again nearer the time.

We gave Wendy and Dean our home address and I said that in addition to having Lucy visit them at their home, the whole family was welcome to visit us, if they wanted to. Lucy's happiness was paramount and I hoped that the more contact she had with her family the easier it would be for her to build relationships and ultimately return home.

Social Services were happy for us to make these arrangements amongst ourselves; there was no need to ask permission, simply to let our social workers know what we were doing, which I did routinely in any case.

The manager gathered up her papers and drew the meeting to a close. I sat there for a moment thinking about what had been said. *I really want to have a word with Wendy on the phone before any visit,* I thought. I decided I would have to suggest, as diplomatically as I could, that Wendy didn't accuse or criticise Lucy to her face again. Hopefully, once the therapy sessions started up, the professional counsellors would give Wendy the same advice.

Lucy hugged her daddy tight then said goodbye but she pointedly avoided any physical contact with her stepmother. It was not difficult to notice this; Dean headed out of the door leaving Wendy in the foyer with Lucy, who swiftly turned on her heel and ran down a corridor, saying she needed the toilet. I went after Lucy, waving bye to Wendy over my shoulder and telling her we'd speak soon.

Driving home I wondered if Wendy was irritated by the fact Lucy had settled in with us. Somehow, I had a feeling she'd have been happier if Jonathan and I had joined in with her criticisms of Lucy, and this bothered me. *Why would you want that? Surely you should be pleased to hear Lucy is behaving herself in foster care and that her foster carers are pleased with how she is getting along?*

Hopefully I'd got Wendy all wrong, but that felt like wishful thinking.

Lucy herself seemed unperturbed by Wendy's harsh words at the meeting, and she focused only on the positive.

'Can I phone Granny when we get back to your house?'

'Of course you can.'

'Good. I want to tell her I saw Daddy and that I'm starting a new school.'

'I'm sure she'll love to hear your news.'

'Yes. And I want to tell her the best news of all. I want to tell her I'm going home in the summer, after I've had my holiday with her.'

'Well, that's the plan,' I said cautiously. 'Everyone is hoping things will be sorted out by then, but we'll have to wait and see because sometimes things take a little longer than everyone expects. I would tell her that is what we're *aiming* for.'

'OK,' Lucy said rather vacantly.

I knew very well that plans could change dramatically and sometimes in ways you could never anticipate. I didn't want Lucy to be disappointed if she ended up staying with us for a little longer, or if she didn't get to stay with her granny in the summer.

Nevertheless, when she called her grandmother, Lucy stuck to the positive news and completely avoided talking about her stepmother or any of the negative things that were said.

'Perhaps I should take a leaf out of Lucy's book,' I mused.

Jonathan raised his eyebrows. 'How so?'

'Focus on the positives. At least Wendy and Dean came

to the meeting and are going to attend the family sessions. Everyone's pulling together, and even though Lucy's been pushed out of the nest she still belongs at home; everyone acknowledges that. I'm sure it will all work out in time, with all the help the family is getting.'

Jonathan said that, as far as he could see, this was a simple but sad case of a little girl who had become a casualty of dysfunctional family relationships. 'Of course there are some thorny issues that need to be worked through – possibly issues we don't know the half of. And Lucy does need expert help to deal with the behavioural problems she has, but that's what the Child and Family sessions are there for, isn't it? Everything is going in the right direction.'

'That's exactly right. And let's face it, we've encountered far worse cases in our time, haven't we?'

We both thought about some of the problems our foster children had contended with over the years: appalling abuse, shocking criminal activity and devastating mental illness, to name but a few. She wasn't in that situation at all, thank God.

'How are you feeling?' I asked Lucy that afternoon.

'Really happy. I know I'm going home soon. I loved seeing Daddy. I'll miss you when I go home, you know.'

I took a call from Wendy later, asking if the whole family could visit on Sunday. I hadn't expected her to call so soon but I agreed and we fixed a time when she and Dean would be able to drive to us, bringing with them all four children

– Josh and Liam, who I now knew were definitely twins, plus Lucy's little sister Milly and stepsister Gemma.

When I told Lucy the news she was thrilled and started asking lots of questions.

'Can I show them my bedroom? How long will they stay? Can they bring anything from home for me?'

I told her she could certainly show them her bedroom and that they were planning to stay for a cup of tea and take her out for lunch. I said she could phone them any time she liked and ask her stepmum or her daddy to bring what she wanted from home.

'Great, but can you please call her Wendy? She's not my mum and it seems strange to call her stepmum. I've got my own mum. I'll ring soon, when Daddy is in from work. I want my sticker album, my coloured pens, my teddy and my pillow.'

'Pillow? I have plenty of pillows. Is it a special one?'

'Yes. My teddy's special too. I sleep better with them. I've missed them.'

'Teddy's special too? What sort of teddy is it?'

'She's a cuddly yellow bear called Honey. I've had her since I was a baby and she's SO soft. I cuddle her so much.'

'She sounds lovely. Tell me when you're ready to call and I'll dial the number for you if you like.'

'Thanks. I can't wait to see them all. Do you think they will be the same or do you think they will have changed?'

I wasn't quite sure how long it was since she'd seen her siblings, though I realised it could have been many weeks, depending if she saw them when she was living in the homes of her two aunties.

'I don't really think they'll have changed too much,' I said breezily.

Lucy thought about this for a moment.

'*She* changed. She used to be my best friend you know. She changed so *fast*. Do you want me to make this?'

I'd bought a new shoe rack for the hallway and it was still in its box. It was one of those wooden-framed ones that snapped together and so I said I'd be delighted if Lucy could assemble it for me. As she began to tear open the cardboard packaging she started to tell me all about Gemma.

'When we were best friends I used to go to her house all the time. That's how Daddy met Wendy. She picked us both up from school when Daddy was working. The twins went to their friends' houses and so did Milly, mostly, but she sometimes came with me and Gemma if Daddy couldn't get out of work early enough.'

'I see. So you spent quite a bit of time with Gemma after school?'

'Yes. I went to her house for tea lots. We were in the same class too – Diamonds.'

She explained in detail how all the classes were named after precious stones.

'I used to be in Ruby class. Diamonds was better though. I liked my teacher. Everything was good, until SHE came along.'

I guessed she was talking about Wendy but I wasn't certain. I wanted to ask how long Wendy and Lucy's dad had been together, and how long it had been since he was with his previous partner, Val. Was it true about all those awful things Lucy claimed she did? Obviously I couldn't ask. I let Lucy steer the conversation around all kinds of topics before she finally returned to the subject of the family.

'Gemma changed, she did. She started being horrible to me as soon as she moved in to MY house. She tells Wendy lies about me. She causes trouble. Wendy blames me for everything but it's all Gemma's fault, you know.'

# 7

## *'I didn't take them! I don't know how they got there'*

Dean phoned first thing on Sunday morning, before they set out, to ask if Lucy wanted her bike bringing over. He also asked rather sheepishly if I wouldn't mind ensuring that Lucy was not wearing her Nike clothing.

'Wendy doesn't want the other kids asking for designer gear,' he muttered, sounding apologetic and a little embarrassed.

Her jogging bottoms and tracksuit top were hardly what you would describe as 'designer gear' in my opinion, but I took this on board and assured Dean I would make sure Lucy wasn't wearing them.

His question about the bike bothered me, but I didn't let it show. I remembered very clearly how Lucy had told Jonathan that her stepmother wouldn't let her have a bike. I tried to recall her words: 'Wendy said I didn't deserve a bike because I was too naughty . . . Wendy was just being mean to me.'

That's definitely what Lucy had said. I couldn't let this go and I thought carefully about how I would tackle this.

Accusing a child of lying is something you have to be extremely cautious about. You have to be crystal clear about the facts before even thinking about suggesting a child has been untruthful, and even then you need to tread very gently because there is often baggage attached to the lies children tell. Nowadays we know that lying – and stealing – are often related to developmental delay, which produces behaviour you would expect in a younger age group. The reasons and causes of developmental delay are manifold and complex. Lies can be shame-based, with the lie shielding the child from the shame of their actions. This is a minefield for foster carers like us, because you need to understand a child's history in order to even begin to work out why they would act in a particular way – a way that they are sufficiently ashamed of to want to hide with lies. One expert says you should ignore the lie but not the child: they have learned to lie from fear and stress. I always bear this in mind.

Lucy was busy tidying her room ready to show to her siblings, but when she heard the phone she came charging down the stairs.

'Was that Daddy?' she asked excitedly. Fortunately she was wearing jeans and a plain T-shirt, so at least that was one issue I didn't have to tackle right now.

'Yes. He was just asking if you wanted him to bring your bike over. I said yes, because I know you said you like cycling, but do you think he's got a bit confused?'

'Er, why?'

'I thought you didn't have a bike? Perhaps he's got muddled up?'

'Oh, no. I do have a bike, I just forgot. It's, er, old though. It was second hand. I wanted a new one and Wendy wouldn't let me, even though Gemma got a brand-new one.'

'OK, well your daddy's bringing it and I guess you can decide if you want to use it, or ride one of ours. They're all coming in his van so there's plenty of room for it.' Dean's van had eight seats with seat belts, and even when all the seats were being used there was still plenty of room for storage.

'Good. I've made space for my things. I'm going to put Honey on the bed. Honey looks out for the tooth fairy, you know. She didn't always come when I lost a tooth, but she did sometimes.'

My heart swelled. Lucy was so sweet and innocent. It was such a shame things had gone so wrong at home for her. I really hoped the visit would go well.

'Shall we make a few biscuits for our visitors?'

'Yes! But first, will you come and have a look at my bedroom?'

'Of course.'

Lucy showed me around her room with pride. She'd tidied up and made her bed and she showed me exactly where she was going to place her pillow and her teddy when they arrived.

'I want Honey on this side of the bed, so I can hug her!' she said.

'What a good idea,' I replied, stepping up close to the bed. As I did so I heard a rustle beneath my feet, and when I looked down I saw that I'd stepped on a chocolate bar wrapper. I bent down to pick it up, only to see several other wrappers that had evidently been pushed under the bed.

'Lucy, what are these doing here?'

'What do you mean?'

'I mean we don't allow eating in the bedroom, and do you remember the other rule?'

She shook her head.

'You have to ask before helping yourself in the kitchen. Do you remember I told you that?'

'But I didn't take them! I don't know how they got there.'

'Well perhaps you could have a think about it. I know they weren't there yesterday because I vacuumed the carpet and I'm sure I would have seen them.'

I didn't want to have a scene just before her family arrived and I certainly didn't want to upset Lucy by directly accusing her of telling fibs, although there didn't appear to be any other reasonable explanation. Maria had been at her grandmother's all day yesterday and, besides, I couldn't imagine she would have had anything to do with this – why would she?

There were four chocolate wrappers, all from a six-pack of biscuits that I always bought from the same supermarket. I hadn't opened the packet yet, so I'd easily be able to see if the biscuits had come from my cupboard.

'Anyway, what sort of biscuits are we making?' Lucy said. 'Do you know how to make custard creams? Do you like ginger snaps? My granny loves ginger snaps. She has them every day.'

I let Lucy change the subject but as she babbled on, asking question after question, I was thinking back and wondering about her eating habits. Was she picking at her main meal because she was having too many snacks and treats that I didn't know about? I needed to get through to Lucy the importance of telling the truth and sticking to the rules we had in place in the house, as they were there for her benefit, to help keep her healthy.

'Come on,' I said, when I could get a word in edgeways. 'Let's make the biscuits. They'll be ready just in time if we get started now.'

Inevitably, there was a wider issue bothering me. In order to help Lucy integrate back into her family it was crucial I knew fact from fiction. As it was, I was becoming increasingly uncertain about the truth of anything Lucy told me. I'd have to talk to her about this, when the time was right. She needed to be truthful. Jonathan and I, plus the therapists and social workers, needed to know exactly what we were dealing with in order to successfully help Lucy move back in with her family.

When the doorbell rang, Lucy shot from the kitchen to fling open the front door.

'Daddy!'

She launched herself excitedly at her dad then hugged her little sister Milly, who was almost the double of Lucy, but slightly shorter and with longer blonde hair. The boys gave their sister slightly self-conscious half-cuddles, as you might expect from nine-year-old boys, while Gemma and Wendy shuffled through the door last.

'Hi!' Lucy said, waving at them and turning away in virtually the same movement.

Dean introduced Jonathan and me to all the children and Lucy asked if she could show everyone her bedroom.

'Of course,' I said. 'I'll put the kettle on. Who would like tea? Or maybe a cold drink?'

While I took the drinks order Lucy asked her dad for her pillow and teddy. He looked at Wendy.

'You were sorting that, love, weren't you?'

'Was I? Oh I'm sorry; there was so much to do this morning, getting everyone ready. I didn't put them in. You'll get them next time, Lucy.'

'OK.'

I could almost feel Lucy's pain, because I had a pang in my own heart, thinking how disappointing this was.

'I've brought your new swimming costume though. I thought you'd want that.'

'Thanks,' Lucy muttered.

She stole a glance at me, but I didn't say a word about the fact I'd just bought Lucy a new swimsuit, or the story she'd told me about Wendy telling her to make do with her old one that didn't fit. Had Lucy told fibs about this, or was she just confused, having been living out of bags and in various different houses for weeks on end? I really wasn't sure, and once again I'd have to find the right moment to broach this topic, and do so very carefully.

All the children were chatty and friendly and there was

a good atmosphere in the kitchen when we had our drinks. There didn't appear to be any hostility between Gemma and Lucy: they seemed to just rub along, like kids do. The shortbread biscuits we'd made went down well and little Milly asked if Lucy could make some more, when she went home.

'Yes,' Lucy said. 'Is that OK, Wendy?'

Her stepmother looked horrified and for a moment I thought it was the mention of Lucy going home that made her stop and stare at the little girl.

'Wendy? I'm MUM to you. I don't want to hear you call me Wendy again!'

Gemma sniggered nervously and Dean shuffled in his seat and looked like he was about to speak, but Lucy jumped in first.

'Yes. I'm really sorry. I just forgot.'

'I expect it's been a little unsettling for Lucy,' Jonathan said, rising to his feet. 'Of course, Angela and I call you Wendy when we're talking to each other about arrangements and so on, and she's heard us use your name. I expect that's the reason.'

I could tell Jonathan was annoyed with Wendy for making a scene about this, but if you didn't know my husband like I did you would never have spotted his irritation. Jonathan spoke calmly yet firmly, and he gave the group a nod and a smile when he'd said his piece, as if to draw a line under it.

The family took Lucy out for lunch and she was buzzing when they dropped her back.

'We had a roast dinner and I had Yorkshire pudding. Do you like Yorkshire pudding? Can you make it? Can you show me how to make it? What did you have for your lunch? Can I phone my auntie?'

They didn't come in. I had been worried about how Lucy would react when she had to say goodbye to everyone, but she was as chatty as ever. It might have just been her way of coping, of course, but even so I was pleased to see she remained in a good mood and was upbeat about the visit.

I told Lucy she could use the phone in the living room so she could talk without being disturbed, but as usual she said she was happy to call her from the kitchen, while I got a few jobs done.

'Auntie Lisa? Yes it's Lucy here. Yes I saw them today. They all came. Sunday lunch? Everything was BRILLIANT! Yes, Gemma came too. You should have seen the size of the puddings! Wendy, I mean Mum, was fine. It was *so* good to see everyone. What? I'm going to be here for a bit longer. I like the foster carers. They're nice. Not long though. I'm going back home in August. Yes, I'll be going into Year Four, in my old school. No, not long. I can't wait. I miss everyone.'

I felt uncomfortable listening to Lucy talk like this. She was so desperate to go home and she was fixated on having a date to aim for. I had too much experience of fostering to share her optimism that she'd definitely be back for the start of the new school year. I wouldn't believe she was going home on any given date until I'd had it agreed, confirmed and signed off by Social Services, at the very least.

*Wendy could certainly throw a spanner in the works*, I thought. The way she spoke about Lucy so cruelly at the core meeting bothered me greatly. I couldn't imagine Wendy being in any hurry to take Lucy back in, but we'd have to wait and see. Perhaps the counselling would work wonders? I truly hoped so. Lucy's place was with her family, and she clearly loved her siblings and her daddy very much indeed. That was a great foundation to build on.

'Bless her,' Jonathan said later that evening, after Lucy and Maria had both gone to bed. 'I know she was full of beans when they brought her back but, really, it must have been very hard for Lucy, seeing the family driving off, all going home without her.'

'I know. I can't imagine how difficult it is.'

'I wished they'd remembered her teddy and pillow,' he added. 'That was such a shame.'

'Yes, poor Lucy. Can you think back to when you were eight years old? How would you have felt, in her shoes?'

Jonathan was the youngest of four brothers and the idea made him shudder.

'I can't imagine it. Devastated by the whole thing, I'm sure.'

'Same here, definitely. It's good that they came to visit, but at the same time it highlights how she's been, well, rejected. I hate to say that, but it's true.'

We both sighed. It was painful to think about it.

We also talked about Lucy's bike. It turned out it was in excellent condition and her dad told us he'd pumped up the tyres that morning so it was ready for her to ride. He also gave us a little toolbox that came with the bike when he bought it new, just a few months earlier, plus he'd brought over her smart and expensive-looking helmet.

'I wonder why she tried to pretend she didn't have a bike?'

Jonathan frowned. 'I think the lie had more to do with her hitting out at Wendy than anything else, don't you?'

She'd told me Wendy had said she was 'too naughty' and didn't deserve a bike, so I tended to agree with Jonathan.

'This feud with Wendy is deep-rooted,' I said. I felt like I was stating the obvious.

'It is indeed, and I suspect there's an awful lot we don't know.'

# 8

## *'I'll be very, very good when I go home'*

On the Monday I had a call about Lucy's schooling. It wasn't good news: the head at St Bede's had decided he could not offer Lucy a place because it seemed that Lucy was not statemented after all. Her previous school had explained that she was given support but it came from a classroom volunteer rather than a paid teaching assistant. The volunteer helped several children with below-average reading skills and there was a question mark over whether or not Lucy was dyslexic, but she had never been officially tested. Her LEA had confirmed there was nothing officially on file stating she had special educational needs, and Mr Morris-Butler had told Social Services that his school was already stretched and could not pay for the extra support Lucy needed without the funding they would have received from the LEA, if Lucy were statemented.

Jess gave me the news, and I could tell she was fed up and also very busy.

'Are you happy for me to put in a call to another school and make an appointment?' I asked.

'Of course. I'll come with you if I can. Thanks, Angela.'

I told her I'd also call our LEA to see if there was anything they could do, given the circumstances.

'Maybe they could make an exception and provide funding for Lucy without a statement?' I said. 'After all, it's only going to be short term, and if we went down the line of getting Lucy tested and statemented she'd miss even more school.'

'You're right, and I'm very grateful. Do you know, I'm taking on three more kids today? Crazy, isn't it? I've never been so frantic.'

I tried to set up a meeting with another primary school but unfortunately they turned us down on the spot after hearing Lucy needed support but had no statement. 'We'd love to help, but it's just not possible. All our classroom assistants are flat out and we simply don't have the budget to take on another member of staff, even on a part-time basis.'

I called our LEA and stated Lucy's case, explaining that by now she had already missed more than two months of school.

'I'm sorry but we are not responsible for any support Lucy may need. You need to contact the LEA in the county she came from.'

'I don't think they will help, because she isn't living in that area at the moment.'

'It's still their responsibility. They should be able to help you.'

I doubted it, and I was right. When I called them I was told it was not their responsibility either.

'Lucy is not living in the county and therefore we're not responsible. Without a statement we wouldn't pay for support even in our own county. I suggest that if she's living with you, you need to look into having her statemented and then your LEA will fund the support she needs.'

'But she's only going to be with us for a few months, and the statement will take time. It could be half term by the time it comes through. Then we'll have gone to all that trouble for what could amount to just a few weeks of support.'

'I'm very sorry, there's nothing we can do.'

I called Jess, who sounded distracted and exhausted, so I filled her in as quickly as possible.

'I'm at the hospital,' she said. 'One of my kids has been involved in an incident. I've got to go to the police station next.'

I could hear ambulance sirens wailing.

'I'm very sorry to hear that. Do you want to call me back when it's convenient?'

'It's OK. I've got it. Leave it with me, Angela. I'll talk to my manager and see what we can come up with. Maybe she can convince the LEA to make an exception for Lucy.'

'I think that's a good idea. Let me know if I can do anything to help.'

'I will. I'll keep you posted.'

When I told Lucy we were having trouble finding her a school place she shrugged.

'I don't mind doing the computer games. Anyway, I'll be back at my old school soon.'

I tried to look on the bright side. At least Lucy was willing to do some work at home. Things could be a lot worse; hearing about the child who had ended up in hospital and involved with the police made me count our blessings.

The following week went well. We went on a couple of good bike rides with Maria when she was in from school and Lucy spent hours doing history and maths challenges on the computer. I bought her a stack of educational books to work through. I sat with her as often as I could, and it was very obvious she struggled with reading.

'The words are jumping around,' she said. 'It's so ANNOYING! All the letters are jumbled up. I'm not doing that. I'm going on to the next page.'

Not being an expert in this field I allowed Lucy to focus on what she wanted to do and what she could do, rather than leaving her to struggle and get frustrated. However, this was something I would flag up with Social Services. If it was going to take a while for Lucy to be properly tested and statemented, I figured that at least her child psychologist should have as much information as possible to work on.

Bella called me to tell me that Wendy and Dean had given permission for Lucy to ride a horse at Diane's. Wendy made the call to the social worker, saying they had no objections at all and apologising for taking so long to get back with an answer – it had slipped their minds, apparently. When I told Lucy the good news she wanted to go to Diane's immediately.

'Let me phone her and see what she can do.'

'Can you phone now? Shall I get my shoes on?'

'Hang on, let me call her!'

As it happened Diane was more than happy to have Lucy over within the hour. Lucy was incredibly excited, so much so that she looked fit to burst by the time she was kitted up with an old riding hat that once belonged to Diane's daughter Clare, who was now thirteen, and some spare boots from another foster child who had outgrown them.

'Can I gallop?' Lucy asked Diane.

'No! Not yet. I'm going to just walk you around the yard for starters.'

'OK. What do I hold? Can I do this? How do I make her turn? Has she ever thrown anybody off? How do I get down? Has she won any medals? What are those for?'

As usual, the questioning went on and on. Diane was brilliant with Lucy and after giving her a lesson for about half an hour she agreed that Lucy could come early in the morning to help muck out.

'That's how you earn your rides,' she winked. 'Is that a deal?'

'It's a deal!' Lucy said. 'Yee-ha!'

Lucy went round to Diane's most mornings after that. She was always up at the crack of dawn, asking me to take her round before Maria had even gone to school. She offered to walk there herself if I was busy with Maria, but even though Diane only lived a few minutes away I wouldn't have let Lucy go there on her own at the age of eight. I always took her, and we often went on our bikes.

'If I were you I'd stay in bed,' Maria muttered to Lucy one morning. 'You're lucky. You should make the most of not having to get up for school. I would.'

Lucy looked baffled. Her idea of hell was to do nothing and stay in bed. She wanted to be on the go all the time.

We were still in limbo with the school situation, but things were ticking along well at home. Going to Diane's gave Lucy's day some structure, and the arrangement whereby the teenage boy Diane was fostering came and did work experience in the shop with Jonathan panned out very well indeed. Matty got on well with Jonathan and came up with some fresh ideas for promotions, which was the area he was interested in working in.

Lucy spoke to her family regularly on the phone and gave them all her news. She seemed very relaxed when talking to her granny or her aunties, but the phone calls home sometimes appeared to stress her out.

'I only wanted to talk to Daddy tonight but I had to talk to everyone!' she often complained. I always tried to leave Lucy to it when she was on the phone but she usually chose to follow me around and make the call from whichever room I was in. Sometimes she even sat on the arm of the chair I was sitting in; she didn't seem to have any idea of how to respect another person's personal space, and at the same time she wasn't bothered at all about having privacy to talk to her family. She chatted away freely, even if Maria was around.

To my ear, the tension between Lucy and her stepmother was always apparent: I could tell when she was talking to Wendy just by the tone of her voice, the things she said and the way she held herself. Her voice flattened, her head went down and she often became monosyllabic. By contrast, when Lucy spoke to her dad she perked up and never failed to sound excited and animated. She told him in detail what she'd been doing and how much she was missing him and looking forward to coming home. She was always happy to talk to her brothers and sister too, but it was hit-and-miss with Gemma. Their conversations usually seemed a bit stilted, and more often than not it sounded to me like Lucy couldn't wait to get off the phone, or talk to her dad or brothers and sister instead – but mostly only her dad.

'Wendy has been decorating the lounge,' Lucy told me one day, after a phone call home. 'She said she's got new pictures on the wall. When am I going home?'

For a moment I thought she meant when could she move back in with the family, but thankfully she was only asking about a home visit. I'd been told by Bella that Wendy and Dean had decided it was best if Lucy didn't visit until they'd all had a few therapy sessions at the Child and Family centre. It seemed sensible, the idea being that progress would have been made and the visit home would be more likely to be a success. Looking further ahead, if the visits home worked out well the next step would be for Lucy to stay the night, as previously discussed.

'I'm not exactly sure when you can go home,' I said to Lucy tactfully. 'I think it will be in a few weeks – not too long!'

'Oh,' she said, sounding disappointed.

She told me her daddy's birthday was coming up and she wanted to go home for the party.

'The party?'

'Yes, Daddy told me they're having a party. Daddy said I could go. I'll be good, you know. I'll be good for you and I'll be very, very good when I go home.'

'I'm glad to hear it, Lucy.'

I smiled but I felt uneasy. Had Dean made a promise he might not be able to keep? I hoped not, because the last thing Lucy needed was to have a carrot dangled in front of her and then see it snatched away. I told Lucy we'd need to wait and hear when the date of the party was, and see if it was possible for her to visit on that day.

'But I can go?'

'I don't want to make any promises, Lucy. Let's see what the plans are.'

She kicked a chair and walked out of the room saying, 'It's not fair if I can't go. It's just not fair!'

Unfortunately, after various meetings and letters, Jess's manager had failed to convince our LEA to fund the support Lucy needed in school and so we were back to square one. Jess was about to go on annual leave for two weeks and so I offered to take over again and do what I could to get Lucy the help she needed in the classroom.

'By all means,' Jess said. 'You have our full backing. It seems the LEAs in both counties are happy to pass the buck on to each other, and meanwhile Lucy's education is suffering.'

'Quite. I'll have a think about where we can go from here. Leave it with me. I'll do my best.'

'I know you will: you always do. We need more Angelas in the fostering service!'

I was very grateful for Jess's kind words. Encouragement from a caring social worker was just what I needed after hearing the disappointing news. I felt supported and valued, and this energised me. Weeks had slipped by and the end of the school year was now less than two months away, but that was not going to put me off. I was determined that Lucy's learning was going to be supported as it should be.

'I'll get her into a school and I'll get her the help she needs. I won't take no for an answer,' I told Jonathan that evening.

He thought about this for a moment, raised his eyebrows and smiled.

'Isn't that what you said to me all those years ago, when you first wanted to get into fostering?'

I laughed, albeit a little wearily. I do have a very determined streak and when I set my mind to something I like to see it through. However, the truth is that Jonathan didn't need much persuasion when I first suggested to him that we could become foster carers, back in the eighties. An advert in the local paper caught my eye and I called the number to find out more. Jonathan supported me all the way as he could see how interested I was, although I must admit that we both expected fostering was something we'd do for a relatively short time, maybe until we started our own family. We never imagined for one moment that we'd end up fostering dozens and dozens of children over three decades. Nor did we anticipate we would never have children of our own, because of fertility problems. Nevertheless, neither of us ever looked back, and it's the same to this day.

# 9

### *'I'm allowed to go to the party!'*

The Child and Family sessions were to be held in a modern council building not far from Lucy's old school. For the first session Wendy and Dean were both to be in attendance. Bella came to our house to give us the details, and she explained to Lucy that the family therapist would talk to all three of them together. She also said that Lucy would sometimes have sessions on her own, either with the family therapist or with her psychologist.

'Will I see Daddy every time I go?'

'I can't promise that,' Bella said. 'You'll certainly see him at the first session, and after that I think it depends when the slots are available and how the sessions are organised. I expect that sometimes your daddy will go to a session on his own, or with your stepmum, and he might have to go when it fits in with his work.'

'I don't like calling her stepmum, I prefer to call her Wendy,' she said sulkily. 'Can you just say Wendy? Anyway,

*I* can go any time. It's not like I'm at school! Can't I just fit in with Daddy?'

My heart went out to her, as it did so many times.

'Let's wait and see what's offered,' Bella said gently. 'It's up to the Child and Family centre.'

As usual, Lucy's focus was entirely on her father. Seeing him was her number one priority, and I thought that if she were told to walk over hot coals to see a glimpse of him for just a few moments, she'd have done so willingly.

Lucy asked if she could go to her daddy's birthday party, and Bella told her that she would have to wait and see.

'I'm sure Daddy or Wendy will let you know,' she said.

Bella and I swapped glances. I knew she felt the same way I did: we wanted Lucy to be invited, but we didn't want to interfere and cause any unnecessary trouble. Wendy and Dean had to make this call, and I really hoped they would. When I saw Bella out I mentioned that Lucy had also asked Jonathan and me to avoid the words stepmum and step-mother, a request we tried to comply with when possible. Bella said she agreed with this tactic, as there was no point in antagonising Lucy every time Wendy was mentioned.

On the morning of the first Child and Family session Lucy seemed very excited. I picked her up from mucking out the horses and she was raring to go, getting herself showered and dressed in record time. Then she sat waiting in the kitchen half an hour before we were due to leave.

'I'll be very, very good,' she told me. 'I won't make Wendy cross with me.'

'I'm pleased to hear you're going to be well behaved, sweetheart. By the way, have you remembered she prefers you not to call her Wendy?'

'Yes. I need to call her Mum. I don't like calling her Mum, but I will. Mum, Mum, Mum.'

Lucy drummed her knuckles on her skull as she said, 'Mum, Mum Mum.'

While Lucy was in her session Jonathan and I sat outside the Child and Family centre and I called a third primary school on my mobile, asking if I could make an appointment to see the head.

'I'm afraid she's off sick.'

I explained what it was about and asked if there was another person I could see in the head's absence, such as the deputy head.

'No, I'm afraid not.'

'It's actually very urgent.'

'I'm very sorry but you will have to call back when the head returns.'

'I see. Do you know when she is coming back to work?'

'No, she's off sick.'

'Yes, I understand. Perhaps I can leave my phone number and you can let me know when she is back?'

'Actually, it's best if you call us back. I'm not here every day because I job share and I can't guarantee the other secretary will get the message. If I were you, I'd try again in a couple of days.'

I was fuming when I put the phone down and I forced myself to count to ten. Jonathan and I have always been very focused on supporting every child in our care with their education, to make sure they get the best foundation in life. We are very vigilant about attendance and lateness. For instance, if we suspect a child is feigning illness to get a day off we don't let them get away with it, despite the fact it usually creates trouble for us, having to negotiate and cajole an unwilling child. Similarly, if a child misses the bus or is going to be late through no fault of their own we always do our best to help them, giving them lifts and explaining the issue to the school. When we take them out for medical appointments and so on we make sure we return them to the classroom as quickly as possible, so they don't miss out on lessons. In short, we value education and are very aware how precious it is. To hear this secretary suggest I call back in a 'couple of days' was absolutely infuriating.

'What if the head is actually back tomorrow and then I don't call for another day or two?' I vented to Jonathan. 'What is the point in that? That would be even more of Lucy's education she'll be missing out on!'

'What are you going to do now?' Jonathan knows very well how to handle me in this type of situation. Instead of joining in with my complaint and stoking my anger he steered me towards focusing on finding a solution. I told him I was going to call the education welfare officer at the LEA.

'Good idea,' he said.

There was no answer at first but I kept trying until I finally got through to someone.

'Sorry, the education welfare officer is out.'

I asked for the name of the officer.

'Can I leave a message for him to call me when he returns?'

'Of course.'

I left my number and explained I was fostering an eight-year-old girl who urgently needed a school place, as she had already missed approximately two months of school. Nobody called me back. When I called again I got an answerphone, and so I left a message. Still nobody called me back.

When Lucy came out of her therapy session she practically bounced over to us.

'Guess what? I'm going home next weekend!'

'Going home next weekend?'

'Yes! It's Daddy's birthday, remember? And I'm allowed to go to the party!'

'Daddy's birthday? And there's a party?'

'Yes. Wendy has invited all the family over. I can't stay the night because there's no room for me. But I'm allowed to go to the party!'

It was still my understanding, from various conversations and meetings with the social workers, that Lucy would only begin to spend weekends back home when she was much closer to moving back permanently. I wondered where she had got the idea from that there was 'no room', but I wasn't left to think for long because Lucy told me that Milly now slept in the bunk bed with Gemma, and Wendy had got rid of the small fold-up bed that used to be on the floor, as Milly had outgrown it.

'It's OK though. They're building an extension on the house. Wendy said they need more space. When the extension is done there'll be an extra bedroom upstairs, the boys will have a bigger room and there will be another room downstairs, at the back of the kitchen. There'll be plenty of room for me!'

Wendy and Dean had already left – apparently they had to dash – and so I told Lucy I'd phone them to talk about the arrangements for the party. I'd call Jess too, to keep her in the loop.

Lucy cheered as she buckled herself in the car. It was the first time she hadn't created a fuss over the seat belt, as normally she made out she couldn't fasten it or asked why she had to bother wearing it.

'Wendy said I've got to behave myself and I will. I promised. I'm going to make Daddy a card.'

Back home, after settling Lucy down with some paper and pens to make the birthday card, I called Wendy, who confirmed in rather a business-like way that Lucy was invited to spend the day at home the following Sunday.

'Are you able to bring her over and her father will bring her back?'

'Yes, that's fine. Maria is out that day. Jonathan and I can both drive Lucy to you.'

'Great. We'll see you then.'

'Great. She's looking forward to it.'

'Well, we were meant to have a few sessions before the visit but I suppose we'll have to stick with this now.'

'How do you mean?'

'I told Dean it was too early to have Lucy over, but you know how soft he is. I just hope she behaves.'

When the day of the party came Lucy was beside herself with excitement and anticipation. I'd helped her make some chocolate muffins to take with her, as she said they were her daddy's favourite. She'd spent all of her pocket money on a poster of her dad's favourite football team. The birthday card she made was incredibly sweet. She'd drawn a picture of her and her daddy holding hands under a rainbow and two bright suns.

'I want to write "I love you and hope your birthday is a very happy, sunshiny day",' she said. 'Can you write that on a piece of paper so I can copy it?'

'You have a go first on some scrap paper,' I encouraged.

'No, because the thing is, I want it to be perfect.'

'OK, well how do you *think* you spell "happy" and "birthday"?'

'Can you just tell me? I'll only get it wrong.'

'No, have a go.'

Lucy told me her hand was aching and she didn't want to waste all her energy on writing words out wrongly and having to re-do them.

'OK,' I sighed, realising I wasn't going to win this one. 'This is how to write your message. Why don't you copy it out in pencil first and then go over it with the coloured pens? That will help you remember how to spell the words.'

'That's a good idea!'

Lucy had no problem with 'wasting energy' when it

came to copying and she spent ages going over the pencil writing in lots of different colours, but clearly she lacked confidence in her spelling skills.

*I'm going to secure her a school place if it's the last thing I do*, I thought. *Lucy can't afford to lose any more of her education.*

I thought about who I could call to rally support and I resolved to try the head of Social Services and the Child and Family psychologist, to enlist their help. It was totally unacceptable that Lucy was being allowed to founder like this, simply because of her family circumstances and the fact the foster service was so stretched she'd had to travel to another county to be cared for.

Lucy chatted non-stop all the way to the party. It seemed there was no topic she didn't want to discuss, no question she wanted to leave unanswered.

'Why do you listen to that radio station? Who's your favourite singer? Do you like Oasis, because my daddy does. He tries to play the guitar but he's rubbish! Do you play a musical instrument? Once I played a trumpet at school. Can you play the piano?'

It was a pleasure chatting to Lucy when she was in this mood. We've had plenty of surly kids in the back of the car and endured many awkward silences and frosty-faced journeys in our time. By contrast Lucy was fun and entertaining, so we didn't mind that there was no let-up in her chatter.

However, once or twice she said things that didn't fully

ring true. For instance, at one point she said Wendy had told her 'exactly' what to wear for the party, but I'd spoken to Wendy myself. The truth was that Wendy had once again asked Lucy not to wear any of her Nike clothing, as the other kids would be jealous and it may cause trouble. She hadn't told Lucy what she *could* wear, and I reminded Lucy that she'd picked out the dungarees and short-sleeved shirt she had on. 'She told me to,' she said, but the dungarees were new and Wendy didn't even know I'd bought them for Lucy just the day before.

I'd been reading up on the topic of lies ever since Lucy's fibs about her bike and swimsuit. The advice was to not say anything immediately, but to pick your moment some time after the event and talk to the child in general terms about how lies make you feel. That way it's not confrontational or accusatory, and there is more chance of the child listening to you and taking on board what you are saying, rather than coming back with excuses or more lies. This made a lot of sense to me and I'd been waiting for the right time to broach the subject.

'I can't wait to tell you *all* about the party afterwards!' Lucy said, and that's when I saw my chance.

'I'm looking forward to hearing all about it. By the way, you know you can talk to me about anything, don't you? You can be honest with me, and with Jonathan, and if there is anything at all you want to talk about, about the party or anything else, we are here to listen.'

'Can I?' Lucy said.

'Of course, as long as you are telling the truth you can

tell us whatever you like, and we are here to listen and help you. The only thing we don't like to hear is any fibs, because if anybody isn't truthful with us it hurts us here.'

I pointed to my heart, following the advice I'd read in a fostering and childcare book, specifically aimed at Lucy's age group.

She nodded, looked beyond me, out of the front windscreen and asked, 'Are we nearly there yet?'

'Not far!' Jonathan said. 'Oh look, there's the estate.'

The family lived on the edge of a very big housing estate. Lucy tried to direct us but we took a couple of wrong turns before we finally arrived at the house, which was on the end of a large crescent of properties facing a play area that looked well-used and in need of revamping.

'We've got the biggest garden of everyone!' Lucy said proudly. 'Daddy's so clever.'

The parking area was up the side of Lucy's house and we could see there was plenty of land at the back. There certainly seemed to be room for an extension, as Lucy had described. She unfastened her seat belt the second the car stopped and was at the front door in a flash. Her father answered, and she flung herself at him.

'Daddy! Daddy! Daddy!'

'Hello, princess. How are you?'

'Happy to see you! Happy birthday!'

Lucy turned to look at Jonathan and me as we walked up the path. She'd left the muffins and her dad's card and present on the back seat of the car in her hurry to get to him, but I'd picked them up.

'I nearly forgot, thank you, Angela,' she said politely, taking them off me and giving me a little smile.

Dean invited Jonathan and me inside. We didn't want to intrude but Lucy said she'd like us to see Dean open his present and so we said we'd pop in for a few minutes. There was a buzz in the air and all the children were milling around. All four were polite and friendly, as they had been last time we met, and Milly told me how they'd all helped to blow up the balloons that were festooned around the room.

'They've done me proud!' Dean said.

'They have indeed,' Jonathan said. 'The decorations look fantastic!'

Dean raved about his football poster and the card Lucy had made. 'I'll put it in pride of place,' he said.

Lucy gave the biggest smile I'd ever seen, but as Dean went to place the card on the mantelpiece her little face fell.

'Where are the photos?'

'Which ones?'

'You know, all our school pictures that were on the wall, there?'

Wendy appeared, said a brisk hello to us and answered on Dean's behalf.

'Oh, they were old. I've done a bit of decorating, d'you like it? I got some new pictures, remember I told you about the decorating?'

Lucy nodded obediently as she looked to the wall Wendy was pointing at, on the opposite side of the room. The new pictures were a mixture of family photos, all in matching frames. The largest one was of Wendy in a silver dress and Dean in a tuxedo. It looked like it had been taken at a Christmas party. Next there was an A4-sized school photo of Gemma, followed by a lovely shot of the twins posing either side of Milly, out in the countryside somewhere. Finally there was a group shot of all seven members of the family, lined up in front of a church. This was in the smallest frame, about half the size of Gemma's school photo.

'Baby Tia's christening,' Lucy commented as she looked at this last picture. There was a note of disappointment in her voice and I stepped towards Lucy and the photograph.

'What a beautiful baby,' I said, my eyes drawn to the pretty little bundle who was dressed in a long, satin christening gown with a matching bonnet.

'Yes, she's my sister's youngest,' Wendy said proudly. 'Proper little smasher she is. I'm her godmother.'

I looked along the line-up. Scanning left to right I saw Josh, Liam, Milly and Gemma grinning broadly for the camera, followed by Dean and then Wendy, who was holding the baby in her arms. Her left elbow was lifted high, slightly obscuring the face of the little blonde girl next to her: Lucy. No wonder she was disappointed. Lucy was stuck on the end like an afterthought, and I had to look twice to be sure it was even her.

We didn't stay for the tea that was offered. Wendy told me they had eighteen people coming over and it was obviously she wanted to get on with the party food and finish the preparations. Dean told us he would drop Lucy back later, around six o'clock. She smiled when he said this.

'Will it just be you driving me?'

He shrugged. 'I'm not sure. If anyone else wants to come, that's fine by me.'

I imagined Lucy would have liked to have some time alone with her daddy, but I don't think Dean thought about that. He seemed like a very straightforward and decent kind of man – a 'what you see is what you get' type of person. Perhaps he wasn't as emotionally tuned in to Lucy as another person may be, but he clearly loved his daughter and was doing his best in difficult circumstances.

Jonathan and I both felt Lucy's pain about that photograph and we carried it with us out of the house.

'Do you think Wendy was just thoughtless, or did she do that deliberately?' I asked.

'I think the fact you are even asking that question says a lot. We don't know Wendy well enough, do we? And with Lucy's tendency to tell fibs, it's very difficult to work out what is really going on.'

'You're right. It's a very tricky situation. It'll be interesting to see how today goes. Fingers crossed.'

We tried to be optimistic and we talked about the positive things. The general atmosphere in the house had been good and all the siblings – including Gemma – were in an upbeat mood and seemed pleased to see Lucy and welcome her home. The house itself was tidy, clean and comfortable, and Wendy was clearly going to a lot of trouble to put on the birthday gathering for Dean. Compared to the many other family homes we'd visited of kids in our care, this one seemed very functional.

'But that's worrying in itself,' Jonathan said thoughtfully.
'What is?'

'The fact everything seemed functional. Or not dysfunctional. I'm still at a loss to really understand how things got so bad Lucy had to move out.'

Move out was a polite way of putting it, I said. I was feeling very protective towards Lucy and that christening image was still burning in my mind.

Jonathan made a good point. None of the typical problems we'd encountered with other families were present in Lucy's case. This was not a family grappling with drug or alcohol addiction, extreme poverty or mental health traumas, to name just some of the common issues we've contended with over the years. Wendy and Dean were raising four other children together, holding down jobs and running a home. For her part Lucy was a healthy, loving little girl who wanted nothing more but to live back with her family, and to belong. She was not afraid of anyone; she wanted more contact with her family, not less.

'Well, I'm sure everything's going to be fine today,' I said as we arrived home. I was trying to remain positive, and there was a lot to be optimistic about. 'The main thing is that Lucy wants to move home more than anything in the world. She's going to be on her best behaviour at the party, I'm sure. Wendy obviously just wants everybody to have a good time on Dean's birthday. She certainly won't want any incidents. I can't imagine anything will go wrong, not today.'

Jonathan sighed and gave a little laugh.

'If only life were that simple! I know you're only saying that because you desperately want things to work out for Lucy, but I'm afraid we both know the truth.'

I looked at Jonathan and reluctantly acknowledged the sense of his words. As usual, he had his feet firmly on the ground and his instincts were finely tuned.

'Let's face it – *anything* could happen,' he said ominously.

I felt a pang in my chest and looked at my watch. Waiting for Lucy to come home was going to seem like days rather than hours.

# 10

## *'I just can't cope with her'*

The whole family came to drop Lucy back to our house after the birthday party. I expressed surprise about this as I imagined the last thing they would all want to do after such a busy day was to spend two hours in the car.

'We like to stick together,' Wendy said firmly. 'Besides, I like to know exactly what is going on.'

She said this with a slightly accusatory tone in her voice and didn't seem very happy.

'How was the party?' I asked. I'd been on pins all day, desperately hoping nothing would go wrong. More than anything else, I wanted Lucy to return with a smile on her face and some hope in her heart. She looked slightly subdued as she stood huddled with her siblings in the doorway, but hopefully that was just because she didn't want to say goodbye to her family. She was probably tired too, I thought.

All the children began chattering at once. It sounded like they'd had a lovely afternoon playing games and eating cake, and Dean said he'd had a 'brilliant day', surrounded by family and friends.

'I'm going to slip out to the pub for a quiet pint with the boys when we get home,' he said, giving Jonathan a wink. 'Think that will top the day off nicely!'

Wendy rolled her eyes and looked even less happy than she did before.

I thanked Dean for driving Lucy back and she gave everyone a cuddle, including Wendy. It was a slightly awkward hug and Wendy didn't crack a smile, but at least it was better than nothing.

'Thanks Lou-Lou. That's a good girl.'

I got the impression Dean had asked Lucy to make sure she gave Wendy a hug and that's what Jonathan thought too. I also happened to notice that Gemma was wearing a Nike T-shirt, which I thought was odd after everything Wendy had said about designer labels. I didn't say anything, of course. I wouldn't dream of it, and in any case Wendy was looking decidedly irritated now.

'I'll ring you later,' she said, ushering the kids back to the car.

I said OK and nodded in agreement, though I sensed trouble.

'There are a few things I need to talk to you about, Angela. Are you in this evening?'

'Yes, we're not going anywhere.'

'Fine. I'll talk to you later.'

The way Wendy spoke filled me with dread: she might

just as well have thrown a bucket of ice-cold water over me. My mood plummeted, my body tensed and I felt stung.

Lucy gave her daddy one last hug and waved her family off. It seemed heartbreaking she had to go through this process of saying goodbye and being left behind at our house. It would surely have been easier for Lucy if the other kids didn't tag along in the van. She watched it disappear around the corner and thankfully didn't seem upset.

'So, how was it?' I asked.

'Brilliant!' Lucy smiled. 'Daddy LOVED the muffins. We had sausage rolls. I love sausage rolls. Daddy let me have two pieces of cake. We played hide and seek. I saw the drawings of the new extension. It's going to be AMAZING, Daddy said. He promised I can help him do some jobs.'

Lucy paused for breath and said sweetly, 'I miss him already.'

We went into the kitchen as I was still clearing up after our Sunday dinner and she carried on talking. 'What do you do on your birthday? When is it? Gemma's got the next birthday in our family. She wants a pony! I told her all about the horses. Can I go on the computer? Wendy said . . .' Lucy paused again and quickly corrected herself. 'Mum said it sounds like I'm having the life of Riley. Who's Riley?'

I told her it meant it sounded like she was having a good life. I know the phrase has critical undertones, suggesting someone is having it easy, but I avoided mentioning this, of course. There was definitely trouble looming with Wendy. She had obviously taken objection to something that had happened that day. I didn't want to ask Lucy any leading questions and she didn't offer any clues, but I'd find out soon enough. I was waiting anxiously for Wendy's call, and I wasn't looking forward to what she had to say.

Lucy was in bed when the phone rang later in the evening.

'I'll get straight to the point, Angela. Lucy was very difficult today, and I mean VERY difficult.'

'I'm sorry to hear that. I thought everything had gone well. She certainly seemed to have enjoyed herself, and everyone looked happy enough when you dropped her home.'

'Well, yes. I didn't want to spoil the day for Dean, and that's why I'm phoning now, while he's down the pub. He didn't see what she was like as he was so busy with our guests, but Lucy behaved like a spoilt little madam all day. I'm not sure I can have her over again for a whole day like that. I don't think it's fair on the other kids, and I just can't cope with her.'

I was very surprised and disappointed to hear this, but I felt a little sceptical too. How could Dean have failed to notice if Lucy behaved like a 'spoilt little madam' the whole time she was there? And how come Dean and Lucy had both used the word 'brilliant' to describe the day. I'd noticed this and hadn't got this wrong. On the other hand, Dean was probably distracted by his guests, and I couldn't always rely on what Lucy told me. I was prepared to listen to Wendy, and she was more than prepared to talk. She wasted no time in listing all of Lucy's faults and failings.

'She broke Gemma's alarm clock. She said it was an

accident but I don't believe her. She bragged about the horses to make Gemma jealous and now I'm being nagged to death about letting her have a pony and riding lessons. She interrupted me every time I tried to have a conversation. She would only eat crisps and cake. Need I go on? I can do without it, I really can. She even came and stood right in between me and Dean when he was trying to say thanks to everyone for coming. She stood on my foot on purpose. It was embarrassing. She really knows how to cause trouble. She's a proper little madam, and she's spoilt.'

I wasn't sure how to handle this. My heart wanted me to scream, 'Wendy, you are talking about a vulnerable little girl who has gone through major disruption and needs to be shown love and understanding. Her self-esteem is on the floor and she craves attention from her daddy. Maybe she has broken something, but how can you be so sure? Maybe you need to consider it was an accident and Lucy is doing her best to please you all? Can't you see she could have stepped on your foot by accident, simply because she wanted to be close to her daddy?'

My head told me to say the bare minimum and remain impartial and professional. Perhaps Lucy *had* caused trouble on purpose. It wasn't beyond the realms of possibility.

'Thanks for passing this on,' I said evenly and politely. 'I can assure you that Jonathan and I are doing our best to teach Lucy to be well mannered, to eat properly and to be kind and well behaved. I'm sorry to hear about the clock. I'll talk to Lucy about what happened.'

Wendy said she should pay for a new one out of her pocket money.

'I'll talk to Lucy,' I repeated calmly, not committing to anything before I'd heard both sides of the story, and refusing to match Wendy's aggravated tone.

'Thanks very much indeed, Angela,' she said. With a huff she added, 'I knew you'd understand. I don't know how you put up with her!'

I brought the conversation to an end. However Wendy chose to interpret what I'd said, I'd been very careful not to accept her version of events or make any promises about what Lucy must do next.

The next morning I sat Lucy down and told her that I'd had a call from Wendy, who was unhappy about her behaviour at the party.

'Why? What did I do wrong? *She* was mean to *me*. I was too hot, you know, and Wendy wouldn't let me take my shirt off, even though I had a vest top underneath. It was boiling. She was horrible. I bet she never told you that! And Gemma was wearing Puma shorts and a Nike top when Wendy said nobody was allowed labels! I think she had it in for me. I think she wanted to wind me up!'

I focused on the broken clock, the alleged interrupting and the standing on Wendy's foot while Dean was talking to his guests, plus the issue with the food and the supposed 'bragging' about the horses.

'What broken clock? I didn't even know Gemma had a clock!'

Lucy dismissed all the other criticisms too, claiming she had no idea she'd interrupted all the time, or stood on Wendy's foot. She was adamant she ate the same food as the other kids and that they all swapped stories about what they've been up to, so how could she be accused of bragging?

'Josh and Liam have started karate. Milly's doing disco dancing. Gemma's in a marching band. She went on about that for AGES. So how come they can talk about their hobbies and I can't? It's not fair.'

Lucy was red in the face and looked very angry. She kicked a cupboard and I had to tell her to stop and take a deep breath.

'I HATE Wendy!' she said, balling her fists. 'She's even WORSE than horrible old Val!'

I told her to take deep breaths and try to stay calm and I suggested that she should stop shouting and to sit quietly for a moment. She ignored me and stomped around the kitchen repeating, 'I HATE WENDY!'

I tried to ignore her in the hope she'd burn herself out. I must admit, after listening to what Lucy had to say, my gut feeling was that Wendy seemed to have blown things out of proportion. I didn't think for one moment that Lucy had behaved impeccably every minute she was at the party, but was she really so bad that Wendy – a mother of a girl the same age as Lucy and stepmother to three other young children – seriously couldn't cope? It didn't really add up to me. Most of it sounded like typical stuff a child might do, especially at a party. The broken clock was potentially an issue, but to my mind nothing else seemed to warrant Wendy's extreme reaction and conclusion.

When I paid her no attention Lucy eventually stormed out of the room and said she was going to her bedroom.

I was doing some ironing and still thinking things through when Lucy appeared at the living-room door about twenty minutes later.

'Sorry,' she said, looking very sheepish.

'Sorry?'

'Yes, I'm sorry. I lied.'

'You lied?'

'Yes. I lied about the clock. I might have broken it. I didn't meant to, but I was trying to make the bell go off and the dial came loose in my hand. I tried to put it back on – it looked like it could be fixed back on – but Gemma took it off me and told me not to bother. I didn't think she was that worried. She just put it back on her bedside table and we went back to the party together.'

'Thank you for telling the truth,' I said. 'I'm very pleased you've told the truth.'

Lucy took a step closer. 'Can I have a cuddle?'

I wrapped my arms around Lucy and praised her again.

'If the clock is broken then we need to offer to replace it,' I said. 'Even if it was an accident, the right thing is to offer to get Gemma a new one.'

Lucy nodded.

'Can I go on the computer now?'

'Yes, in a minute. As you're being very honest with me,

Lucy, I'd just like to check with you, is there anything else you need to tell me about the party?'

She shook her head.

'No. I liked it. I didn't do anything else wrong, I swear. I don't know why Wendy phoned you like that. It wasn't like that. She's made up so many stories! I tried really, really hard to behave myself. We all had a good time.'

'Are you absolutely sure there is nothing else you need to tell me? You won't be in trouble and we can sort things out, but only if I know the truth. I'm pleased with you for being honest.'

Lucy shook her head.

'Is there any chance that you were trying to annoy anyone or that you did any of the things Wendy said you did, the things that annoyed her?'

'No. I swear. No, I didn't.'

'What about the interrupting? Or the standing on her foot?'

Lucy grinned a little mischievously.

'Well, maybe I did interrupt a little bit. But I didn't *mean* to annoy anyone. I didn't stand on Wendy's foot on purpose though. I definitely didn't. I wouldn't do that.'

'OK, thanks again for being honest. Do you think it would be a good idea to say sorry to Wendy for the things you did do?'

'I suppose so.'

'Good. I'm sure Wendy will appreciate you being truthful, and hopefully next time you see her you can get off to a better start because there won't be any old arguments hanging over you.'

'Yes. OK. I'll say sorry.'

'Thank you, Lucy. We'll call Wendy later. Let's get you a programme set up, shall we? I thought you could have a go at the history CD-ROM today. It's a really good one. Do you know anything about the Romans?

Lucy struggled to concentrate or settle at anything that afternoon. She got fed up of the CD-ROM after about ten minutes, said Julius Caesar was 'boring' and asked if she could do something else.

'Can I help you, Angela? What about the garden? Is there anything I can do? I'm bored. Can I go to Diane's? Can you show me how to make this? What's this for?'

I was trying to get all the ironing done and I had several little sewing jobs to do, like replacing buttons and shortening a pair of trousers.

'Can you teach me how to do that? I want to learn to sew. Can I make a pair of trousers too?'

As ever, Lucy's enthusiasm for being busy with her hands knew no bounds.

'I didn't make the trousers,' I explained. 'I bought them in a sale and they're too long so I'm taking them up.'

'Oh. I bet I could do that for you. Can you show me?'

I set Lucy up with a needle and thread and showed her how to sew on a button.

'Do that to begin with. You need to start with the simple things and work your way up. That's what my mum taught me.'

'Is your mum good at sewing?'

'Brilliant. Much better than me. She can also knit and crochet and she does embroidery too.'

'Will she teach me?'

'I'm sure she would. We'll ask her.'

I was thinking to myself that I'd ask Mum sooner rather than later, in fact, as I was looking for as much help as I could get in keeping Lucy occupied. Mum was away visiting a friend that week, but once she was back I'd invite her over. She was also very good at playing board games and cards with the kids and always had much more patience than me when teaching them the rules, or when games went on for ages. Over the years she even taught some of our foster children how to play chess to a really good level.

Jonathan and I decided to take Lucy and Maria swimming in the early evening, after the shop was shut. Lucy did more than twenty lengths and I was worn out trying to keep up with her. After we got home and had something to eat Maria was happy to watch a bit of TV and just relax in the living room with us, but Lucy seemed to find it impossible to sit down or concentrate on a programme for more than five minutes. She began to pace around and stare at each of us in turn, as if trying to provoke a reaction. Maria snapped first, inevitably.

'For God's sake! Stop staring at me!'

'I'm not!'

'Yes you are! Jonathan, can you tell her to stop staring at me?'

'Lucy, please don't stare. It's not nice. None of us like it. Why don't you relax and watch television?'

'I don't feel like watching television.'

'Well why don't you find something else to do?'

'Like what? Will you play this with me?'

She took our game of Monopoly down from the shelf at the back of the room.

'No, it's too late to start that now. A game of Monopoly can go on for hours.'

'Oh, can it? Can I phone my granny then?'

'Yes, of course you can. You can use the phone in the kitchen if you like. Do you remember how to use it? Remember, her number is on the pad next to the phone.'

'Yes, I can do it.'

Lucy chatted to her granny for about fifteen minutes and seemed to perk up.

'Can I call Daddy now?'

I said that she could but suggested I would make the call and talk to Wendy first, as she was waiting to hear back about the clock and the other issues she'd flagged up. Ideally I wanted to leave this until the next day because I was tired and in no rush to talk to Wendy, but I couldn't avoid it if Lucy wanted to call home.

'Do I have to talk to Wendy?' Lucy asked, eyes narrowing.

*I know how you feel*, I thought.

'I think it would be a good idea if you explained what happened to the clock and apologised for that. Also, don't forget she likes you to call her Mum, will you?'

Lucy rolled her eyes but agreed.

Wendy was polite and friendly to me on the phone. I said we would take a small amount out of Lucy's pocket money each week to pay for a new clock for Gemma.

'Thank you!' Wendy said. She sounded almost triumphant. 'I'm glad you've got through to Lucy. She needs to know how much trouble she causes. Thanks for supporting me.'

'It's right that Lucy pays for the clock, as she broke it,' I said. 'I'll put Lucy on now. I'll speak to you soon.'

As I stepped out of the kitchen I heard Lucy apologising.

'I'm sorry for annoying you. I'm sorry about the clock. I didn't realise I was so annoying. I won't do it again, I promise. I don't mean it. I'll try my hardest. Can I talk to my daddy?'

By the time Lucy had finished on the phone it was time for her to get ready for bed. Maria had already gone up, and I asked Lucy to please be quiet as she got herself ready and used the bathroom.

'I don't want to go to bed.'

Lucy stared at me.

'Oh, don't you? Well that's a shame, because it's bedtime. And if you don't get to sleep at a reasonable time you'll be too tired to muck out the horses early in the morning.'

'I won't. I always get up. I never oversleep.'

'I'm not saying you won't get up, or that you'll oversleep. But you will be tired. You need your sleep, to make the most of the day tomorrow.'

'What's the point? I don't have to do anything after I've been to the stables. I don't have to go to school. Who cares if I'm tired? I don't.'

Jonathan was reading the paper, patiently waiting for a moment to intervene.

'Lucy, the fact is that you are eight years old and we are responsible for looking after you,' he said. 'You must do as we ask. We're not asking you to go to bed for the good of our health. You need your sleep and we are taking care of your needs. Now please go up and get ready for bed. It's been a long day and we're all tired.'

'I'm NOT TIRED.'

Lucy stared at Jonathan and then at me. I picked up a magazine and started doing a word-search puzzle.

'What are you doing?' she asked accusingly.

'A word search.'

'I mean, why aren't you telling me off?'

'Well, to be honest, we've told you what we want you to do and we've told you why. I have nothing else to say. What's the point in repeating myself?'

'But you can't just leave me standing here while you do your stupid puzzles and read the paper!'

'Lucy, Angela loves doing word-search puzzles. She doesn't think they're stupid, in fact she finds them very relaxing.'

After about half an hour Jonathan made a cup of tea, sidestepping Lucy who was sitting on the floor next to the door, looking angry and hostile. She was staring at me intently while I refused to be riled and stayed calm and tried to appear completely unperturbed. I assumed Lucy was trying to make me lose my temper or provoke any kind of reaction other than the one I was giving her, but I was determined not to let her win. Jonathan and I had used this tactic before. Another foster carer had told us about the 'power of indifference', as she called it, many years earlier. It's very simple: the child wants to cause trouble and you remain indifferent and don't let them get to you. If it all goes to plan, the child gets bored and gives up their campaign.

'Aren't you bothered about me sitting here? Why don't you send me to bed?'

'I've already told you to go to bed. What's the point in me repeating myself? I'm not going to carry you upstairs, am I?'

This went on for the next hour or so. Jonathan went to bed eventually, as he had to be up earlier than I did the next day to open up the shop. I remained seated, and I began reading a book from the shelf.

'Are you going to just sit there reading?'

'Yes.'

'Don't you want to go to bed?'

'I'm not in a hurry. I like reading. It's been ages since I had the chance to start a new book.'

I could hear Lucy sighing loudly every time I turned a page but I refused to look at her. I just carried on silently reading. We had a dimmer switch in the living room and Lucy began to fiddle with it, turning it up very brightly then down so low that I couldn't see the page. I got out of my chair, switched on the table lamp beside me and carried on reading.

Lucy then began biting her nails and spitting bits of them on the carpet. *Nothing I can't clean up tomorrow*, I told myself through gritted teeth.

'I'm bleeding,' she said.

I looked up and couldn't see any blood.

'Look! Don't you care!'

Lucy started poking the side of her thumb on the white-painted doorframe, leaving specks of blood. It was a tiny amount, and I thought she'd probably torn a bit of skin around her cuticle as she bit her nail.

*Nothing I can't clean up tomorrow*, I thought again.

After another twenty minutes of similar behaviour Lucy said, 'You're useless, Angela! You can't even tell me off. What kind of foster carer are you? I'm going to bed, and I'm going to tell my social worker on you.'

'Night night.'

'Don't you care? I'll tell her you sat there reading a book while I was bleeding to death!'

With that Lucy stomped out of the room.

'Make sure you give your hands a good wash,' I called after her. 'And don't forget to clean your teeth.'

'What do you care?'

'I care very much,' I said. 'Night night, Lucy.'

# 11

## *'I think she's a bit of a control freak'*

The following morning Lucy knocked on our bedroom door very early, long before we were due to wake up.

'What is it, sweetheart? Are you OK?'

'I need a clean sheet.'

My very first thought, in my half-awake state, was to remember her dabbing blood on the doorframe the night before.

'What's happened?

'Erm. It's wet.'

'OK, I see,' I said, instantly relaxing. 'Don't worry. We can sort that out very quickly.'

Lucy had already put a pair of dry pyjamas on but I could still smell urine on her. We went up to her room and I changed the bed as quickly as possible, tucked her in and told her to try to get another couple of hours' sleep.

'You can have a nice shower in the morning and I'll put the washing machine on and get all this sorted out. Don't worry.'

The bed was undamaged as the children's mattresses are always covered in waterproof sheets. I reassured Lucy that having an accident like this was not a problem at all. I've changed hundreds of wet sheets over the years.

'Do you think she was upset by talking to Wendy last night?' Jonathan asked me when I went back to bed. 'Was that also why she was playing us all up, d'you think?'

'I'd say it's very likely, but who knows? It could just be coincidence I suppose.'

I made a note of the bed-wetting and would mention it to Social Services, just to make sure everyone was kept in the picture. I hadn't been told of any history of bed-wetting, so I thought it was important to pass this on.

The school situation was still no closer to being resolved. I'd left messages at the Child and Family centre, in the hope that Lucy's psychologist might be able to put something in writing to support us, but I hadn't heard back from her yet. I'd also asked the head of Social Services to get involved. Her secretary had asked me to put Lucy's case in writing, which I'd done, and I was waiting for a reply from her too.

In the end it took well over a week to hear back from Social Services, and the response was not what I wanted. We were advised to contact the schools directly, which is exactly what we'd already done.

'I don't believe it!' I said. 'This is ludicrous!'

The psychologist then called and told me she would need to talk to her manager before responding but would do so that day. Her helpful letter, supporting Lucy's need to be in school, arrived about three days later. With nowhere else to turn I decided to try to set up appointments with two other schools, take the letter along and plead Lucy's case.

The head teacher of one of the schools, Mr Tripp, called me back within the hour.

'I hear you have a child who needs a place urgently,' he said. 'Please tell me the details, Mrs Hart.'

I explained the situation and read some extracts from the psychologist's letter.

'Though Lucy is not statemented, in my professional opinion she does have some special educational needs,' I quoted. 'She would benefit greatly from being back in a school environment. This will aid her reintegration into the family unit.'

Mr Tripp sounded kind and wise.

'I can see you've been given quite a run-around but have refused to give up,' he said. 'Luckily, we do have space in school, and in the circumstances I'm happy for Lucy to start as soon as you can arrange it. It's very unsatisfactory that you've had to go round in circles like this.'

Mr Tripp told me he had plenty of volunteer parents and would make sure Lucy got some support at least, and he told me he would contact the LEA and see if they could provide some interim funding for a SEN classroom assistant, using the psychologist's letter to 'fight our corner'. I was delighted and told him I was very grateful. It was the first time I'd found an ally within the schools system who seemed to be on Lucy's side and was prepared to put common sense above red tape and concerns about funding.

Lucy seemed very pleased when I gave her the news.

'I don't want to be horrible, but I'm bored.'

'You're not being horrible. It's perfectly natural for you to feel that way. You should be in school like all the other girls and boys of your age. I'd have hated missing so much school when I was your age.'

This school – St Joseph's – was a good half-hour car ride away from our house, which was not ideal. It meant that either Jonathan or I would have to take Maria to school and the other would have to drive Lucy: dropping Maria off en route was not possible, as at that time her school gates didn't open until 8.30 and Lucy needed to be in the yard by 8.50 at the latest. In situations like this Social Services sometimes pay for a taxi, but I didn't want to create any additional problems that might cause Lucy to lose any more days of her education. For the time being at least, I'd ask Barbara to open the shop up every day and Jonathan and I would do the two school runs.

Lucy embraced her new school life. She was up early every morning, getting herself ready, packing her book bag and helping me make her packed lunch. She always went off with a spring in her step, chattering away about what she might do that day and asking lots of questions. True to his word, Mr Tripp managed to secure some interim funding, from Social Services in Lucy's home county, and before long Lucy benefited from having a SEN assistant to help her in the classroom. This was no mean feat without a statement, and considering she was living 'out of county'. I was hugely grateful.

Lucy wanted to carry on seeing the horses and so we fixed up a few visits to the stables after school. By now we'd started to pay Diane as she was giving Lucy proper lessons as well as loaning her all the equipment.

Lucy seemed in her element. She was tired in the evenings and for a while we hardly saw any of her aggravating behaviour. We thought she was probably just too busy and worn out to bother getting involved in any silly tiffs with Maria, or to cause any scenes like the nail-biting and staring we'd had in the past.

She still phoned home regularly but Wendy hadn't come on the phone since the birthday party. I'd mentioned to both Bella and Jess that Wendy had warned she couldn't have Lucy over for a visit again but I'd heard no more from anybody about whether or not she was going to stick to this.

Lucy had asked me many times when she was next visiting her family and I had to be honest and say I didn't know. Then one evening, after she called her dad, Lucy came running out to find me in the garden.

'Guess what? Daddy said I can go and see him on Saturday!'

'Really? Well that's nice. I'll give him a call.'

'How many sleeps is that? Let me see . . . one, two! Just two sleeps. I miss Daddy. I want to show him my new uniform and my book bag.'

I left a message for Dean to call me back but had no reply.

When I dropped Lucy at school on the Friday morning she announced excitedly, 'One more sleep until I see Daddy! Yipeeeeeee!'

I still hadn't got hold of Dean and had a bad feeling about this. Unfortunately, when I got home there was a message on the answerphone from him, saying something about things being a 'bit tricky' for Saturday. Jonathan played it back to me and we both stared at the phone, feeling sorry for Lucy. Dean said he had to work and was very sorry but he wouldn't be at home all day as he'd expected. He stuttered and stumbled over his words, and it sounded like he was making excuses. He ended the message saying perhaps it would be best to move it to another day, and then he'd get more time with Lucy.

'Do you know what, I think we should just drive Lucy over as planned. She'll be devastated if the visit is cancelled. Even if she has to wait to see her dad, or even if she can only see him for a short time and just show him her new uniform, that is going to be far preferable to cancelling completely.'

Jonathan agreed. We both hate it whenever parents cancel plans or change contact sessions or visits like this. It always seems so unfair. We played the message again and decided that it could be interpreted as Dean simply warning us he wouldn't be around all day and *suggesting* we could move the date. We decided not to call back but take a chance and drive over anyway. If all else failed Lucy would see her siblings, and we'd just have to contend with Wendy. As Jonathan pointed out, at least Wendy wouldn't have to 'cope' with Lucy for a whole day. Our decision was sealed when Lucy came home from school and showed us her homework. She was asked to write a page about her weekend, and she had already written the title: My Weekend With MY DADDY!

When we arrived at the house Dean answered the door. Lucy threw herself into his arms as we'd seen her do on the previous visit.

'Hey, Lou-Lou! How are you, princess?'

'I'm fine! I like my new school. I've brought my homework book to show you. And my new sweatshirt. You can have a look if you like?'

'I'd *love* to,' he said.

It sounded like he was trying his best to be enthusiastic but was actually on the back foot a little, and was having to make a bit of an effort.

'You didn't get my message then?' he said, looking up at me.

'Oh yes, you have to do some work and can't be here the whole time? Yes. Got that. It's no problem for us, we can collect Lucy any time you like, or are you planning to drive her back?'

'Can you collect her? There's no point in you driving home and back again, is there? I can only have her for a couple of hours.'

Lucy wasn't worried about this; we'd already prepared

her for the possibility it might be a short stay and that not everyone might be around. The fact her daddy was there, right in front of her, was all she cared about.

'That's fine,' I said. 'I was thinking we'd go and explore up at that big new shopping centre.'

'Oh yes. Wendy loves it there.'

As Dean spoke Gemma appeared at the door.

'Mummy's got a new job in the wedding shop,' she announced. 'And did you know, when Mummy and Dean get married, she'll get staff discount on her dress!'

Lucy's jaw dropped and Dean looked shaken.

'Er, we haven't got any plans in place, not yet!' He tried to laugh it off, but Gemma persisted. 'You should go and see her if you're going shopping. She can show you all the styles and the one she likes best. She'd like that. Her shop is the best!'

'Sounds good,' I said, not wanting to commit to calling in on Wendy. 'We'll come back in a couple of hours then. Have a good time, Lucy.'

Jonathan and I walked swiftly to our car and drove off before Dean could say anything else.

'Do you know what I think?' Jonathan said.

'Yes. You're thinking exactly the same as me. You're thinking that Dean tried to cancel because Wendy wasn't going to be there.'

'Yes. And the reason for this?'

'It's not that Dean can't cope. It's that Wendy likes to be in control. I think she's a bit of a control freak. I think she told him to cancel Lucy because she's got this job and knew she wasn't going to be there.'

Our instincts told us to steer clear of the wedding shop, so as not to alert Wendy to the fact we had brought Lucy over after all. Of course, we had no evidence to prove our suspicions and we would not have speculated like this with anybody else. But Jonathan and I were of the same opinion, and we both felt we were on the right track. We also wondered if perhaps Wendy was jealous of Lucy, because she and Dean had such a close bond. Again, we were only going on gut feelings, but it was certainly something to bear in mind.

We decided to go for a walk and have a coffee in a garden centre instead of going to the shopping centre.

When we returned to collect Lucy she was in a great mood. She was holding her special pillow and her cuddly yellow bear, Honey, which she had finally retrieved. It seemed they'd been forgotten before because they'd been put out of sight, in a cupboard in Lucy's old room. She found them when playing hide and seek, which made her day.

'We had the best game EVER!' she told me. Her brothers and Gemma all agreed: Milly was out at a dance class and 'missed all the fun', they said. They'd found some great new hiding places inside the house and in the garden, and Lucy had also helped her dad to set up a new potting table in his greenhouse. She asked him if she could show us their handiwork.

'Of course,' Dean said with a shrug. 'If you want.' He was

such an easy-going man, and he led us through the house to the garden where he showed us not just the new potting table but gave us a tour of his vegetable patch and a rose bed he was particularly proud of. The kids had swings and a slide and there was a badminton net set up at the far end, tethered between two old trees. It all looked lovely – a perfect garden for the children to enjoy.

'Guess what?' Lucy said. 'We're going camping when I'm back! Did you know, we've got a ten-man tent? It's GINORMOUS! Do you know how to put up a tent, Jonathan? I do.'

'Hold your horses Lucy-lu!' Dean said, before explaining to us that he was *hoping* to take the family on a camping trip at some point that year though nothing was yet organised.

Lucy gave everyone a hug when it was time for us to leave. Not surprisingly, her dad got the biggest hug of all, but even Gemma got quite a bear hug this time. There was a good vibe between the two girls and as we left Gemma asked when Lucy was visiting again.

We all looked at Dean. 'Oh, I don't know yet, but we won't leave it too long, eh?'

'Can I come next week?' Lucy asked.

'I'm not sure, princess. Let me talk to Mum and we'll sort something out.'

As we drove away Lucy said, 'Why does Daddy have to talk to Wendy? She'll be at work again.'

Jonathan and I swapped glances. 'I expect he just wants to make sure it fits in with everybody. He wouldn't want to make a mistake and agree to a visit that wasn't possible, because that would be disappointing, wouldn't it?'

We had no idea if Dean was going to work later that day, when Wendy got home, or whether he'd just used his work as an excuse to try to put off Lucy's visit in Wendy's absence. He didn't refer to it and we didn't ask. The main thing was that Lucy had spent a couple of hours with her family, and her visit had been a success. Perhaps this was the way forward for the time being, limiting her visits to short slots?

Lucy sat quietly in the back of the car and after a few minutes I realised she was engrossed in filling in her homework book. Her writing was not neat at the best of times and I knew it would be even less tidy than usual if she worked on her knee in the back of the car, but I didn't want to stop her. By the time we got home she'd filled the whole page of her news book with writing and added some lovely pictures around the border. It was messy and her spelling was very poor but I understood what she was trying to say. Overwhelmingly, Lucy's words were happy and positive, and that is what stood out for me. Anyone reading her work would be able to tell she'd had a lovely time and packed in lots of fun and activities that morning. At the bottom of the page she'd drawn her dad as a tall stick man with a speech bubble coming from his mouth. 'Where's Lucy???' he was saying. Next to him she'd drawn a tree with a small stick girl hiding behind it, who was shouting, 'I'M HERE!!!' Her mouth was disproportionately large to show a huge smile.

'Well done,' I praised. 'Your teacher is going to be very pleased.'

In the middle of the following week I had a phone call from the school. My heart leaped and I wondered if Lucy had been in trouble. The office manager cut straight to the point, 'I'm afraid it's about the funding of Lucy's support. Social Services has stopped paying, due to the legality of who should be responsible.'

This was terrible news. Thanks to Mr Tripp, Social Services in Lucy's home county *had* agreed to pay for the support she needed, despite the fact it was not technically their responsibility, so what had gone wrong?

'As you know,' the office manager said, 'money should normally come from the LEA, not Social Services, but because Lucy wasn't statemented it meant neither county's LEA was keen to foot the bill. Thanks to Mr Tripp's intervention, Social Services across the border did agree to pay, but I'm afraid a senior manager over there has now decided to object to the arrangement, questioning the legality of it, particularly as Lucy is now living out of the area. He feels our LEA should be paying.'

I was upset and angry on Lucy's behalf and expressed my disappointment.

'Mr Tripp has asked me to invite you in for a meeting, at your earliest convenience.'

'I can come in any time. I want this resolved without delay.'

The office manager said she'd get back to me as soon as possible, explaining that Mr Tripp wanted representatives from Social Services to be there, along with two teachers. She called back that afternoon to set a time and date the following week, when Jonathan and I would attend the meeting with Mr Tripp, Lucy's form teacher, a special needs assistant, our social worker Jess and Lucy's social worker Bella.

'It's quite a big meeting,' I remarked to Jonathan. 'I wonder how much it's costing for all these people to attend? I don't know why money gets wasted on red tape instead of being used on educating the children. It's absolutely ridiculous!'

Jonathan nodded in agreement even though we both knew that my comments were unrealistic. Of course things had to be done legally and officially. Mr Tripp was doing everything correctly in order to help Lucy, but it was maddening that the system was so long-winded and difficult to navigate. Lucy wasn't the first child in foster care to cross a county border, so why weren't policies already in place that would help everyone concerned to deal more efficiently with scenarios like hers?

'At least she's in school,' Jonathan reasoned. 'They are not going to send her home, are they? I know it's not ideal not having the help she needs in the classroom, but at least she's still being educated, and she seems happy to be there.'

Jonathan was right. He's always very good at pointing out the positives and helping keep my feet on the ground. I said I had a good mind to contact our local MP and that I'd write to the Prime Minister if need be, but Jonathan told me to calm down and wait to see what happened at the upcoming meeting.

Unfortunately, the school meeting was very disappointing. Despite Mr Tripp strongly objecting to their U-turn, Social Services in Lucy's home county was still adamantly refusing to pay for the support she needed at St Joseph's. The fact she didn't have a statement was the root of the problem. As we already knew, nobody was taking responsibility for having her statemented, even though the psychologist recommended it and she clearly needed help in the classroom. It was so annoying, because if she had the statement the LEA would be forced to pay for Lucy wherever she went to school, and Social Services would not need to be involved. It was a catch-22 situation.

Mr Tripp kindly suggested that Lucy could continue being supported by parent volunteers now her SEN funding had been cut. He also said he was not giving up and would continue to fight Lucy's case until she was statemented.

'She can have two sessions a week with our reading volunteer, Mrs Ethel. She comes in on Monday and Wednesday afternoons and listens to children read. She's a great asset to the school. Reading levels have risen across the school since she joined us last year.'

I agreed that this was better than nothing but said I was very concerned about the effect it would have on Lucy, to have no support on a day-to-day basis in the classroom. Mr Tripp was doing his best, though, and I tried not to show how annoyed I was.

'We'll continue to support her at home,' I added. 'I'll keep encouraging her to practise writing more neatly and I'll take her to the library so she can choose some books.

She likes horses. I'll see if we can find a few books that capture her imagination.'

The special needs teacher said this was a good idea and the two social workers agreed to keep the school informed of any developments, and of any change to Lucy's circumstances. Privately, I started to seriously think about contacting our local MP.

Lucy was brought in at the end of the meeting and had all of this explained to her. She didn't seem bothered either way and just nodded.

Thankfully, once she was back in the classroom, Lucy didn't complain about the lack of help and whenever I asked her how her work was going she said everything was fine. Her form teacher, Miss Heather, made a special effort to check in with me at the end of the week. She said Lucy seemed happy and engaged most of the time, although she'd recognised that when she wasn't busy she had a habit of annoying the other pupils. Miss Heather had made her a 'pet monitor'. This entailed looking after some mice kept in a cage in the classroom.

'She's much happier and better behaved when she's busy and she's a very willing helper. If I can see she is losing focus I give her extra jobs to do, like going to the staff room to fetch fresh water for the mice.'

I thanked the teacher and told her I deployed similar tactics at home. I also told her about Lucy's progress with the extra reading and writing work I was still encouraging her to do, whenever I saw the opportunity.

'I find her attention span is very short and she gets

frustrated easily, but when she's in the right mood and is looking for something to do she's very keen and willing. She's reading a book on transport at the moment. She likes books with lots of pictures and diagrams. I think she's definitely going to do something practical when she's older. She loves making things, working with her hands and is fascinated by machinery and building things. She loves being outdoors too.'

Miss Heather nodded. 'I agree,' she smiled. 'In fact, you could have taken the words out of my mouth. That's Lucy to a T.'

There was a session arranged for the following week at the Child and Family centre, for Dean, Wendy and Lucy to have some counselling together, and also to discuss how they thought things were going. Lucy had had a few therapy sessions on her own by now and Wendy and Dean had too, on one occasion taking Gemma with them. It was my understanding that feedback from this session with Lucy would be passed to Social Services. If things were on track, the social workers were hoping they could finally move towards Lucy staying overnight at the family home. Wendy had said no more to me since her outburst about not being able to cope with Lucy for a 'whole day' and I took it that she'd calmed down and progress had been made, particularly after the very successful visit home Lucy had when Wendy was at work.

Jess told me that if Lucy stayed overnight and things went well, she would hopefully be able to progress quite quickly to staying weekends, as per the initial plan. Jess was very hopeful that we'd then be well on the way to helping Lucy move home at the end of the summer, as she so desperately wanted to.

'How do you feel things are going?'

'Really well,' I told Jess. 'Jonathan and I are very pleased with Lucy's progress. I'd say she's generally happier in herself since starting school, and she's less inclined to be irritating or to misbehave than when she first arrived, as she's got a lot to keep her occupied. Her last visit home helped no end, I'm sure. She had such a lovely time and I think it did wonders for her relationship with Gemma. Come to think of it, she's been asking me less about when she is going home. I guess she's less anxious now that things are on track. The bed-wetting only happened a few times, all in the same week, and has stopped now.'

Jonathan came in on the tail end of our conversation. 'I'd say she's certainly less anxious,' he said. 'There's good and bad in that, in my opinion. She's calmer because she's absolutely certain she's going home in August, and it worries me because that's not so far off now, and I know a delay could set her back.'

We also told Jess that Lucy had seemed particularly happy after her last individual visit to her psychologist.

'She came out in a great mood, chattering about what she wanted to do next time she got to play in her garden at home, and how she was pleased she was friends with Gemma again. That said, I've noticed Lucy is generally in a good mood on the days she goes to the Child and Family centre.'

'Really?'

'Yes. Lucy says she likes the fact her school friends are jealous when she gets taken out of school!'

Jess laughed and said this was no bad thing, as sometimes children are embarrassed to be taken out of the classroom and refuse to attend such appointments. 'Good for Lucy!' she said. 'The success of the sessions are key, and if she's in a receptive mood then it can only be a help.'

Lucy called her daddy when she got home from school on Friday night. It was five days before the joint session at the Child and Family centre. I heard her say, 'I can't wait to see you!' and left her to chat while I went upstairs and helped Maria choose an outfit for a birthday party she was going to that weekend.

By the time I came down Lucy had finished on the phone and was grinning and skipping around the kitchen, looking very excited.

'Guess what? Daddy said I can go over on Sunday!'

'Oh, that's great! That's something to look forward to, isn't it?'

'Yes. I can't wait! AND I'll see him next week too.'

She was absolutely thrilled to bits. I wondered what the arrangements were and was just thinking about whether to call Dean and fix a time when the phone rang.

It was Wendy, sounding tired and a bit down.

'About Sunday,' she said. 'I know it's short notice but can you drop Lucy off and pick her up?'

She explained that they already had some other commitments that day and that the visit would have to be quite short. 'Dean's a big softie, you know. Lucy can wrap him round her little finger.'

I told Wendy we could manage both lifts, even though I was thinking it would mean Jonathan and I spending hours in the car and asking my mum to come and babysit Maria either side of the activities she had planned that day. However, if that's what it took we were prepared to go the extra mile – or miles!

'Are you sure, Angela? Don't worry if you can't. We can always rearrange Lucy's visit for another time, and we are seeing her next week anyhow.'

'It's absolutely fine,' I said. 'She's already looking forward to it.'

Wendy called back at about ten o'clock that night, sounding harassed and very apologetic.

'Is everything all right?'

'Look, I'm sorry to do this. Dean shouldn't have invited Lucy over on Sunday. We've got too much on already and now I'm not feeling well. I just won't be able to cope. I'm sorry to mess you around.'

'Oh dear, I'm sorry to hear that,' I said, though my main concern was that Lucy was the one being messed around.

Wendy muttered something about Dean being a 'typical useless man'. 'He means well, but you can't trust them to get anything right, can you?'

Then she rushed off the phone, leaving me with a heavy heart and a dread of having to break this to Lucy the next day.

When I told her over breakfast the next morning she just stared at me for a moment before forcing a smile onto her face.

'It's OK,' she said bravely. 'I'll be home *all* the time soon, anyway.'

## 12

### *'I'll miss her when she's gone'*

Jonathan and I drove Lucy to the Child and Family centre for the joint session. On the way she said she was going to ask her daddy about the camping trip he hoped to take the family on; she'd mentioned it several times since.

'I helped cook the sausages last time we went camping. It was fun. Daddy said I was a champion camper. Do you go camping? Do you like barbecues?'

We told her we both love staying on campsites and that we had a touring caravan.

'Where is it? I haven't seen it!'

'We store it in a big garage, not far from where we live. We only get it out when we're ready to go away.'

'Oh well, so I won't get to see it.'

'You never know, you might. We often go away for weekends and in the school holidays.' We didn't have our next camping trip in the diary although we did have a summer holiday booked and were going to stay in a log cabin with Maria.

'No, I won't. I'll be back home. Do you think they will tell me today when I can move back in with Daddy?'

'We don't know,' Jonathan said firmly. 'We know as much as you, Lucy. Let's wait and see.'

When we arrived at the centre Lucy was taken into a meeting room immediately. Jonathan and I said we were going to get petrol and would come back and wait in reception.

Lucy waved us off. She had a spring in her step as she entered the room, and we heard the therapist telling her that her family had already arrived.

'Bless her,' Jonathan said. 'She wants nothing more than to go home. I wish her all the luck in the world.'

I smiled. 'I think we're getting there, slowly. Let's hope so. Mind you, I'll miss her when she's gone. That part of fostering never gets any easier, does it?'

We were just on our way out the door when the therapist reappeared and called us back. She looked concerned and I wondered what was going on.

'Lucy's father would like you to be in the meeting.'

Jonathan and I were not expecting this at all, and I told the therapist this. 'My manager is in the room. Shall I ask her to step out and explain?'

'Well, yes, if you don't mind. We thought it was more of a joint session for Lucy, Wendy and Dean, that's all.'

It turned out that Dean and Wendy had arrived early, having arranged a meeting with the manager before their session with Lucy. I had no idea what had been said, but apparently they needed Jonathan and me to join them, as they had 'things to say.'

When we walked in the room I thought, *You could cut the atmosphere in here with a knife*. Dean was scowling, Wendy was sitting with her arms folded defensively across her chest and, to my surprise, Gemma was in the room. As well as the manager of the Child and Family centre there were two therapists present.

Lucy was sitting on the opposite side of the table to her family, flanked by the therapists. Jonathan and I took the two available chairs at the far of the table. Nobody smiled and it felt like everybody stared as we took our seats. I felt self-conscious and on alert. Jonathan and I were well used to attending core meetings, review meetings and placement meetings – all names used for the various routine meetings we have regularly with social workers, teachers and Social Services officials. But this was different. It was unprecedented to be asked to join in a meeting like this, at a therapy centre. Something was wrong, but I had no idea what.

Introductions were made, and the manager looked at Dean.

'Mr Harrison, can I ask you to repeat what you just told me?'

It sounded like we were in a courtroom rather than an NHS centre. Lucy was hunched over so much her chin was on her chest and she looked like a frightened little mouse, while Gemma was owning her space at the table, elbows planted wide and a high and mighty expression on her face.

'Yes.' Dean hissed the word. He looked furious. 'When Lucy came over for my birthday she called Wendy a fucking bitch. Pardon my French. And she also called her "Wendy the witch". We can't have it. I'll not stand for it any longer.'

'I didn't!'

Lucy's cheeks were flushed. She uncurled herself from her hunched position and jutted out her chin in fury. Then she sprang to her feet and kicked the table leg.

'Sit down,' Wendy snapped.

'No!'

'You'll do as I tell you. SIT DOWN NOW!'

Lucy looked both stung and frightened and she sat back down. Meanwhile Dean balled his fists and shook his head.

The manager intervened and filled us in on what we'd missed earlier. Apparently Lucy had used this term to Gemma when the two of them were alone together at Dean's birthday party.

'I didn't like it and I thought everybody needed to know,' Gemma explained dramatically. 'It's not fair on my mum. I don't want Lucy in the house again. None of us do. She's just not wanted. It's better without her!'

'Daddy, I never said that!' Lucy gasped. She was still red in the face and looked distraught.

'Be quiet, Lucy. You've said enough. You've gone too far this time, causing all this trouble. You're well out of order, do you hear me? You're a little liar. That's what you are.'

'But I'll be good, Daddy! I didn't say those things. Honestly, I didn't.'

'You're such a big liar!' Gemma spat.

'I'm not! I didn't lie. THIS IS SO UNFAIR! YOU HAVE TO BELIEVE ME!'

Lucy was on her feet again and she banged her little fists on the table in temper and frustration. I wanted to go to her, to her calm down. Jonathan instinctively put his hand on my knee, as if to hold me in my seat.

Neither Dean nor Wendy reacted and it was left to one of the therapists to step in and steer Lucy back to her seat. She sat on the edge of the chair, staring at Gemma intently and grinding her teeth.

'You see, this is what she's like,' Wendy said triumphantly. 'Look at her. She's like a wild animal when she gets mad.'

The manager interjected, thank God, because if she hadn't I think I'd have given Wendy a piece of my mind.

'Clearly, there is a difference of opinion here. Nothing is going to be resolved like this. Please, can everybody stay calm? Angela and Jonathan, have you talked to Lucy about what happened at the party?'

I was very glad to have my say. I explained about the broken clock and about the fact that Wendy had made a few complaints about Lucy afterwards, but that we had ultimately straightened everything out, or so I thought.

'As I recall, Wendy believed Lucy had been bragging, deliberately interrupting conversations and that she was difficult with her food. This was many weeks ago and I thought we'd moved on. Lucy's last visit went very well. Milly was out at a dance class, I believe, and Wendy was at work. Dean, the boys, Gemma and Lucy got on very well.

They had a great time, in fact, playing happily together in the garden. They all enjoyed Lucy's visit.'

I shot a look at Gemma, remembering how Lucy had given her a bear hug as they said goodbye.

Gemma was asked why it had taken her so long to speak out about what happened at the party.

'I didn't want to upset people, especially Mum, and I didn't want to snitch on Lucy. But then I didn't like keeping the secret. I couldn't keep it in any longer. Now I don't want Lucy back home. I'm scared of what will happen.'

'I'm scared too,' Wendy piped up, unfolding her arms and banging her hands down on the table. Her hair looked blacker than ever and she was wearing dark red lipstick. I thought she looked very intimidating; I dreaded to think what Lucy made of her.

'I'm *very* scared, actually,' Wendy intoned. 'I think Lucy could harm me. She hates me. It's obvious. I don't trust her and what she might do to me. She's got a screw loose! I don't want her near my daughter. I don't want her in the house. She's a poisonous little madam.'

A feeling of dread came over me; I was in shock.

'OK, please let's stop there,' the manager said with authority, rising to her feet.

It was too late. The words had been spoken. Lucy looked like she might cry and she began protesting pitifully that she had not called Wendy 'those horrible names'. I felt heartbroken for Lucy. How could a grown woman talk about a little girl like that? And how could another little girl

– a girl who had once been Lucy's best friend – be so hard-faced and unkind?

Jonathan and I had never heard Lucy use the 'f' word and I was not certain I believed Gemma's version of events. It didn't ring true to me, but of course Lucy had a chequered history when it came to telling the truth and so it was very difficult to know what to believe.

Dean said he wanted to end the meeting there.

'I've had enough of this. I'm going outside for a fag!'

He stood up and walked out of the room. Wendy followed him. 'Good idea,' she said. 'I'm coming with you.' As she left the room, with Gemma hot on her heels, she shot Lucy an icy look.

'See the trouble you cause? See what you're doing to your father, to all of us? You need to learn how to behave young lady.'

The manager thanked us for joining the meeting and I said I'd talk to our support social worker.

'Lucy was hoping to go home at the end of August,' I said.

'Perhaps that's a little ambitious,' one of the therapists said.

The family left without saying goodbye.

On the way home I sat in the back of the car with Lucy. She still didn't cry, but she didn't speak either. She looked dazed and wounded and she hooked herself on to my arm, as if it were a crutch. I was furious and incredibly sad, all at the same time. I knew I had to be very careful what I said and how I reacted. Kids repeat to family what you say, and clearly it wouldn't help matters if I were seen to take Lucy's side, although that is how I felt.

After we all sat in silence for a while I talked to Lucy. I told her that Jonathan and I were upset about what just happened, and I made it crystal clear we had no idea in advance that Gemma was coming to the meeting, or about anything the family had to say. I also reiterated the fact Jonathan and I had not expected to be called in to the meeting with the family. It was very important Lucy was able to trust us and rely on us to protect her and look after her. I also told her she could talk to us and that we were here to support her, and that she could say whatever was on her mind. She didn't say a word, and I left it there. We carried on in silence for a while, and then Jonathan put a Sheryl Crow CD on, one of my favourites.

I tried to listen and relax a little but I found it very difficult. What I really wanted to do was vent my anger about how Wendy, Dean and Gemma had carried on in the meeting. I couldn't help thinking about what I'd like to say to Wendy and Dean, if it were possible.

*Why did you tackle Lucy like that? Can you imagine being in her shoes? How do you know Gemma is telling the truth? Even if she is, do you think handling the situation in this way was helpful? Or more likely to damage all the progress we've made since the party? Don't you want her back where she belongs?*

When we arrived back at our house Lucy went straight

to her room, and she said she wasn't hungry when I tried to talk to her about dinner a little later on.

'You can help me if you like? I'm doing macaroni cheese. Maria doesn't like tomatoes on the top so I usually make two separate ones. How about you?'

'You *know* I eat tomatoes. I had them last week. Can't you remember?'

She said this in an accusatory way. I could tell it wasn't going to matter what I said or did; for the time being, Lucy's back was up and she was probably going to be in an aggravating mood.

Dinner was an awkward experience. Lucy stared at Maria and picked at her food.

'What are you looking at? Angela, will you tell her to stop staring at me?'

'They're my eyes. I can do what I like with them.'

'Lucy, please focus on your food and don't stare at Maria. She doesn't like it.'

'Like I say, they're my eyes.'

'Can I get down?' Maria huffed.

'Have you had enough to eat?'

'Yes. *She's* put me off my food.'

Lucy was very annoying and irritating for the rest of the evening and it made no difference what anybody said to her, she came back with a retort designed to aggravate. Maria sensibly kept out of the way while Jonathan and I walked on eggshells around her.

I was relieved when it was time for Lucy to go to bed. I'd been watching the clock because the atmosphere in the house was so tense. I was tired, and I wanted the day to draw to an end.

When I told Lucy it was her bedtime she snapped, 'I was going anyway! There's no need for you to tell me. Are you trying to wind me up?'

'No, not at all.'

'I don't believe you. Now you've said that, I don't want to go to bed.'

'But it's bedtime. Aren't you tired? I know I am.'

'No. And I'm NOT going to bed.'

'Really? Well I'm not going to force you up the stairs.'

Her eyes narrowed and I imagined she was remembering the night she bit her nails and put blood on the doorframe.

'I'm going to finish watching this documentary now and then read my book. If I were you I'd just go to bed. There's nothing exciting going on down here and you'll only be tired at school tomorrow.'

'I don't care. You're more bothered about school than I am. What's the point of it? They don't want me there, do they? Daddy doesn't mind. He let me miss loads of school. Why do *you* care? What's in it for *you, Angela*? You just want me out of the way during the day, don't you?'

'I care about you going to school because I want you to have a good education, so that you will have more choices open to you in the future. Do you know what you might like to do, when you are grown up?'

'No. It's ages away.'

'I'm not surprised you don't know. Most people don't

have a clue what they want to do until they are much, much older.'

'So why are you asking me stupid questions?'

'I'm asking you to try to help you. I want you to see why school is important. I know plenty of people who didn't do very well at school and wish they could go back and try harder.'

'That's so dumb. You just don't understand anything!'

Lucy marched off to her room shouting, 'I'm going to bed!'

She was probably too young to take all this sensible, grown-up advice on board but I felt I had nothing to lose in trying to get through to her. Anyway, at least I wasn't going to have another bedtime battle on my hands, although that felt like a very small blessing right now. The fact was, Lucy was deeply disturbed by what had happened at the Child and Family meeting. You didn't have to be an expert to see that. She was in shock and she was distressed, and she was taking it out on us.

No sooner had Lucy gone upstairs but Maria came downstairs, complaining about the noise Lucy was making in the bathroom. As soon as I opened the living-room door I could hear the pipes making a long, low whistling sound, and I knew this was another of Lucy's attempts to wind us up. She had worked out that if you turned the taps on to a certain point then no water came out, but the pipes made a racket.

'She's done this on purpose to piss me off!' Maria shouted.

'No I didn't!' Lucy yelled back from the other side of her closed bedroom door.

I told Maria off for using bad language and added, 'If you're right and she is trying to wind you up, then the best thing to do is not to let it get to you.'

I tightened the taps, cutting off the noise instantly. Maria scowled and went back to her room.

'I think I'm going to phone Wendy and let her know what's going on here,' I said to Jonathan, when I was confident Lucy was in bed and asleep.

'What, now? Do you think that's wise? Shouldn't you sleep on it?'

Jonathan is generally more calm and considered than I am, but he always hears me out.

'I thought that and I'm really not in the mood to speak to Wendy, but she needs to know what effect it's had on Lucy, having to sit there and listen to all that criticism. I really don't want this to happen ever again. This is a huge setback. Who knows what damage has been done?'

'I think you need to tread very carefully. She might well accuse you of interfering and then we could have another kind of setback on our hands.'

'I know, but at the end of the day I want Lucy to go home. That's more important to me than anything. If Wendy thinks I'm being a busybody I don't care, frankly, as long as I get the message across that Lucy can't be subjected to this kind of treatment ever again.'

I started to get upset and angry once more, and Jonathan

managed to convince me to leave the call until the next day and get some rest. Given the way I was feeling, this was a very good idea. I do find things always seem clearer the following day, when I've had time to think things through.

I woke the next day to find that Lucy had wet the bed after a long stint of being dry. She was still in a terrible mood too, complaining about everything, dragging her feet and trying to annoy Maria by pretending to flick breakfast cereal at her and generally getting in her face.

As we left the house she turned to me and said, very seriously, 'I didn't call Wendy those names. Gemma is lying, I promise. Why would I do that? I want to go home. I want to live with my daddy, and everyone.'

I wanted to believe Lucy and I felt sure she was telling me the truth, even though I knew she didn't always. This was too important to her, so why would she jeopardise going home by saying those things? That was what my instincts told me, but still I had to accept that I couldn't be one hundred per cent certain she was being honest with me.

'Lucy, it's very important you're telling the truth, do you understand?'

'I'm not lying! Gemma's the liar this time!'

Lucy then clammed up and spent the car journey to school making an annoying humming noise and kicking the back of my seat. I felt like I'd already done a day's work when I got home from the school run. I had a cup of coffee and a buttered crumpet with strawberry jam to give myself a boost and then I picked up the phone to call Wendy. It wasn't going to be an easy conversation but it had to be done: I owed it to Lucy.

Thankfully, she answered the phone straight away; I was ready for this and I didn't want to talk to anybody else or have to wait for her to get back to me. Wendy sounded polite and friendly, to the point where you would never have guessed this was the same woman who had behaved so unpleasantly the day before.

'How can I help you, Angela? Thanks very much for coming into the meeting yesterday. We needed you there. I was *so* upset by what Lucy had been saying about me.'

I inhaled and decided to just go for it, with no beating about the bush.

'Actually, that's why I'm phoning. I found the meeting very upsetting I'm afraid, the way you all spoke about Lucy in front of her.'

'Really? We were only stating facts, making sure everybody is fully in the picture.'

When she said that the image of the christening photo, with Lucy obscured by Wendy's arm on the end of the family group, flashed into my mind. It said everything to me about how she felt about Lucy. I had never seen her treat Lucy the same as Gemma or the other kids. At best she kept her at arm's length, at worst she was actively elbowing her out of the way. I felt rage rise in my chest, but hopefully I managed to keep an even tone.

'I found it upsetting that Lucy had to listen to you and Gemma saying she wasn't wanted at home,' I said boldly.

'They're harsh words for a little girl to hear, aren't they? Her family is so important to her and she wants nothing more than to be back home again. She talks about it all the time. It's her goal in life.'

I told Wendy that Lucy had told me that morning that she definitely had not called her those names at the party.

'To be honest, Wendy, I do tend to believe Lucy,' I ventured. 'She is absolutely adamant those words never came from her mouth, and I know how desperate she is for things to work out. I can't see why she would derail things in that way.'

There was a pause, and then Wendy said flippantly, 'Oh yes, you're right about that bit. Gemma has admitted she made that up.'

I was absolutely flabbergasted.

'She made it up? But why? When did you find this out?'

'Last night. She told Dean. I don't know why she made it up. We're talking about eight-year-old girls here, aren't we?'

'Yes, but this has done huge damage. Does she realise the implications?'

'All I know is that I totally believed Lucy was capable of saying those things. She doesn't like me and she's never going to accept me as her mum. I was really angry and upset that Lucy could have said those things about me.'

'But she didn't . . .'

I was stunned and I wanted to ask Wendy why she hadn't got to the truth before creating so much pain for

Lucy, but I sensed it was time I held my tongue or this could descend into an argument.

'No, but she could have, and it doesn't mean all the other things aren't true about her.'

This was beginning to sound like a playground spat. I told Wendy I was going to tell Lucy that Gemma had admitted she lied.

'I'd just leave it if I were you, Angela.'

'Why?'

'It's just going to cause more trouble.'

'I don't agree. It's not fair on Lucy to be left in the dark about this, and if the two girls are being truthful with one another then surely that is the best foundation to move forward on?'

'But Gemma only did it because she was trying to help!'

'Trying to help? How could that help?'

By this point Jonathan had appeared at my side and was miming at me to stay calm and wind things up, but I wasn't letting this go. First Wendy had told me she didn't know why Gemma had told lies and now she was changing her tune.

'Bless her, she thought I wasn't ready to have Lucy home, which I'm not, because she does scare me at times. Gemma thought that if she made something up like that then I would be pleased, because then Lucy couldn't come home. Shows how young they are, doesn't it? Quite sweet really, looking out for her mum.'

How could Wendy say this in such a blasé and sentimental way? Gemma's lies had had a devastating effect on

Lucy and there was nothing 'quite sweet' about it. I swallowed hard and told myself to remain polite and even-handed as I described to Wendy how Lucy had behaved since the meeting.

'Well, it just goes to show that she isn't ready to come home, doesn't it? We're a long way off. Dean says he can't stand all the aggro, and it takes a lot to get him riled. Anyway, Angela, I appreciate you calling. You really do deserve a gold medal, putting up with all this. I must go now. Bye!'

I was taken aback at how rapidly she ended the call and I only just managed to say goodbye before I heard the phone go dead. I slowly began to relay her words to Jonathan and tried to make sense of the conversation. As I described what she'd said I felt like I'd missed something. Could Wendy not see how unfairly Lucy had been treated? Did she not think Gemma's behaviour must be addressed rather than explained and tolerated, or brushed under the carpet? As for Dean, I sincerely hoped he was not still blaming Lucy for the latest 'aggro'.

'Unbelievable,' Jonathan said.

'Totally. I'm calling Lucy's social worker and our social worker. Everybody needs to know about this. Lucy's future is at stake here.'

I left a message for Bella to call me back but she didn't. When I phoned again I was told she was on annual leave. I eventually got hold of Jess and told her everything. She said she'd try to arrange the next placement meeting as soon as possible, calling together everybody involved in Lucy's care.

'Thanks Jess. When do you expect it will be?'

'I'll make it my priority to fix it up as soon as possible, but I'm afraid it could take a few weeks as I'm taking some annual leave.' *Not you as well*, I thought.

It was exasperating. I would have liked the meeting within days, not weeks, but of course that was unrealistic, even without the social workers taking holidays. I thanked Jess, but when I put the phone down I felt very pessimistic. What were the next few weeks going to be like for Lucy? We were all going to be in limbo. Jonathan could see how worried I was and gave me a hug.

'It'll all work out in the end,' he told me.

'Will it? We were supposed to be helping Lucy move back home, and now she's even further away from that than she was at the start of her placement.'

# 13

### *'Why should you care?'*

'Mrs Hart? Can you come into the office when you collect Lucy this evening? I'm afraid we're having a few problems.'

It was the school on the phone.

'I'm sorry to hear that. What sort of problems?'

'Disruptive behaviour. Name-calling. Annoying other pupils. Miss Heather has kept a log this week and would like to talk to you.'

We weren't particularly surprised to have received a call from Lucy's school, because ever since the disastrous Child and Family meeting her behaviour had deteriorated even further at home. Telling her about Gemma admitting to the lies was not pleasant at all. Lucy pulled her own hair and kicked the wall, then she ran around the house yelling, 'I told you I'd never said those things! It's the same here, nobody listens to me! I hate it here!'

I tried to be as positive as possible, telling her it was brave of Gemma to tell the truth in the end, but Lucy was having none of it. 'She won't get into trouble, I bet you! It's always OK for her to tell lies, but it's not OK for me to even tell white lies.' I didn't know what to say to that, because she was probably right. From what I'd heard, Wendy wasn't going to discipline her daughter, and I couldn't imagine Dean wading in and contradicting anything Wendy said.

Lucy had begun to make it a nightly habit to set the taps at the point where they made the pipework whistle and clank, just to annoy us. She did this all around the house and Maria reacted every time. One night they'd tussled on the landing, pulling each other's hair and calling each other names. Jonathan had to step in and separate them.

'Can't you get rid of her?' Maria complained nastily. 'Can't she go back to her family? Oh sorr-ee. Her family doesn't want her.'

'Yes they do! It's *your* family who doesn't want *you*. At least I visit mine. You are only allowed to visit your gran!'

'Ha! When are you seeing *your* gran? I'm seeing mine tomorrow, so there!'

'Girls! That's quite enough,' I said sharply. 'Both of you – stop talking! I don't want to hear another word.'

I had no idea what Maria knew about Lucy's circumstances, or vice versa. I certainly never discussed any child's personal details with anybody else, let alone another child in the house. I could only assume that, despite their differences, the girls must have spoken at some point about their families and how come they were in foster care.

We sent them to their rooms to simmer down. I thought

how sad it was that the two girls had so much in common yet clashed so much. I wished they could have been a support to each other rather than falling out like this, but I knew it was probably just wishful thinking.

When children have suffered trauma and upset in their life it can take many years to repair the damage and for those children to display anything like 'normal' behaviour. Being empathetic is something a lot of children in care struggle with, because so much of their energy has gone into survival and self-preservation.

Sadly, we've seen a lot of kids who never manage to escape the legacy of their past and find it impossible to form healthy relationships with other people, even those they have a great deal in common with, and even when they are adults. I accepted the chances of Maria and Lucy becoming friends were always going to be slim, but still we couldn't have them fighting like this.

At that time we were taught in our fostering training sessions to send kids to their rooms to cool off and so this is what we did. Nowadays the advice has changed and 'time out' is not as commonly recommended as it once was. The current thinking is that isolating children with behaviour issues might alienate them even more, while inclusion, distraction and encouraging communication are often far more effective ways of getting through.

In addition to fighting with Maria, Lucy was constantly giving us cheek and backchat.

'Can you go and clean your teeth now?'

'I've already done them.'

'No you haven't because I know for a fact that the tooth-paste has run out in your bathroom. Here, take this new tube up and please do as I ask.'

'It's like living with private detectives! Are you and Jonathan spies in real life?'

'What do you mean "in real life"? You are funny, Lucy! I just want to make sure you clean your teeth, and I am making no secret of that.'

'Like you care! You won't even *know* me when I've got all my adult teeth! Why are you bothering to nag me? You wouldn't even care if I had to have more fillings.'

'Lucy, you know that isn't the case. I care about you a lot and I want to make sure you are well looked after.'

'But why? Why should you care?'

Before I could answer again she began babbling, firing questions one after the other. 'Why did you buy *that* tooth-paste? Why didn't you get the one we had last time? Why does it matter if I clean my baby teeth? They are falling out anyhow. The tooth fairy doesn't care how clean they are. What's the point? Did you have fillings when you were my age? How come Jonathan has got a gold tooth? Did it cost a lot of money? How much did it cost? If I have bad teeth, can I get gold ones instead of grey fillings?'

She went on and on like this on every topic under the sun.

'She'd test the patience of a saint, that one,' Jonathan commented on a daily basis.

'If I had a pound for every time you said that I'd be a rich woman!'

I suppose the call from school saying they were having 'problems' was inevitable, given how Lucy was behaving at home. Jonathan came with me as Maria was going straight to a friend's house from school and the girl's mother said we could collect her at six o'clock, which was helpful timing. Lucy was kept back after school when all the other children were collected, and Miss Heather invited Jonathan and me into the classroom.

'Take a seat,' she sighed, ushering us to sit around a child-sized table on tiny chairs.

The pretty young teacher looked exhausted; she had dark circles under her eyes and when she sat down she hunched over the desk and couldn't suppress a yawn. It looked to me like she had the weight of the world on her shoulders: I didn't envy her at all, dealing with a class of thirty-one seven- and eight-year-olds all day long as she did. In that moment I felt very sorry that Lucy had added to her burden.

Lucy had been to the toilet and she joined us at the little table. She didn't say hello; she just sat and stared at the tub of pencils in the centre of the desk, refusing to give anyone eye contact.

'I'm afraid to say that Lucy has been involved in a number of incidents this week. She has been calling other pupils rude names, using bad language and refusing to stay quiet when asked.'

Miss Heather looked down at the notes she had made.

'On four occasions I've had to keep her in at break time. When we did work with compasses she scratched marks on the table and damaged the cover of her textbook. When we worked with marbles Lucy dared another pupil to swallow one.'

Now it was Lucy's turn to yawn and she did so loudly, failing to cover her mouth. Miss Heather asked her to put her hand over her mouth next time she yawned and Lucy sighed, gave the faintest nod and gazed out of the window.

'This could have been a very dangerous situation, had one of the other children not alerted me to what was going on with the marble,' Miss Heather continued. 'When I've spoken to Lucy about her behaviour she has been rude to me and used inappropriate language. It seems to me that Lucy is unhappy and doesn't want to learn. I want to help change that, but when I've put incentives in place – such as earning more time as the pet monitor or gaining stars to win some "golden time" in the games corner – Lucy has not seemed interested.'

'That's because I'm not,' Lucy piped up. 'I'm not staying in this school anyway. I don't care about your stupid pets or your crappy gold stars and golden time!'

'Lucy!' I said. 'Please don't use language like that and please do not be rude. Miss Heather is trying to help you, just like Jonathan and I are trying to help you.'

'I *said* I don't care. I hate this school. I want to go back to my old school. I don't want to be here. I want to go home!'

Miss Heather gave me a sympathetic look. She could see Jonathan and I had a lot on our plate and she probably imagined Lucy's comment would be mortifying for us. The truth was, I wasn't hurt by Lucy's words because I was concerned only with her feelings, not ours. We've had so many children tell us they want to go home and they don't want to be with us, and who can blame them? When I was a child I wouldn't have wanted to live in any other home but my own and I hated it when I had to go and stay with someone else for a while when my mother was ill. I missed my mum like mad and those feelings are still very strong in my memory. I never take it personally when children say they don't want to be with us, or even that they hate us both, and our home.

Jonathan changed the subject. 'We find that Lucy enjoys using her hands and being outdoors, isn't that right, Lucy?'

Lucy nodded at the table.

'I wonder, Miss Heather, if there is anything Lucy could work towards that she *does* enjoy? I mean, if golden time or pet monitor time isn't the right incentive, perhaps she could earn time helping in the school garden or greenhouse, or something like that?'

Miss Heather looked unsure. I imagined she had expected us to support her by putting some sanctions in place at home, perhaps, rather than suggesting rewards. Nevertheless, she listened carefully.

'What do you think, Lucy?' Miss Heather asked. 'Would you like to earn greenhouse or garden time instead of golden time?'

The greenhouse was a popular new addition to the school and all the classes took turns using it for projects like growing seeds and learning about bugs. Miss Heather said that the caretaker and a couple of volunteer parents were in the process of putting together shelving and storage units to help keep it neat and tidy. She suggested Lucy could help them, if her behaviour improved.

'I'll try,' Lucy said. 'But I don't do bad behaviour on purpose, you know. I just get bored. I don't like being in the classroom.'

In the circumstances this seemed as good a response as we were going to get. Miss Heather looked quite relieved, I think, and Jonathan and I gave her an appreciative look. 'We all want what is best for you, Lucy,' he said. 'I'm glad we are all working together on this.'

Lucy managed a small smile before saying goodbye to her teacher. *Fingers crossed*, I thought. I wanted this to work but I must admit I had my concerns. Knowing her home with us was temporary – however long temporary may be – made it extremely difficult for her to apply herself and settle into this school, especially as she still had no SEN teacher supporting her. The fact the end of term was now looming and the summer holidays were in sight didn't help either: even the best-behaved kids start to lose focus at this point in the school year. For Lucy, it was doubly hard.

I took a call from Wendy a few days later, telling me she had instructed a solicitor to 'fight the authorities' over the funding for Lucy's education. My initial reaction was to be happily surprised, and impressed. *Good for you*, I thought, thinking perhaps I should hold fire on writing to our MP as

I intended to, should Mr Tripp not resolve the problem. In the next breath Wendy revealed her motive.

'I don't want Lucy coming home when it suits Social Services. It has to suit all of us and she is not welcome, not at the moment. She needs to stay in St Joseph's and your LEA needs to pay for her.'

*Talk about a sting in the tail*, I thought.

Wendy's words sounded so cruel but I didn't tackle her about this. I simply told her I was grateful she was fighting for Lucy's funding, as her education was very important. I mentioned that we'd been called in to talk to Miss Heather, because I thought the fact the teacher was struggling with Lucy's behaviour might help support Wendy's case with the LEAs. However, instead of taking this information from me with good grace, Wendy used it to spit, 'I'm not surprised, little madam!'

I told Jonathan I felt like piggy in the middle, and it was not a comfortable place to be.

There were some things I instinctively didn't tell Wendy, such as Lucy's reaction to finding out Gemma had lied, because this would only stoke up trouble. 'It's so tricky,' I said. 'It would be easier not to tell her anything at all, but that would cause trouble too.'

'It would. You did the right thing telling her about us going to school because that information has to go in Lucy's notes and we have no idea what goes back to the family after we've let Social Services know what's going on. We *are* stuck in the middle, but I guess that's our job.' With a jokey smile he added, 'I'd prefer to call us diplomats rather than piggies in the middle.'

He was right about our role, and I realised Lucy's case was quite unlike any other we'd dealt with before. We were not just looking after the child, we were part of the team helping the whole family to reunite, and so our relationship with Wendy and Dean – and the kids, to a lesser extent – was extremely important. It could make or break Lucy's return home this summer.

'I guess we also have no idea what might go back to the family after Lucy talks to her granny and aunties on the phone,' I said.

'Exactly. Regardless of how Wendy behaves, we have no choice but to be civil with her and share key news.'

I didn't write to our MP, having decided that the diplomatic thing was to see how Wendy got on first, with the help of the solicitor.

One evening we had a barbecue in the garden. My mum came and I invited Diane and her family over to say thank you for everything they did for Lucy. She was still enjoying her riding lessons and Diane gave her far more time than we ever paid for, as well as continuing to let Lucy help with the mucking out whenever possible.

'Lucy's a pleasure to have around,' Diane said. 'She's a smashing little worker. Don't know how I'll manage without her when she moves back home!'

It seemed Lucy had informed Diane that she was definitely going home once the schools broke up for the summer.

I didn't say anything, because maybe she would, and in any case I would never talk about a child's personal care plan.

The barbecue was really enjoyable. Lucy helped Jonathan light the fire and keep an eye on the burgers and kebabs, and we all had a game of giant Jenga and garden-sized pick-up-sticks, which a friend had given me when she moved from a large house into a flat that only had a small patio. Lucy showed great dexterity and won several rounds of both games, beating Maria hands down.

'Stupid game,' Maria muttered, but that was the closest we came to having any cross words.

The sun was warm, the food was delicious and we all ate mounds of strawberries Mum had bought in town.

'Why didn't you grow them yourself?' Lucy asked.

'I'm trying,' Mum said. 'But the birds have got through the netting this year. I don't think I'm having much luck!'

Lucy offered to go over and have a look at Mum's strawberry patch.

'We're growing them in the greenhouse at school,' she said. 'I can teach you how to do it, if you like.'

'Thanks,' Mum said graciously, resisting the urge to tell Lucy she'd been growing strawberries for decades, with so much success she normally produced pounds of strawberry jam at the end of the season.

That evening Lucy was expecting a call from her daddy. He told her he was working across town and would call when he got home, but the phone never rang. Lucy asked if she could phone him, in case he'd forgotten.

'Of course,' I said, although I had a nagging voice in my head telling me this might not be a good idea.

Jonathan shot me a wide-eyed look as if to say, 'This could be asking for trouble,' but what could I do? I couldn't refuse to let Lucy call home, though I could stall for time.

'Why don't you give your gran a call first? It might be that your dad is late home from work.'

'But then I might be on the phone when he gets in.'

It was a fair point but I managed to convince her it was best to give her dad more time and that she could call him straight after she'd finished speaking to her gran. Thankfully, she agreed. To my relief she had a fairly long chat with her gran, telling her all about the barbecue and what she was doing at school with the greenhouse work. As usual I tried to leave her to talk privately but Lucy insisted on making the call from the kitchen while I was unloading the dishwasher.

I couldn't help notice that when Lucy spoke about school she gave nothing but good news.

'My teacher's lovely. I like Miss Heather lots! She's got lovely blonde hair. She never tells me off. She gives me all the best jobs too. She says I'm doing very well and I'm a very good girl, but I still want to go back to my old school.'

Lucy ended the call by telling her gran, 'I love you too.'

She was beaming when she came off the phone.

'I love my gran! She's the best granny in the whole wide world. I'm phoning Daddy now.'

'Shall we leave it just a bit longer, in case he's still not back?'

'No. I'll just try him now.'

I couldn't stall her any more, and no sooner had Lucy dialled the number but her dad was on the line.

'Are you OK? Have you had a busy day at work? Oh. I see. Where have you been then? I like it there. Can you take me there when I come home? Oh. OK bye. Love you!'

The call lasted for about thirty seconds and Lucy looked crestfallen when she put the phone down.

'Everything OK?'

'Yes,' she said, trying to smile but not quite succeeding. 'He didn't go to work today. He must have got muddled up when he told me he was working. They went to the picnic fields, the ones by the stream, where you can go fishing for tiddlers. I love it there. Daddy promised he'd take me next time! Daddy said he couldn't wait for me to go home. Daddy says he misses me. They all miss me. We're going to go to the picnic fields the next time I go home.'

I felt incredibly sad. It was so obvious Lucy wasn't telling the whole truth, as she simply hadn't been on the phone long enough for all of those things to have been said. Dean had clearly been in a huge rush to get off the phone and I didn't know what was true and what wasn't, but hurt and disappointment etched on Lucy's face spoke volumes.

'Ow!' she said suddenly, and began rubbing her eyes.

'What is it?'

'I think I've got something in my eyes.' She rubbed them again and I saw that they were bright red and glassy-looking.

'Let me have a look, sweetheart.'

Her face started to crumple and her lip wobbled.

'No! Leave me alone.'

She stomped up to her bedroom and I realised she had been trying not to cry. Moments later the phone rang again.

'I think it would be better if Lucy didn't call us, for the time being.'

The words stung me, and I felt so glad that Lucy was out of earshot.

'Why, Wendy?'

'Because we are all getting over the recent upset, that's why.'

I wanted to remind Wendy that the 'upset' had been largely created by Gemma when she made up lies about Lucy, but my conversation with Jonathan, about us being diplomats in the middle, was fresh in my mind.

'I see.'

'Good. We all need some time. We don't need any aggro. Me and Dean think it's best for everyone if we don't have any contact with Lucy until the next placement meeting, when there are professionals there to sort all this out.'

'Right. I'll let the social workers know the situation.'

Wendy didn't like this and asked me why I had to be so fussy about reporting 'every little spit and comma' of what was going on to Social Services, especially as this placement meeting had now been booked and was only about ten days away.

'It's my job, and the fact you are cutting contact, even for a short time, is important information.'

I knew the blunt way I said this would not please Wendy

but I wanted her to know that I was not going to just accept her making up rules behind the backs of the social workers. I felt very protective towards Lucy and I had to stand up for her rights.

We ended the call on a civil note, with Wendy reluctantly accepting what I said and saying as politely as she could muster, 'We look forward to seeing you at the placement meeting, and thank you for understanding.' I didn't understand, but I let this go.

'What's the matter?' Jonathan asked when he walked in the kitchen, carrying the blackened barbecue grill and a large cooking fork.

I filled him in and his jaw dropped open.

'What on earth? This is so unfair. Have they forgotten that it was Gemma who caused the so-called "aggro"? How are they going to repair their relationship if they insist on demonising Lucy and cutting her off?'

I shook my head. I had no words. Wendy was clearly a very controlling woman by nature, but why did she have to be so unkind with it? And why did Dean let her call all the shots when his relationship with his own daughter was at stake?

# 14

### *'My throat hurts. Thanks a lot!'*

Lucy wet the bed again that night but didn't tell me. When I stripped the sheets off, a small, curved knife fell to the floor, making me jump in surprise as it hit my ankle. I'd never seen the knife before and I wondered where it had come from and, more importantly, what Lucy was doing with it in her bed.

Jonathan was in the shop and as soon as I'd put the washing machine on I went in to see him.

'Do you recognise this?'

'No. Never seen it in my life before. It looks expensive, doesn't it?'

On inspection the steel handle had an intricate design on it, and when I looked closer I realised the pattern was made up of tiny horseshoes.

'Diane,' I said. 'It must have come from Diane's place. Look – it must be used on the horses.'

Jonathan nodded and suggested it might be a special kind of knife used to clean out horseshoes, because of the shape. I thought he was probably right, though I knew next to nothing about looking after horses. We both agreed we'd sit Lucy down after school and ask her to tell us all about it. She'd gone to school in a bad mood with a very grumpy expression on her face and I wasn't looking forward to the conversation, but we had to get to the bottom of this: it was a knife, after all, and she'd had it in her bed. Like all foster carers Diane was trained to be very vigilant about keeping sharp or dangerous objects out of reach of children and I was certain she wouldn't have given permission for Lucy to bring the knife home. My suspicion was that Lucy had helped herself to it, but we'd have to see what she said and, as ever, be very careful not to make any accusations based on opinion not fact.

I had another call from the school that day. Lucy was being kept behind for kicking a younger boy in the shins. I was asked to collect her ten minutes later than usual, and to call into the classroom to have another word with Miss Heather.

'You don't need to be Einstein to work out the pattern,' Jonathan commented.

'I know. The worse things are with her family, the worse Lucy's behaviour is.'

'Exactly,' he said thoughtfully. 'FT=LP squared.'

'Pardon?'

'You know. $E=mc^2$. The theory of relativity. Except in Lucy's case it's Family Trouble equals Lucy's Problems squared.'

'OK, Einstein,' I laughed. 'But I'm not sure "squared" has it covered. More like multiplied by a hundred, I'm afraid.'

We often have silly conversations like that as a way of diffusing our angst about a situation, but there was nothing remotely amusing about Lucy's predicament. We both knew that she was only going to be truly happy when she was finally accepted back into her family's life, and loved and nurtured unconditionally.

Miss Heather had a concerned expression on her face when we arrived in her classroom. Lucy avoided looking at us. She was sitting at a desk and when we installed ourselves next to her she suddenly seemed very interested in a blank piece of paper that was in front of her.

'I think one thing that might be contributing to Lucy's behaviour problems is that she is not getting enough sleep,' Miss Heather said.

I looked at Lucy. She blushed and stuttered as she tried to explain that she had told her teacher about how she helped with the horses.

'Lucy does spend quite a lot of time with the horses but I don't understand how this has anything to do with her sleep,' I said. 'We do make sure she gets enough sleep. Lucy is a naturally early riser, but she always goes to bed at a sensible time and she sleeps well.'

Lucy was scarlet by now.

'Can I go to the toilet please?'

'Just a minute, Lucy. What have you said to Miss Heather about the horses?'

'Oh, I think I got a bit muddled up.'

It turned out that Lucy had told Miss Heather she got up at five o'clock every morning to help muck out Diane's horses before school. She had given the impression that she was obliged to do this in order to be allowed to have riding lessons.

I told Miss Heather that Lucy had indeed got 'muddled up' and that the truth was she was allowed to ride regularly, regardless of how often she helped out. She never helped in the mornings before school, as there wasn't time: Lucy typically got up at seven in the morning and went to bed at eight o'clock. I estimated she had ten hours sleep on average per night, which was the recommended amount for her age.

Miss Heather asked Lucy why she had 'told tales'.

'I don't know. I didn't mean to. I was in a mood because you told me off.'

'Thank you for being honest now,' the teacher said. 'Now, do you think you can explain what happened with Joey in the playground? He has a nasty bruise on his leg.'

'He started it. He said I smelled of piss.'

'Lucy! Please don't use language like that.'

I thought back to the wet bed that morning and wondered if Lucy had showered properly, as I encouraged her to do each morning before school. Miss Heather thanked Lucy for telling the truth and told her that if Joey called her any more names she was to report him to a teacher immediately and not lash out, under any circumstances. The same went for anyone else.

Unfortunately, it was a very hot and stuffy day and when

we drove home I could detect the faint smell of stale urine on Lucy. I hadn't noticed it that morning. She had definitely told me she had showered and I heard the water running in her bathroom, and she was dressed in a set of clean clothes when she left the house. I didn't know she'd wet the bed until she was already at school and I stripped the sheets and found the knife, but I still felt guilty for not noticing she wasn't as clean as she should have been. We've had many children tell us fibs about showers over the years, and a lot of kids seem to be a dab hand at running the water and making out they've washed when they haven't.

I made a mental note to check Lucy's bed while she was having breakfast in future, and I had a gentle word with her about hygiene, which she seemed to take on board without a problem.

The horse knife was something else we needed to talk about.

'Why don't you go and have a shower,' I said. 'It's a very hot day and I think you need to freshen up. I'm making some milkshake, so afterwards we can sit in the garden and have a drink.'

'You can't make me have a shower.'

'That's true, but I'm requesting that you have a shower as you need one.'

'Well I'm not having one.'

'OK, well that's up to you. Don't have one. But if I were in your shoes I would like to smell fresh and clean.'

'OK I'll have one, but only because I want to have some peace and quiet!'

She ran upstairs and half an hour later she came down dressed in clean shorts and a striped top, asking for her milkshake.

'Do you feel better?' I asked.

'Yes. I'm sorry. I love you, Angela.'

She gave me a hug.

Jonathan joined us in the garden. We'd bought a swinging chair that summer and Lucy and I sat side by side, gently swaying back and forth. Her legs dangled over the edge and she took a deep breath.

'I like the smell of cut grass,' she declared, looking at our freshly mown lawn. 'You've done a very good job, Jonathan! Nearly as good as Daddy!'

He smiled and glanced at me. I could tell he was thinking the same way I was. It seemed a shame to spoil the moment by bringing up the subject of the horse knife, but of course it had to be done. I mean, we had only guessed that it must have come from Diane's and that Lucy had helped herself to it. We had to hear what she had to say.

'We need to talk to you about something,' Jonathan started.

'What?'

'Angela found a knife in your room when she made your bed today. Can you tell us where it came from?'

'What knife? I don't know what you're talking about. Someone must have put it there. I bet it was Maria, trying to get me into trouble.'

Jonathan fetched the knife and showed it to Lucy.

'It's this one. Now can you tell us where it came from?'

'No. I've got no idea. Oh! Wait a minute.'

Lucy put on an act of furrowing her brow and looking like she was thinking very hard, trying to uncover a memory buried deep inside her head.

'Oh, I remember that! It was a present, from Clare. I've had it ages. I forgot all about it.'

'Clare, as in Diane's daughter?'

'Yes.'

'Does Diane know Clare gave you the knife?'

'How should I know? Can you stop asking all these questions? Aren't I allowed to have a present?'

I explained that we had to be very careful about sharp objects in the house and that we certainly could not let her keep it in her bedroom.

'You've got knives in the kitchen!' she said. 'If I wanted to get a knife I could get one out of the drawer!'

In reality I kept all the sharp knives locked away and always have done; only blunt cutlery is within reach. It's what we've been taught and it's second nature to us. Jonathan told Lucy that he was going to have to look after the knife and would keep it safe. In the meantime he said we'd have to phone Diane and make sure she was happy that Clare had given it to Lucy.

'OK,' she said. 'Do you have to?'

'Yes.'

'I'm going to my room. It's too hot out here.'


'So that's where it went!' Diane exclaimed. 'No, Clare certainly didn't give it to Lucy. It was a gift to Clare from one of her godmothers, and she's been upset about it going missing.'

Diane reassured me that as a fellow foster carer she understood these things happen, which was kind of her in the circumstances. She wished me luck in dealing with the situation and told me she once had a similar scenario herself, involving a child she fostered who stole a trinket box from her best friend's house.

When I confronted Lucy with the facts she bit her lip and stared at the floor.

'Lucy, sweetheart, why did you take it when it didn't belong to you?'

'I don't know. I didn't even want it. I don't know why. I don't know why I made up the story, I just got confused and forgot what happened.'

'But now you know you shouldn't have taken the knife? And you won't take anything else that doesn't belong to you?'

She nodded her head and whispered, 'Yes.'

'OK, thank you for being honest now, at least. We'll return it to Clare tomorrow, and I think it would be a good idea to buy her a little something to say sorry. What do you think?'

'If you *say* so.'

'Yes, I do. You can't take things that don't belong to you, and Clare has been worried about losing her knife. It's precious to her. Let's take her a bunch of flowers, shall we?'

'Do I have to pay for them?'

'I think you should contribute £2 from your pocket money.'

'£2! That's loads! That's not fair!'

'I think that's fair. Now please go and get ready for bed.'

Lucy stamped her feet then ran away. To my horror she began howling like a wolf as she ran around the house, making a terrible racket that set Maria off. She started complaining and shouting down the stairs and when Lucy ran past her door she bellowed, 'SHUT UP YOU! YOU'RE MAD! SHUT UP YOU STUPID CRAZY GIRL.'

'Lucy, what on earth are you making that noise for? Maria, please go into your room and don't get involved. I don't want to hear you being rude to Lucy.'

'I'M SURPRISED YOU CAN HEAR ANYTHING! LUCY STOP HOWLING!'

Lucy got louder and louder and ran faster and faster, up and down the stairs, in and out of every room and around the garden.

'What do we do now?'

Jonathan scratched his head. 'Leave her to tire herself out? Hopefully she'll get fed up if we don't pay her any attention, like she has before.'

I agreed, and the two of us settled down to watch a film on video while Maria put her earphones in and turned her music up. Meanwhile Lucy continued to howl and rampage around the house. She must have come in and out of the living room half a dozen times, trying to annoy us, but we refused to react and simply paused our video every time until she charged off and continued howling in another room. In the end she kept up her campaign for two hours before she finally stomped into the living room and demanded to know why we were letting her make so much noise.

'It's your choice,' I said. 'It's your voice and your throat. I thought you'd get fed up sooner. I'm glad you've stopped now.'

'I'M GOING TO BED!' she yelled furiously. 'YOU TWO ARE SO ANNOYING! OW! My throat hurts. Thanks a lot!'

Lucy wet the bed again that night and didn't tell me. Thankfully I checked with plenty of time to spare before school so I could make sure she didn't leave the house again without having a good wash. When I gently tried to tell her that it was OK if she wet the bed and that she could always tell me, she exploded.

'Do you know what *she* used to do? *She* used to rub my nose in the wet sheets!'

'Did she?'

'She did, but I don't want to talk about it any more, OK?'

I wasn't sure if she meant Wendy or Val, or perhaps someone else. She could even have made it up, but I couldn't press Lucy if she didn't want to continue the conversation.

'Sweetheart, I am very sorry you're upset. I would never do that to you. I can't tell you how many wet sheets I've changed in my time. It happens. I am only concerned that you're clean, your clothes are dry and your bed is fresh every night, so you can have a good night's sleep and always smell nice.'

'OK, OK! I'll tell you if it ever happens again. There's no need to nag me. I've got it.'

She barged past me and began putting her shoes on. Lucy then sat frowning in the back of the car and refused to buckle her seat belt. When I insisted we weren't driving to school until she was safely strapped in she said she 'couldn't care less'.

'You're the one who'll get into trouble, not me. You get paid to look after me and take me to school. You're not doing your job properly.'

'I'll have to phone the school and tell them what is going on if you don't wear your seat belt.'

'FINE!' she said, finally clicking it in place. 'Are you happy now? Anyway, I don't know why you're bothered what the school think. I'm not staying there.'

I didn't respond to this and Lucy and I then sat in silence for the first half of the journey.

'Do you think I should have gone to the police when she did that?' Lucy suddenly blurted out. 'It's breaking the law!'

'Gone to the police? What do you mean?'

'My stepmother. Rubbing my face in the sheets. She put poo in my face too, when I had an accident. I told you that, didn't I?'

'No, I don't think you did.' I remembered that Lucy had said Val had put dog muck in her hair, but I didn't say it out loud.

'She was evil. When Daddy found out what she was like he got rid of her, really, really fast. Poof! She was gone. "Good riddance," he said. "Good riddance to bad rubbish."

He told me I did the right thing telling him about everything that happened. She – that Val – she said I was lying but he didn't believe her. He believed *me*. She was a really horrible old cow!'

'Language, Lucy! I'm very sorry to hear what you're telling me. And I'm glad you talked to your daddy.'

'So am I, because he believed me, and she had to go.'

I thought back to what else Lucy had said about Val. 'She put salt in my tea and pins in my bed.'

I couldn't be sure of the truthfulness of Lucy's stories. They sounded a little bit far-fetched to me, but then again I've learned that as a foster carer you never stop being shocked, and you never stop expecting the unexpected. Unfortunately, sometimes the tallest and most improbable tales do turn out to be true.

'Good riddance to bad rubbish,' she repeated. 'Wendy's horrible to me too, but Daddy doesn't see it. Daddy doesn't believe me!'

She left this last statement hanging in the air. She gave no specific examples about exactly how Wendy was horrible to her, as she did with Val, but I understood her inference very well. It seemed clear to me that Lucy was thinking Wendy was 'bad rubbish' too . . . or at least that's what she wanted her daddy to believe. An alarming thought struck me. *What if Lucy is deliberately trying to aggravate Wendy in the hope history will repeat itself? Does she think her dad will automatically side with her if it comes to her word against Wendy's, and that he'd get rid of her, like he did with Val?*

I sincerely hoped I was over-analysing the situation and had got this very wrong, but inevitably I couldn't help thinking back to the awful meeting we'd had. I'd been shocked at how strong Wendy's antipathy towards Lucy had become, and how it had spread to Dean and Gemma, both of whom made it clear they didn't want Lucy back in the family home any time soon. I'd been left confused, because the Lucy I saw in my home was not the same little girl who was being described that day. What did they say? Wendy had called her a 'poisonous little madam' and claimed she was scared of her. Gemma had said 'I don't want Lucy back home. I'm scared of what will happen' and Dean had effectively taken their side and said 'I'll not stand for it any longer'. It had been so upsetting, so baffling and so traumatic, especially for Lucy. When I'd called Wendy to complain, my focus was on how the family had spoken out in front of Lucy and the effect that had on her. But what if I only knew half the story? It still wouldn't justify their crass handling of the situation, but what if Lucy was a Jekyll and Hyde character, turning nasty when she was at home to deliberately cause trouble and provoke Wendy, in the hope it would break up her relationship with her daddy?

# 15

### *'Why, exactly, is Lucy in foster care?'*

Wendy called.

'I've got good news,' she told me.

'Good news? What is it?'

'The solicitor says Lucy *should* be statemented, and if she isn't there is a case to answer.'

'A case to answer?'

'Yes. It means if your local authority doesn't pay to have her statemented we will have a strong case if we take them to court to force them to pay. Like I say, it's good news. It's a clear-cut case. The authorities should be paying for her – for the statement, for all her educational needs.'

I was very pleased to hear this. 'It's great news for Lucy,' I said. 'This will make life much easier for her in school.'

'Should have happened a long time ago,' Wendy went on. 'Thank God it's getting sorted out and she can stay at St Joseph's.'

I told Wendy I'd pass this on to my social worker and

that no doubt we'd talk about it at the upcoming placement meeting.

Lucy came in the room at the end of the call, and when she realised I was talking to Wendy she asked if she could speak to her daddy.

'Sorry,' Wendy said bluntly. 'He's out at work. Won't be back for ages.'

Lucy decided to call her grandmother instead, and after their conversation she was grinning from ear to ear.

'Granny said I can stay with her this weekend if some-one can take me. Can I *please*?'

Lucy had an inset day from school the following Monday, which I assumed was how this idea came about. All her friends seemed to be going away on trips and long week-ends but we hadn't booked anything, partly because Maria didn't have an inset day and partly because it was an extremely busy weekend for the shop, with several large summer wedding orders to deliver. We'd thought about taking the girls out for a picnic on the Sunday, but we didn't have any plans set in stone.

'Let me see,' I told her. 'I'll have to check.'

I spoke to Ivy to make sure she was OK with the visit and then I called Social Services, who said that if Wendy and Dean were in agreement it was fine by them. We'd have to work out the travel arrangements between us, which I real-ised probably meant Jonathan and I would have to take her and pick her up. This was just about manageable, we reck-oned.

I called Wendy back and to my surprise Dean answered.

'Oh, hi Dean, are you just in from work?' I said.

'No, I've been off today. I've hurt my ankle. How can I help?'

I explained about the trip and Dean said it was fine by him, but they would not be able to help with lifts.

'I'm housebound at the moment and probably won't be able to drive by the weekend and Wendy is working. If you and Jonathan can take her, that would be great. Oh, sorry, I've got to go now. Thanks. Bye.'

I could hear Wendy in the background, asking who was on the phone. I'd have loved to have been a fly on the wall in their house when she realised she and Dean had told me very different stories about what he was doing that day. It was puzzling and made me wary of Wendy. *Maybe she was the one who had Jekyll and Hyde characteristics?* I thought. *Maybe she meddles and Dean doesn't see it?* It was very difficult for me to get to the truth of the matter; I didn't entirely trust Wendy or Lucy, and I was struggling to understand precisely what was going on between them, and how it had caused such a rift in the family.

Jonathan and I agreed to juggle things so that we could drop Lucy at her granny's on the Friday night after school and collect her on Monday. It meant booking Barbara in for some extra hours and asking my mum to collect Maria from a school friend's house on the Monday, but we decided it was worth the effort. The return journey was 230 miles and we both wanted to accompany Lucy, and share the driving. Wherever possible we try to avoid travelling alone with a child even on shorter trips, just in case anything untoward happens. Social Services prefers two adults to travel in a car with a child, to safeguard all parties, and the rule is that even if there is only one adult in the vehicle the child must sit in the back. Obviously it wasn't possible for us to all travel together when we took the girls to their separate school every morning, but we did our best to both be there on all other journeys.

Lucy gave me a hug when I came off the phone after making all the plans. She immediately went to pack a bag, even though it was only Wednesday.

'It's great to see Lucy so excited,' I said to Jonathan. 'This could be just what she needs.'

For the next couple of days Lucy was as good as gold, and she didn't wet the bed.

'What's wrong with Lucy?' Maria commented after we'd all eaten dinner together on the Thursday night.

'What do you mean? She seems in a perfectly good mood to me.'

'That's what I mean. She's being too nice. She's not staring at me and she's not being a pain.'

I let this go and gave a gentle laugh. 'I think she's in a good mood because she's spending the weekend with her granny, and she hasn't seen her for a while.'

As I cleared the plates off the table I tried to work out how long it had been. Unbelievably, it was coming up for three months. The time had flown.

Lucy was bouncing in her seat when we arrived at her grandmother's. School had finished a little earlier than usual that Friday and we'd been lucky with the traffic, so we'd arrived in very good time.

'Come here Lucy,' Ivy said, opening the front door. 'Come and give your old granny a big hug.'

Lucy cuddled her granny as if her life depended on it.

'Look at you! You've got your front teeth I see. You're looking very grown up.'

Ivy invited me and Jonathan in for a cup of tea and said she was very happy to fetch us something to eat, if we were hungry. We declined, not wanting to be any trouble, but she still brought out a tray laden with a homemade sponge cake and a pot of tea. Her house was pin-neat and the elaborately wallpapered walls, the brass mantelpiece and every inch of the burgundy-painted windowsills were filled with photographs of her family.

'This is me,' Lucy said proudly, showing me a picture of herself as a toddler, pushing a toy wheelbarrow around a garden. 'And this one.'

The second picture showed Lucy on her christening day, being carried by her dad, next to the font. There was a young woman next to him, with her arm around him, smiling. She was the spitting image of Ivy and I assumed it was Lucy's mother.

'Me and Daddy,' Lucy said, making no mention of the woman. 'I had a hat that matched my christening dress but I hated it, didn't I Granny?'

'You did. You pulled it off. Nearly landed in the font!'

Ivy caught my eye. 'Yes, that's my daughter Noreen, Lucy's mother.'

Lucy didn't react in any way to this reference and Ivy swiftly changed the subject.

'Let me show you to your bedroom, Lucy. I've changed the curtains since you were here. My leg's a lot better so I've been able to do more, thank the Lord.'

Ivy explained that when Lucy had stayed with her earlier in the year she had been recovering from an operation, which of course did not help one bit when she unexpectedly found herself trying to look after an eight-year-old who was miles from home, out of school and upset by all the disruption she'd gone through.

I could see that Ivy still looked a little unsteady on her feet, but she reassured us she was in much better health now.

'Are you sure you can manage the whole weekend?' Jonathan asked.

'Yes, I'm looking forward to it. I was in the Land Army, you know. It might not look like it but I'm made of strong stuff.'

Lucy's eyes widened 'You were a soldier?'

'Not quite. I'll tell you all about it when we have time. Now, what was I saying? Oh yes, I've already got the shopping in so that's done. And Lucy's a good little helper, as I'm sure you've found out.'

Jonathan and I said we had indeed.

Ivy liked to chat and we went on to talk about her experiences as a foster carer several decades earlier. 'How things have changed,' she mused, raising her white eyebrows. 'In my day it was all orphans or unwanted children born to unmarried mothers. Now it's all about dealing with poor souls with syndromes and disorders that the parents can't cope with. I don't know how you do it.'

Jonathan and I swapped glances. Lucy was listening to every word and I felt uncomfortable about that. I hoped she wasn't wondering which category she fitted into. She certainly wasn't an orphan, and she wasn't put into care by an unmarried mother. Neither was she an unwanted child and nor did she have 'syndromes and disorders', as Ivy put it. Lucy had some behaviour issues, of course, but we'd dealt with far worse. *Why, exactly, is Lucy in foster care?* I thought. It was a very complicated question, and I wasn't sure I knew the answer.

Jonathan did what he always does very well, taking the conversation in a different direction and lightening the atmosphere.

'Orphans. Now that's a word you don't hear much nowadays,' he said. 'Makes me think of *Oliver Twist.* Speaking of films, have you seen *Toy Story*? The animation is meant to be out of this world. I'm really looking forward to seeing it.'

Ivy said she hadn't been to the cinema for ages and didn't have a video recorder. Lucy started to tell her all about it, having watched it recently with my mother, and while she nattered away I couldn't help returning to my question, because it was playing on my mind.

*What, exactly, was Lucy doing in foster care, when all her siblings lived at home?*

The more time passed, the more I was starting to think

that *Wendy* was the problem with Lucy, but that was something I had to keep to myself. The reality was I didn't know the half of what had gone on in Lucy's family home, or what went on in Wendy's life, or Lucy's head. 'You never know what's really going on in somebody else's life,' Jonathan and I often say, and this helps us both to stay open-minded and non-judgemental, as we need to be.

Nonetheless, I thought about how unfair Lucy's lot seemed. Her place in the family, the dynamics of her family unit and the personalities of Dean, Wendy and Gemma had contributed massively to her current situation, I felt in no doubt about that. Yet all of those factors and circumstances were beyond Lucy's control. She was eight years old. Surely she should be living with her family, and shouldn't those closest to her be doing their utmost to make that possible? Instead, they seemed to be looking for trouble and coming up with excuses to keep her out of the home. Not everyone, of course. Wendy was certainly like that, and so was Gemma, to a lesser extent. I wasn't sure about Dean. I didn't think he was actively trying to derail the family reunion, as I feared Wendy and Gemma were, but his lack of backbone made him complicit. I wished he'd follow his heart and stand up for himself, and for Lucy, but I didn't know whether he had it in him.

'Angela, Granny is going to take me to the cinema this weekend!' Lucy blurted out, after helping Ivy carry the cups to the kitchen.

'That's good. What are you going to see?'

Ivy chuckled and said she had no idea what was on, but it would be a great treat for both of them, she was sure.

Driving home, we both felt optimistic about the weekend.

'It's great to see Lucy looking so happy,' Jonathan said. 'Fingers crossed she behaves herself and it all goes well. It could be a great turning point for her.'

# 16

## *'Where's my daddy?'*

When we went to collect Lucy on the Monday she was full of beans, enthusing about what she'd done, what she'd seen at the pictures and how she'd helped her granny to cook, tidy up the garden and even paint an old wooden bench that Ivy loved to sit on when the sun lit up her patio in the afternoon.

'Come and see!'

Lucy led us outside and proudly showed off the bench. It was painted navy blue and looked fantastic.

'I sanded it down and everything,' Lucy said. 'Granny said she didn't recognise it when I finished it.'

Ivy waved us off at the door, having given Lucy a warm hug and a kiss on the forehead. She reminded her to keep in touch and told her to look after the booklet: she'd given Lucy a precious piece of memorabilia from her Land Army days.

'It's been so lovely to see you,' she said. 'I'm worn out

now, but I'll get over it! I look forward to seeing you soon. I hope to see you in the summer holidays.'

Lucy looked at me hopefully.

'I hope so too,' I said, not committing myself to anything I didn't have the power to deliver.

Lucy slept in the car on the way home, only waking when we stopped off for petrol and food. We treated her to a McDonald's and she was as good as gold, although that does tend to be the result when you take any child to McDonald's! When we got home she had an animated chat with my mum and Maria, telling them all about her trip. I don't think I'd ever seen her looking so happy and relaxed.

When the girls were in bed Jonathan and I reflected on the weekend. We were very glad we'd made the effort to drive her there and back, although I think we were almost as worn out as Ivy!

'I think the weekend's done Lucy the power of good,' I said. 'Ivy didn't have one single complaint, did she?'

'No. And I think she would have let us know if there had been any problems, don't you? She's a good person, a straight-talking woman.'

'She is. I'd love to ask her what she really thinks about Wendy and Dean, I really would. And I'd like to ask about Lucy's mum. I wonder if Ivy is in touch with her? I wonder what went wrong? It would be helpful to know. I mean, all we know is that she abandoned the family when Lucy was, what? Four?'

We'd been told that right at the start of the placement but heard no more.

'That's right. Lucy was four and she's never seen her since. Very sad, isn't it?'

Lucy was still in an upbeat mood the next day and when I collected her from school Miss Heather came out to find me in the playground, just outside the classroom.

'Mrs Hart, I'm glad I've caught you. I wanted to say that Lucy has been a joy to teach today. She's been kind and helpful and very well behaved. She's listened and tried hard, and she's produced a lovely piece of artwork. We have been looking at Japanese culture and Lucy loved learning about origami. Do you have time to come on in and see what she made?'

'Of course. I'd love to.'

Lucy was holding a tiny little swan made of paper. It was sitting in the palm of her hand and she held it up so I could have a good look.

'I'm going to give it to Granny for her birthday. Do you like it?'

'I do. It's very clever indeed. I'd love to learn how to make one of those. Can you teach me?'

'Yes! I'll make one for you too, if you like.'

Miss Heather told Lucy she could take a few sheets of paper and card home with her.

'Thank you very much,' I said. 'That's very kind of you.'

I gave Miss Heather an appreciative smile and hoped she realised I was thanking her for so much more than the art paper. This was exactly the kind of encouragement Lucy needed. She was very skilful with her hands, and praising her when she produced work like this was great for her self-esteem.

'Bodes well for the session tomorrow,' Jonathan commented when I told him about Lucy's successful day at school and continued good behaviour.

'Let's hope so. I really want it to go well for her this time.'

This session was an extra counselling slot that had been fitted in at the Child and Family centre for Lucy and her father. Wendy had been invited too but couldn't attend as she was working, apparently. Bella had pushed for the session in advance of the upcoming placement meeting as she thought it would be helpful to get things back on track before everyone gathered to make decisions about the next steps. It hadn't been easy to get Dean to attend on his own, I learned, but he had been persuaded. I was very pleased about this. Maybe I was clutching at straws, but I felt sure that he and Lucy would make some good progress together, without Wendy's influence.

Lucy was very excited about the session and she talked about her daddy all the way to the centre, telling us about all the gardening projects he'd done in the past, including the time he won an award from the council for revamping part of an inner-city park. She made no mention of Wendy or Gemma or any of her siblings. It was all about Daddy today, and Lucy was making the most of it.

'He's very kind, my daddy. He makes me laugh. He's the best daddy in the world. Did you know, he can ride a motorbike? He's got one in the garage he's been building for ages and ages. He said he'll teach me to ride it one day. One time he let me squirt the oil on the spooks.'

'Spooks?'

'No! Not spooks. What is it? You know, those wheel thingies.'

'Spokes!' Jonathan and I chimed.

'Yes! Spokes. I like that word. Spokes!'

'I do too!' Jonathan said, and then he told Lucy all about the motorbike he once owned, before we got married.

Lucy listened intently and thought it was hilarious that Jonathan used to ride a motorbike. He said he'd show her photos to prove it and she threw her head back and giggled at the prospect. She was happy and in an incredibly receptive mood. I took a deep breath and looked out of the window just in time to see a beautiful green field full of golden yellow crops drift by. In the distance the horizon was bright and sunny: I hoped it was a good omen.


As we walked into the reception area of the Child and Family centre I felt my throat constrict. One of the therapists was waiting for us and I could tell she was worried, even though her mouth was nailed into the shape of a smile.

'Lucy!' she said with unconvincing cheerfulness. 'Great to see you! It's just me and you today. Daddy can't make it I'm afraid, but never mind. It means I'll have more time to focus just on you! Now you go on in and take a seat in there. I need to have a quick word with Mr and Mrs Hart.'

'No,' Lucy said. 'I want my daddy! Where's my daddy?'

She sounded winded and forlorn. I wanted to hug her and tell her everything was OK but it wasn't, and I had to let the therapist deal with this.

'Like I say, he can't make it today. He's sent a message.'

'Is he poorly? Can I speak to him?'

Lucy's voice had a desperate edge to it.

'I'm sure you can try to call him later, after your session,' the therapist said, flicking me an anxious look. If Dean hadn't turned up here I didn't feel hopeful he'd pick the phone up. I think the therapist shared my doubts.

'Can I, Angela? Can I ring him?' Lucy stared at me, her eyes begging me to give her the answer she needed to hear.

'We can certainly try to get him on the phone, sweetheart. Now why don't you go in and take a seat. The sooner you do the sooner the session can start and . . .' I wanted to say, 'the sooner we'll be home and you can call your daddy,' but I stopped myself and let my sentence trail off. God forbid, I didn't want Lucy to suffer any more disappointment.

Thankfully she did as I asked and went and sat down in the side room the therapist steered her towards. As soon as she was out of earshot the therapist told us that Wendy had called to say that Dean was no longer attending the sessions. 'He thinks they are a complete waste of time, she said. He is not coming today nor ever again, it seems.'

We were gutted. We'd seen this as a golden opportunity for Lucy and her dad to work together and build on their relationship. She was in great spirits. She'd had a fantastic weekend with her granny and had been praised by her

211

teacher, and she'd been counting down the minutes until she could see her daddy. I'd thought Bella had played a blinder fixing up this father and daughter session, but now it had all turned to dust.

I felt incredibly sorry for Lucy and I asked how on earth we were going to tell her that her daddy had thrown the towel in like this.

'Let's see how the land lies after today,' the therapist said wisely. 'He might change his mind, or Wendy may have got it wrong, somehow. We need to speak to Dean himself and there is no point in upsetting Lucy until we know for certain exactly what's going on. I'll change the session to do some one-to-one work with Lucy and hopefully we can get back on track in due course.'

Lucy was calm when she emerged from the forty-five-minute session. The therapist had done a good job in the circumstances, we thought. In the car on the way home Lucy remained quiet and well behaved, asking politely when she could talk to her daddy.

'We'll try him when we get in,' I said, looking at my watch. 'Let's hope he's in, but I guess it may be a bit early. He might be at work.'

'Yes. I know he's busy. I know he loves me. I know he would not want to upset me on purpose. He's a busy man. He's good at his job and he works very hard for the family, you know.'

Her words didn't sound very natural to me and I didn't think she'd have come up with those statements all by herself. I guessed Lucy was echoing some of the positive and reasonable things the therapist had said, and that gave me an injection of optimism. I found myself daring to hope that Wendy had exaggerated how Dean felt about the meetings, and that he would attend the next session, having got over this blip. Lucy was right, after all. Her daddy loved her, and surely that would trump everything else?

By the time we got home I had convinced myself that Dean couldn't possibly mean what he said about the sessions being a waste of time. Even if he did feel that way at the moment, it surely couldn't mean he'd given up completely, because how could he? Lucy was his own flesh and blood. He had to fight for her, not run away or wash his hands of the situation.

As soon as we got home Jonathan headed straight back out again as he needed to get to the wholesaler's before collecting Maria from school. It was too late to take Lucy back to school, and in any case I couldn't imagine she'd be in the mood to learn. I left her to make the call to her dad in private, and she picked up the phone in the hall. I went in the kitchen and put the kettle on but before it had boiled I heard a loud crash in the hallway. When I ran to investigate I saw the phone on the floor, where presumably Lucy had thrown it. She must have done this with some force because part of the plastic casing had fallen off the handset. Lucy was running upstairs and when she saw me she shouted, 'I hate Wendy! She's a cow! I hate her! I want my daddy! I want my daddy. I WANT MY DADDY!'

I heard her bedroom door slam and, after picking the

phone up and putting what was left of it on its cradle, I went up and knocked gently on Lucy's door.

'Can I come in, sweetheart?'

There was no reply.

'Lucy, are you OK? Can I talk to you?'

'No! Talk to Wendy!'

'Talk to Wendy? So it was Wendy on the phone just now, not Daddy?'

'Yes. Talk to Wendy!'

Seconds later I heard the phone ring. I thought about leaving it but I sensed I needed to get it, so I dashed to my bedroom on the floor below and answered it.

'Angela? Is that you? We've had enough, we have.'

'Wendy? What do you mean?'

'I mean we need a total break from Lucy. I've spoken to Social Services. Me and Dean can't be doing with all the stress she causes. We – he – needs a break. He thinks those sessions are a complete waste of time and he's not going again. We're nowhere near ready to have her back home. There's trouble every time. We – he – wants a complete break, and then we'll see how we feel.'

'Have you told Lucy this?'

'Yes, I've explained the situation to her.'

'What exactly did you say, because she's very upset?'

'I told her we'll see her next in the summer holidays, hopefully. If she behaves.'

'Summer holidays? When in the holidays, exactly?' My immediate thought was that the school summer holiday was more than six weeks long, but I could hardly think straight. 'Do you mean at the start of the holiday, when the schools break up?' I stuttered.

My head was banging. I wondered how Lucy would cope, having her life put on hold like this. It was still June – July or August would feel like an eternity away to Lucy. And now it was only going to be for a visit, not for a move home as she hoped. We were back to square one.

'No, we're away at the start of the holiday,' Wendy said breezily. 'We're taking the kids to Spain. We'll be back around the middle of August. It'll have to be after that.'

*Lucy's one of the kids*, I thought.

'Did you tell Lucy this?'

'Yes and she was very rude to me. She said I was mean to not let her come on holiday with us. She called me "mean and horrible" and blamed me for everything, which just goes to show that she's not ready to move back in with us. She can't control her mouth. She's disruptive. Nothing has changed. We know that, and that's why Dean can't be bothered with those useless meetings any more. We think it's for the best, Angela. Dean's tried his best and he didn't want it to come to this, but unfortunately it has. He's in complete agreement with me, and supported me when I called Social Services to tell them our decision.'

I was lost for words. I felt heartbroken for Lucy and suspicious of Wendy. Her last statement smacked of manipulative behaviour. It didn't surprise me in the least that Wendy was the one calling Social Services to report on her and Dean's supposedly joint decision. My instincts told me Dean had been led to this point by Wendy. She wore the trousers, that's for sure.

'I need to go to Lucy,' I said. 'Like I say, she's very upset. She was hoping to move back home for good in the summer. This is a major setback for her.'

'Well I don't know where she got that from! We're a million miles away from having her home.'

I wanted to say, 'That's what we've all supposedly been working towards for the past few months. That's what we all agreed with Social Services. Her placement was meant to be for two to three months, remember? That's where Lucy got that impression from!' Of course I bit my lip. Wendy was not being reasonable and I didn't want to get into an argument.

I swallowed hard and told Wendy I had not expected this at all. 'I hoped today would be a good day. I hoped Dean and Lucy could have a good counselling session and get things moving forward again.'

Wendy adopted a sympathetic tone but what she said showed no empathy or understanding and was actually unreasonable to the point of delusion. 'As I'm sure you know better than anyone, Angela, you have to be honest with kids and you can't give them false hope. That's all today would have given her had Dean turned up, and that's not fair, is it? We don't want Lucy to be disappointed or upset. This move home simply isn't going to happen overnight. She's not ready to move back in any time soon. There's a lot of work to be done. We'll see her in August, after our holiday, and take it from there. I can't stop her phoning her dad but I think it would be best if she didn't. It's best for everyone to go cold turkey I'm afraid, Angela. It's the only way. I've already told the kids and they're OK with it.'

Wendy had lapsed into speaking so dispassionately it was as if she were cancelling a standing order at the bank rather than stopping Lucy from seeing her daddy and siblings for the best part of two months.

I was extremely angry but I couldn't afford to get on the wrong side of Wendy. I brought the phone call to an end as quickly as possible. I needed to draw breath and think about how best to cope with this turn of events. What would I say to Lucy? I'd have to talk to Jess, as soon as possible. She was back from her annual leave and the placement meeting to review Lucy's case was now in the diary at long last. I wondered when Wendy had called Social Services with this bombshell, and what their response would be.

Jonathan was still out at the wholesaler's and I really wished he were home. I wanted to discuss this with him more than anyone else, and I also needed a hug. It's at times like this I realise how much I appreciate that we share our fostering responsibilities, and how much I admire carers who work alone or don't have the support that Jonathan and I give each other.

I went back upstairs, feeling shaken and stunned. Lucy refused to open her bedroom door when I knocked and called her name.

'Has she told you?' she shouted. 'They're going on holiday without me! I can't go home! I'm stuck here! I want my daddy! I just want my daddy!'

217

'Can I come in and talk to you?'

'No. No you can't.'

'Please, Lucy. D'you need a hug? I know I'd like one.'

'No.'

'OK. I'm going to do some cooking now, sweetheart. Please come down and help me if you feel like it. Or just come down and talk to me, when you're ready. I'm making quiche for our dinner later. You can make something with the leftover pastry, if you want to. I quite fancy some jam tarts.'

Lucy appeared after about twenty minutes, just as I was thinking I'd better go and check on her.

'Urgh! What's that smell?'

'I don't know. Is it the chopped onion?'

She walked over to the kitchen counter where the diced onion was piled on a plate, sniffed dramatically and gave an exaggerated look of disgust.

'Urgh! Urgh! That totally reeks. Can I make jam tarts? I don't want to go anywhere near those smelly onions.'

I was very happy to set Lucy up with a ball of shortcrust pastry, a floured board and a collection of pastry cutters. She looked in the cupboard and picked out a pot of jam my mum had made the previous year, put on an apron and washed her hands without me having to remind her. Then she worked diligently, chatting about this and that and asking sweetly if we could go swimming again soon, and if she could visit my mum. This was something she really enjoyed. Lucy would help her with the garden, even using the lawn mower under supervision, and Mum was very pleased with all the help and said her garden was all the better for it.

Lucy didn't say a word about Wendy or her dad and I didn't press her: it was best she broached the subject, if she wanted to talk about it, and so I simply reminded her she could talk to me about anything, any time. When the jam tarts were in the oven she asked if she could call her granny. As usual I said she could use the phone in another room, but she sat at the kitchen table while I cleared up and put the quiche to one side, to cook later, when Jonathan and Maria were back.

'Yes Granny. I had a lovely time. Can I come and stay with you in the summer holidays? No. I'm not going on holiday with Daddy. It's OK. How long can I stay with you? OK. I've just made jam tarts. I miss you Granny. Bye. Love you too.'

Lucy informed me that she was spending 'all the summer holiday' with her granny and then asked if she could go over to Diane's before dinner, as they had a new pony she wanted to meet. I called Diane, who readily agreed, and then I dropped Lucy over to the stables, promising her she could have forty minutes before I'd need to collect her. While she was out I managed to get hold of Jess. She hadn't heard a thing and said she'd find out who Wendy had spoken to when she called Social Services.

'Leave it with me,' she said. 'And well done, Angela.'

'Well done?'

'Yes, well done for how you've handled this. It can't have been easy having that conversation with Wendy. Like I say, leave it with me. Obviously I'll get back to you before the placement meeting. Given the circumstances, are you and Jonathan happy to keep Lucy on for a longer-term placement?'

'Of course. Jonathan's been out this afternoon and doesn't know what Wendy's said to Lucy, but I'm sure he'll be in agreement. We both want the best for Lucy. I'll speak to him this evening.'

'OK. I'm sure Bella will be in touch too; she'll need to talk to Lucy. Do you think Lucy would be happy to stay with you for longer?

'Yes, I think so. We do get on and we're very fond of her. She's comfortable with us, and I think we cope quite well with her aggravating ways. The irritating behaviour we see when she's not busy certainly wouldn't put us off looking after her.'

'OK, that's good to know. Thanks, Angela. It's just as well you are so laid back and easy-going.'

I was surprised to be described in this way and gave a thin laugh. I don't really consider myself to be particularly laid back and easy-going, but I took the compliment as it was meant. I think it's probably more accurate to say I know how to keep my feet on the ground and my head cool in times of trouble and change. Jonathan's the same – we've joked many times that we're like swans on the water. On the face of it we're serenely gliding through even the most difficult of waters, yet under the surface we're paddling away furiously. I guess having a 'laid back' facade is something we've grown into, as it's never helpful for the children to see us flapping or fretting. They need to have complete faith in us and to view us as competent, reliable adults they can rely on at all times, come what may.

I made myself a coffee and sat in the kitchen, reflecting on the twists and turns of the day. My heart was full to the brim with worry about Lucy's future. I had spent the last few months working so hard to help her return home sooner rather than later. That was our role: we were to help integrate Lucy back into the family unit. We'd taken on that role and trusted in the plan, but now it had been derailed and everything was in the air. Worse still, I began to wonder if moving home was actually the right thing for Lucy at all.

What would happen when she eventually moved back in, whenever that may be? Would Lucy and Wendy ever get along, and if not, how would a permanently tense or even hostile environment impact on Lucy? She needed to be shown love and kindness and her self-esteem needed building up, not knocking down. Now, after the brusque and, frankly, cold-hearted way Wendy had spoken on the phone, I was beginning to wonder if Lucy was ever going to get the affection and understanding she needed from her stepmother. I had no doubt her daddy loved her, and her siblings too, but was that enough? Dean allowed Wendy to rule the roost. What chance did Lucy have if her stepmother continued to think so lowly of her and take every opportunity to score points and make criticisms? All Lucy wanted was to belong. Why couldn't Wendy help her fit in?

When I spoke to Jonathan he immediately agreed that we would continue to care for Lucy for as long as necessary.

221

'Absolutely, one hundred per cent,' he said. 'She needs all the stability and support she can get.'

Lucy seemed happy and relaxed when I brought her back from Diane's and was talking nineteen to the dozen about the new pony. However, at bedtime her mood suddenly dipped. She kicked Maria's bedroom door for no apparent reason and when Maria complained, Lucy told her she was a 'cry baby', which of course infuriated the older girl.

'What's your problem?' Maria said. 'Why are you always the one causing trouble? You know what you are, don't you? You're a stirrer! You're a wind-up merchant!'

Jonathan dashed up the stairs and managed to defuse the situation. He told both girls that if they behaved themselves we would visit a newly opened leisure centre across town at the weekend. It had all kinds of fancy slides and a range of diving boards and he said he'd heard that the main pool was fantastic for doing lengths, as it was Olympic-sized.

'Why do we have to wait until the weekend?' Lucy asked.

'Because it'll give you both time to behave and earn the treat.'

Lucy kicked her own bedroom door and told Jonathan he was boring and mean while Maria stayed quiet.

'Kicking the door is not going to get you anywhere. I suggest you stop now and go and calm down.'

'What are you going to do about it if I don't?'

'Nothing. We won't be going swimming at all if you continue with this behaviour.'

'Says who? How about I'll carry on causing trouble until you take me?'

She kicked the door again. She was trying to provoke a reaction but Jonathan didn't rise to it and took a step back.

'I bet you'll give in. I bet if I wind you up enough you'll give in and take me anyway, just to get me out of your hair!'

Jonathan shrugged. 'It doesn't work like that, Lucy. If you don't work with us and behave yourself then you will be the one who loses out. I am very serious. Behave yourself, or you will be the one who loses.'

'Says who?' she goaded, adding sneakily, 'It's worked for me before, don't you know.'

I'd followed Jonathan up the stairs and I was standing shoulder to shoulder with him now. Maria was standing outside her bedroom door, looking with amusement at Lucy being told off by Jonathan.

'I'll scream and scream and scream until I'm sick!' Maria said mockingly. She'd recently watched an old scene from *Just William* on TV and I instantly knew she was trying to shame Lucy by comparing her to Violet Elizabeth – the spoilt little girl who was William's nemesis.

Fortunately Lucy didn't get the reference. She frowned at Maria and told her to shut up, but Maria said it was time for Lucy to shut up. 'You should know them by now,' she cautioned. 'They won't be taking either of us swimming if you carry on.'

'Bet they do.'

'No, Lucy. You need to stop now. Blackmailing isn't going to work. Haven't you learned anything since you've been here?'

Jonathan interjected before either girl spoke again.

'I've just thought, Angela, if we don't go swimming at the weekend, you and me could go to the cinema together. There are a few films I'd like to see. Do you think your mother would be able to babysit?'

'I'm sure she would. I know she's free this weekend.'

We smiled at each other.

'I'm going to bed!' Maria snapped.

'So am I!' Lucy said, and they slammed their doors in unison, leaving Jonathan and me to walk along the landing talking very loudly about how lovely it would be if the girls were extremely well behaved and we could all go to the swimming pool *and* the cinema together.

At midnight there was a knock on our bedroom door.

'Angela, please can you change my bed?'

It was Lucy, looking very sorry for herself. 'Sorry. Didn't do it on purpose.'

'It's OK, sweetheart. It's an accident. Come on, we'll have it changed in no time.'

'Thanks,' she whispered.

I'd shown Lucy where the linen was kept and encouraged her to help herself if she ever needed fresh sheets but she must have forgotten or decided she'd rather I did it for her. I didn't mind.

'You're nice and kind.' Lucy muttered the words very

softly as we padded along the landing, and then she took hold of my hand very gently. As quiet as the words were, they rang loudly in my heart. I squeezed her hand tenderly back, telling her she was very nice and kind too.

# 17

### *'Grown-ups always change their minds'*

With it now looking likely that Lucy would be with us all summer, and beyond, I decided to call the travel agent and see if we could potentially take Lucy with us on the holiday we'd booked before she came to stay. I was told it would be no problem at all: the log cabin we'd reserved already had a double room for Jonathan and me and a twin room the girls could share. It would just be a formality to add Lucy to our party, and we could do this any time. This was something I'd mention at the meeting, as Wendy and Dean plus Social Services would need to approve this, provided Lucy wanted to join us.

The placement meeting to discuss Lucy's future was delayed twice, first due to staff sickness and then because of a diary clash. It felt like we'd been waiting for it forever.

Lucy's behaviour was very mixed in the aftermath of her conversation with Wendy. But she was often sweet and kind, offering to help with tasks I felt were above and beyond the call of duty. She wanted to do everything – rearrange the shed, repair punctures on the bikes, wash the car, you name it – and all of this was after she'd done a full day at school, been riding or mucking out the horses or enjoyed a day packed with activities at the weekend.

We did make it to the new swimming pool and to the cinema with both girls. Lucy set herself the challenge of swimming twenty lengths and achieved it, albeit through gritted teeth for the last few lengths, as the pool was longer than any she was used to. I was impressed by how strong she was for her size. Lucy was still very slim and slight and her eating habits had not changed a great deal since she arrived. Junk food of any kind was still her snack or meal of choice, but I was satisfied she ate enough nutritious food too; I made sure of that by continuing to encourage her to cook and shop with me and also to choose healthy recipes and pick fresh fruit and vegetables from my mum's garden.

I was confident I'd stopped Lucy from helping herself to junk that would spoil her meals, and from eating secretly in her room. Something that worked really well was a tip I'd picked up from another foster carer at a training session. She advised us to put a tuck box in the kitchen filled with a few limited treats Lucy could help herself to during the week. The rule was that she could take from the tuck box provided she was also eating decent meals. When the snacks were gone they were not replaced until the following week.

Lucy liked the idea of having a special box with her name on and it worked very well. Unfortunately, when Maria saw that Lucy had a tuck box she wanted one too, which wasn't ideal. I say this because Maria had access to a seemingly never-ending supply of junk food, fizzy drinks and snacks whenever she visited her grandmother, which she did regularly. It would have been better for her to go without treats completely in our house, but I couldn't deny her a tuck box if Lucy had one. I did my best to make Maria's snacks and treats as sugar-free and low calorie as possible, and I think I got away with it!

While we continued to wait to hear from Jess about when the meeting would take place we had good news about Lucy's statement, which St Joseph's had helped to arrange after Wendy contacted the solicitor. Lucy had finally been tested and the statement had come through at long last, which meant her school place was secure and she would have the help she needed in the classroom without any further fighting over funding, or the lack of it.

It turned out Lucy suffered from dyslexia, as I suspected, and she also had below average maths skills for her age, although at the time that was all the information we had. The head advertised for a teaching assistant, they had a good response to the advert and eventually a teaching assistant was employed to work directly with Lucy.

I was delighted Lucy was finally statemented although I also recognised that now her education was on track at our local primary school, this could potentially give Wendy more ammunition in her arguments against having Lucy home.

'It wouldn't surprise me if she said Lucy has to stay with

us until she's finished her primary education, now everything's set up at St Joseph's!' I joked.

'I doubt she'll go that far,' Jonathan said. 'And in any case, you can't worry about what-ifs.'

'I know but, joking apart, after all that's gone on I can't help being wary when it comes to Wendy. I don't think she ever puts Lucy first. I think she puts herself and Gemma first.'

Jonathan nodded. 'It certainly seems that way, but we can't judge, can we? All we can do is carry on looking after Lucy as best we can, building her self-esteem and taking the lead from Social Services. It'll be interesting to see what comes out of this long-awaited meeting. You never know, maybe we'll find that Wendy was having a bad day when she had her outburst, or maybe Dean will take charge and fight Lucy's corner for once?'

In the meantime Lucy attended another session at the Child and Family centre, on her own.

'They should just call it the child centre,' she said unhappily, looking at the sign.

The logo of the organisation showed a family of stick people holding hands in a circle. *Poor Lucy*, I thought. *She must feel so pushed out. It isn't fair.*

The good news was that the psychologist thought she was making great progress and told me they had an excellent session that day. I wondered if the fact that Lucy had no expectations of seeing her family for the time being was actually helping her deal with the situation. I couldn't discuss this with the psychologist as everything was confidential, but I put this theory to Jonathan.

'You could be right,' he said. 'At least she can't be disappointed or have any hopes dashed.'

'Sad but true. Poor Lucy. It's like she's had all her hopes and dreams taken away.'

The review meeting eventually happened in July, near the end of term, after being re-scheduled yet again due to building work at the Social Services office. Wendy had sent a message to confirm she and Dean were not attending, as they 'didn't see the point'. Bella would need to talk to Lucy after the meeting and so she had to come with us and wait outside with a support social worker, but we made absolutely sure she had no expectations of seeing her daddy that day. She seemed fine with this, perhaps because she'd taken Wendy's word as gospel when she told Lucy they would next see her at the end of August.

The meeting was brief and straight to the point. Jess confirmed that Wendy and Dean had refused to have Lucy back for the time being, or to take her on their family holiday. I was very glad Lucy was not present and was being looked after in a waiting room along the corridor.

'They would like more time to prepare for her return,' is how the social worker diplomatically phrased it.

Wendy and Dean hadn't put a time frame on when they might be ready to start again with Child and Family meetings and resume work towards Lucy's return home, but Jess suggested that it would be a good idea to hold another placement meeting in about six weeks, so we would all know what was happening in advance of the new school term in September. Jess also said that steps had been taken to contact Lucy's birth mother, to let her know her daughter was in foster care. It's possible Ivy had already told Noreen what was going on, but to my knowledge this was the first time Social Services had stepped in. As far as I was aware, because the aim of Lucy's placement with us was to return her to her father and the rest of the family, involving her birth mother had not been part of the initial plan. Things were different now, however. With all this disruption and uncertainty, it seemed sensible to investigate other potential options for Lucy.

'Are you happy to have Lucy stay with you over the summer?'

'Yes,' I said. 'We've already looked into the possibility of taking her on holiday with us, though we haven't mentioned it to her yet, of course.'

I explained our plans and said that Maria would be coming too. Bella said she thought this was a good idea, and said she'd have a 'wee word' with Wendy and Dean. 'I can't see them objecting at all,' she said. Nobody disagreed with Bella's prediction, and everyone assembled gave a little murmur or nod of approval.

Bella had spoken to Lucy that morning to ask if she would be happy staying with us for longer, and Lucy had said she would be, 'but only because I know I can go home soon.' After the meeting Bella had another word with Lucy and explained the situation.

'I don't mind staying with Angela and Jonathan a bit longer but I don't want to go on holiday with them.'

'Why not?'

'Why would I want to? My own family is going on holiday.'

'But you know you're not going with them.'

'They might change their mind. Grown-ups always change their minds. And if they don't, I won't have a holiday. I'd rather stay with my granny. I want to spend the school holiday with my granny. She said I can. Then I'll go home. Daddy will be back from Spain then.'

Bella relayed this conversation to me. 'I think she's a bit muddled up and is in denial, bless her.'

'I know. Don't worry, Jonathan and I will tread carefully and be sure not to make any promises that can't be kept in terms of what will happen in the future.'

After the review meeting Lucy's behaviour was at best awkward, at worst belligerent and aggravating. We were called into school several more times in the last couple of weeks of school. She shouted at a teacher, spat at another little girl and threw mud at a classroom window. Her teaching assistant ended up in tears one day when Lucy refused to do as she was told, called her a rude name and ran out of a lesson howling and screaming 'like a wounded animal'.

Lucy pointedly refused to acknowledge the reality of what was happening with her placement. For example, when she spoke to her granny she always carried on as if everything was fine, talking about her daddy as if she'd seen him yesterday and they were not temporarily estranged at all. She invented stories about supposedly recent games she'd played with her siblings, and if anyone pulled her up on it she'd say, 'Oh I got muddled up. I meant when I was playing with my friends at school', or, 'It happened last year, sorry, what did I say? I got confused.'

One day Lucy talked about how the extension to the family home was being built specifically to create an extra bedroom for her when I knew this was not the case: it was to create more space for the family generally, and nothing had been promised in terms of a new bedroom for Lucy.

I flagged all of this up to Social Services as I felt it was something Lucy's psychologist needed to know, in case she wanted to discuss it at Lucy's therapy sessions. Of course I never found out what was said, or indeed even whether Lucy kept up the pretence with her psychologist or shared her true feelings and understanding of her situation.

Lucy's one-to-one sessions at the Child and Family centre came to an end shortly after the schools broke up for summer. As she was staying with us for longer than antici-pated and was now doing therapy without her family, it was decided she should be referred to a CAMHS centre in our area.

Once the summer holidays got underway Lucy's behaviour improved, probably because she was doing what she wanted to do instead of struggling with academic work. Even with the help of a teaching assistant she still found it difficult to concentrate and focus, and it was clear she found it a trial to be in the classroom. I hoped the break from school would be a real tonic for her; it had been a tough few months.

The weather was fantastic and Lucy began spending more and more time with the horses. By now Diane had taken in another teenager who also started helping out in the florist's. It was a good arrangement and everyone was happy, especially Lucy.

'I'd rather be in the mud,' she commented when Diane asked her how she'd enjoyed herself when she'd helped out in the shop, which she soon lost interest in. 'I get bored stuck inside. I'd rather see flowers growing in the soil than dead in a pot.' Diane and I laughed: we got the gist.

As eight-year-olds go Lucy was very good at keeping herself busy. Jonathan's shed had never been tidier, the bikes had never been polished so brightly and I'd never seen so many Lego models built, destroyed and re-designed over and over again. When I thought back to how she used to follow me around, invade my space and clip the back of my heels I realised we'd made some excellent progress. She still did those things sometimes, if ever she slowed down long enough to get bored, but mostly she was on the go, making something, getting her hands dirty, riding her bike or trying to be helpful and joining in activities with other kids.

One day Lucy helped Diane's husband replace the netting on their garden pond. Jonathan collected her and she came in covered in mud and slime, grinning like the Cheshire cat.

'Don't worry,' she said, when she saw my jaw drop. 'I'm not coming in. I'm going to play football on the field.'

One of the neighbours had organised a five-a-side game on the rec behind our house.

'Don't you want to get changed?'

'No point. I'll only get muddy again.'

Lucy glugged a glass of water and ran off down the side passage, leaving a trail of mud behind her.

'At least by the time she gets on the field her trainers will be *less* muddy,' I remarked.

'Yes, there's a first!' Jonathan laughed.

At that moment my mum arrived, as she was having dinner with us that night. She'd brought her knitting and some crocheting and she said, 'If Lucy's at a loose end I can start to teach her, if she still wants to learn.' She put a large bag of wool and needles on the kitchen table and I smiled.

'Thanks, that's kind. I'm sure she'll want to learn at some point but Lucy's out playing football now. I don't think she's been at a loose end for a single minute of the summer holiday!'

'As it should be,' Mum commented. 'I wish you'd been more like that when you were little, Angela. You were such a clingy child, always following me around. People said you were like my shadow. And you needed a rocket behind you sometimes.'

'Mum!' I said, wincing.

Jonathan stifled a laugh and I thought about how I used to nag my mum to be a foster carer when I was a child, as I had a friend whose mum took in foster children in the holidays. With my brother – my only sibling – being much older than me I felt like an only child growing up, and I liked the idea of being surrounded by other kids my age. Mum always said she didn't have the patience, which I disputed. She was a very patient woman indeed, but now I thought perhaps I knew the real problem: she wouldn't have had the tact!

# 18

## *'What's happened to her?'*

The next morning, after Lucy had gone out for the day with Diane, I took a phone call from Lucy's social worker.

'Hi Angela,' Bella said in an uncharacteristically stern voice.

'Good morning, how are you?' I replied breezily, thinking she was probably stressed about her workload or had too many plates to spin that day.

Bella seemed to hesitate before she began to reply, and an uneasy feeling began to creep over me.

'Angela, I'm afraid I'm going to have to come straight to the point, there is no other way of me saying this . . . I've been racking my brain to see if there is, but there isn't. It's the first time I've been put in this situation. It's new to me, I hope I never have to do it again, it's a horrible feeling.'

'OK' I said, wishing she *would* get to the point. I was now feeling extremely uneasy and worried. 'Has something happened? Is it one of the girls?'

Lucy had been invited to watch Diane's daughter Clare

compete in a gymkhana and they would still be on the motorway at this time, while Maria was over at a friend's house and was going swimming that morning before spending the afternoon with her grandmother.

'I've had a phone call this morning about . . .' Bella hesitated and I could hear her swallowing hard. 'It's about Lucy.'

My stomach turned over. 'What's happened to her?'

It seemed an age until she replied to me. My heart was thumping and I began to get a pain in my stomach, something that always happens when I'm feeling very worried about something.

'A complaint has been made about Lucy's care.'

I was taken aback and extremely concerned. There was a momentary silence before I could think what to say.

'What is the complaint, exactly?'

'Alleged mistreatment.'

'Alleged mistreatment,' I repeated, shocked by the words. 'Who . . . who has mistreated her?'

My mind raced. Had something happened to Lucy when she was last with her family? Had something happened to her at the stables or at school, or at a gymkhana?

'The complaint is against you, Angela.'

Bella's words cut me to the quick. I was astonished, and I felt frozen with shock. I'd never understood that expression until that day. My mouth went numb and I had pins and needles tingling around my lips.

'You can't be serious?'

I'd done nothing wrong and I was in no doubt about

that, but still the whole idea of a complaint of this nature filled me with fear. I'd heard too many stories over the years, of foster carers whose lives had been turned upside down by false or malicious allegations. If you have children of your own, they can be removed if the complaint is serious enough. That's how the investigation system works: safeguard the children, then ask the questions. I knew all too well that even when those accused are fully vindicated the damage is often irreparable. The process is usually long-winded and while an investigation is carried out you're not allowed to talk to anyone in Social Services, not even your support social worker. You can talk to the Fostering Network, that's all. Many foster carers have buckled under the stress and given up fostering altogether because of the immense strain on their family life and health.

'Is Lucy there?' Bella asked.

I gulped, and felt my throat tighten. I explained about the gymkhana and said Lucy would be out all day. Bella then asked about Maria, and I told her she was due home after tea at her grandmother's.

'Do you have to remove the girls?'

'An emergency meeting has been called for this afternoon. I'm afraid I don't know if we'll have to remove them, the decision will be made then. I'm going to have to come out and see you all after the meeting. I'll know more by then.'

The call ended. I was stunned. Jonathan and I had been fostering for nearly ten years and never known anything like this. We'd had the odd complaint from a parent about something minor, which was never pleasant to deal with, but this was on another level. Social Services was holding an emergency meeting to discuss whether to remove our placements. Lucy and Maria could be taken away from us: it didn't seem real.

Jonathan was in the shop and I went straight through the second I put the phone down.

'I need to talk to you urgently,' I said, trying not to look as shaken as I felt. I must have put a brave face on because our assistant Barbara jokily raised her eyes to the ceiling and said, 'Yes, Angela, of course I'll hold the fort!'

'Thank you,' I said, forcing a smile. 'What would we do without you, Barbara?'

'Flattery will get you everywhere,' she chuckled.

We really were very lucky to have Barbara, not just because she understood we needed her to be flexible with her hours, but also because she was very good-natured and easy to get along with. We'd been friends for years and she'd worked in the shop for so long now that she was like part of the fixtures and fittings. She also understood the need for confidentiality, and knew never to ask questions about our placements.

Jonathan and I made our way to the kitchen; I didn't want anyone overhearing what I was about to say to him. When I relayed the conversation I could scarcely believe what I was saying.

'Who has made the complaint?' Jonathan stammered.

'I don't know. In fact I don't even know what the

complaint is about. What can possibly have happened to warrant any complaint about the care I give Lucy?'

'Can't they give us any more details?'

'No, apparently not. Bella will get in touch after the meeting, to explain what's going to happen next.'

It was a beautiful sunny day but it felt like the north wind was blowing through the house and my blood had turned to ice in my veins. Jonathan and I looked at each other in disbelief: it felt so surreal, like we were in a scene in a film or TV drama. The colour had drained from his face and he put his hand over his mouth and shook his head.

'They'll have to take her away,' I said robotically. 'And Maria. That's what happens when a complaint has been made, regardless of whether it's true or not, isn't it?'

'Yes.'

'Oh my God. This is unbelievable.'

Tears pricked my eyes. 'This can't be happening. Tell me this isn't happening?'

Jonathan was lost for words. He took me in his arms and hugged me tight. Neither of us spoke for what felt like a very long time. It was bad enough for Jonathan and me to go through this ordeal, but how would the girls cope with being taken away from us like this?

# 19

## *'It doesn't make sense'*

We sat at the kitchen table for a while, drinking hot tea and picking over Bella's phone call.

'Look,' Jonathan concluded reasonably. 'We know these allegations – whatever they are – are nonsense. There's nothing you've done to warrant any complaint being made against you.'

'I know you're right, but that's not the point. There's a process to go through. We know what happens next. The girls will have to be moved out while an investigation takes place. They'll have to be interviewed, won't they? It's going to be so disruptive to them. And what if . . .'

'What?'

'What if it's one of the girls who's said this? They've both been known to tell fibs, Lucy especially. What if she's made something up and told tales to someone, just for attention or because she's got "muddled up" as she does sometimes? Maybe she's said something to a teacher . . . or to a member of her family?'

Jonathan's eyes widened and he acknowledged that Lucy could have done this as a way of trying to get home to her daddy.

'We know she'd move hell and high water to be with her daddy, but surely not this?' I said.

'No,' he replied, 'I don't believe it. She wouldn't do that, would she? I can't see it, I really can't.'

I desperately wanted to phone Jess to find out more but of course I couldn't. She wouldn't be allowed to speak to me, let alone tell me anything. We had to sit tight and wait for Bella to get in touch after the emergency meeting. We imagined she'd have to talk to the girls as soon as they got home – before we'd had a chance to speak to them – so we expected to hear from her within the next few hours. We didn't know if she'd call us first or simply turn up at the door, and all we could do was wait.

I decided I wanted to work in the shop, to keep myself busy. Barbara was finishing at lunchtime and there were lots of bouquet orders to make up. Besides, I couldn't think of anything worse than being in the house on my own, waiting for the phone to ring or for Bella to knock on the door. Social Services had the shop number and my mobile, so I didn't have to stay in.

'Come on,' I said to Jonathan. 'Let's get to work. It'll keep our minds off this and Barbara will be waiting to go.'

It wasn't easy trying to carry on as normal in the florist's, and it seemed every conversation was designed to remind me of our predicament.

'Hi Angela,' said one of my mum's old friends. 'I'm after

a nice, bright bunch of flowers for Maureen. Something to cheer her up.'

'Oh, is she OK?'

'Not really. Stuck at home waiting for the phone to ring.' *I know the feeling*, I thought as the lady went on to explain her friend was waiting to hear from the hospital, about when she was getting her cataracts done.

Another customer was Diane's next-door neighbour, Gail, who came in to pick up a bunch of flowers for a friend's birthday. I knew Gail well and she was a kind-hearted person, although she did like to chat about other people's business and share her opinions. 'I'm surprised to see *both* of you in here,' she said, looking first at Jonathan and then at me. 'I've met Lucy at the stables a few times. She's a little live wire isn't she? I don't know how you have the time or the energy for fostering as well as running the shop. I wouldn't have the patience to put up with a child like that; she'd drive me around the bend! You've still got Maria too, haven't you?'

'Yes,' I said. 'Would you like me to put some ribbon on these?'

'Yes please. Honestly, Angela, I really admire you and Jonathan, doing what you do. How long have you been fostering now?'

'Oh, it's coming up for about ten years. Which colour would you like?'

'Let me see . . . the pale pink looks pretty, thanks. Is it really that long? Well I never. I bet you can't remember what life was like before fostering. You probably wouldn't know what to do with yourselves without the house full of kids! Where are the girls today then? Off out somewhere?'

Jonathan came over and joined in the conversation, trying to wrap it up before Gail quizzed me any more. He knew I'd be feeling uncomfortable and thinking to myself, *Yes, but will we be foster carers for much longer? Maybe this is the beginning of the end of our fostering careers? Maybe Lucy and Maria will be moving out tonight, and the house will feel empty?*

We waited with anticipation for Bella to call, but the phone didn't ring.

The girls were dropped home to us as planned that evening. They'd both had a good day and told us all about what they'd been up to. To our relief everything seemed perfectly normal and, as far as I could see, they both seemed very happy. Maria's grandmother and Diane both chatted to us, as they had done many times before, and clearly had no idea about the complaint.

It had been a long day for Lucy at the gymkhana and she was very tired. She had a snack and drink and went straight to bed and Maria wasn't far behind her. Jonathan and I sat in the living room wondering what on earth was going on. Nobody had called as we expected. We double-checked all our phones for messages and we hadn't missed anything.

'This is really odd,' I said. 'Why hasn't Bella contacted us like she promised? It doesn't make sense. If we're under investigation, surely they wouldn't want the girls being here with us as if nothing's happened? Surely they need to be talking to Lucy?'

'I'm as stumped as you are. Unless . . .'

'Unless what?'

'Unless one of the girls had already spoken to Social Services *before* we got the call from Bella? Maybe Bella has found something out since our conversation and now no longer needs to talk to the girls when they get home? Maybe they aren't coming back at all?'

I immediately said I thought this was very unlikely and Jonathan agreed with me: we were both tired and were in danger of stressing ourselves out by adding two and two and coming up with five.

We went to bed and tried to get some rest. Jonathan dropped off eventually but I couldn't sleep. I ran every possible scenario and explanation through my head and in the end I got up and made myself a camomile tea. When I went back to bed Jonathan was awake. He's normally a better sleeper than I am but he said he'd been tossing and turning.

'What time is it?'

'Four o'clock.'

'Oh God.'

At six o'clock there was a knock on our door.

'Lucy, is that you?'

'Yes. I'm wide-awake. Can I get up now?'

I was exhausted.

'No, it's too early. Try to get a bit more sleep and if you can't then you can find something to do quietly, but it's too early to get up.'

'OK.'

She let me steer her back to her bed. Her bedroom light was on and Lucy was wearing a pair of short pyjamas with a vest top. I couldn't help scanning her arms and legs, to check for marks, in case the allegation was about her being physically harmed. There wasn't a blemish on her, though I wasn't really sure what I was looking for. Mistreatment could mean anything: physical abuse, verbal abuse – I didn't want to think about all the possible reasons you could be accused of mistreating a child.

'Night night,' she said. 'I love you Angela.'

*At least she's her usual self*, I thought. *That's a blessing. That's the main thing.*

Unbelievably, it took another two days before we heard any more about the 'investigation.'

I couldn't stand the wait any longer.

'I'm going to call Bella, she should have called us by now,' I said to Jonathan before he started work that morning.

'What are you going to say?'

'Ask what's going on, of course. How can they keep us hanging around, waiting in limbo like this?'

I called Bella and was told that she was on sick leave and had been for a couple of days. Dismayed, I left a message for someone else to call me from her office, but nobody did. A few hours later I took a call from Jess. I was surprised to hear her voice, as I understood we were not allowed to talk to our support social worker while the complaint was being looked into.

'Angela,' she said. 'How are you? I'm so sorry you've gone through all this worry.'

'What's going on Jess? Bella said she was going to visit me after the meeting. It's been two days and we've heard nothing.'

'I'm so sorry, but this has all been a false alarm, I didn't realise she'd not contacted you. The allegations have nothing to do with you, or Lucy. There's been a mistake.'

'A mistake? What do you mean?'

I was flabbergasted and confused.

'So who were they about? Has Lucy been mistreated? I don't understand. How can a mistake like this happen? We've been worried sick.'

'I'm still waiting to hear the details. There appears to have been a mix up between you and Wendy.'

Jess went on to explain that a complaint had apparently been made about Wendy by a neighbour, but unfortunately the caller had said 'the child who is in foster care' when really she meant Gemma.

'Consequently the complaint got passed to the wrong office. Rest assured you are not under investigation. You and Jonathan should never have been involved in the first place. I'm sorry I've got to go now as I've got a meeting, but I hope I've put your mind at rest.'

I could feel the stress very slowly leaving my body but nevertheless I still felt very wound up. I felt like I hadn't slept for a week because I'd found it very hard to concentrate on anything other than this 'investigation'.

I told Jess I was relieved and grateful for her call but not happy at all. A swift apology like this was no compensation for the angst we'd gone through.

'You have put my mind at rest, but we've been through a horrible ordeal. We've been dreading a knock on the door. For all we knew both girls were going to be removed. It's been an absolute nightmare, and what about our records? I hope there won't be anything on our file that could be misconstrued in the future? I want this to be wiped off completely.'

I couldn't help reacting this way. I'd been on pins for days and I couldn't say nothing and let Jess dash off the phone. Somebody needed to stand up and be counted here. How *could* this have been allowed to happen? I also wanted to ask about the situation with Wendy and Gemma, but I knew better: Jess would not be able to discuss the details. We would have to trust Social Services to carry out their investigations and inform us if the outcome of their investigation into Wendy affected Lucy in any way.

Jess apologised again, assured me this would not tarnish our records and then said she really did have to dash, grumbling about the number of meetings she had to attend that day.

When I passed everything on to Jonathan he let out a long, deep breath and then went very quiet.

'Un-be-lieeeeve-able,' he said. 'I've got no words. Whoever's responsible for this needs to have a long, hard look at themselves. Have they got any idea what they've put us through?'

We heard nothing more for quite some time but clearly it wasn't serious because the children all stayed with Wendy and Dean. At least Wendy wasn't mistreating any of the kids; that was the only positive thing I could think of. The children were being properly cared for and that meant, when the time was right, Lucy would still be able to go home.

# 20

*'D'you think he'll have forgotten what I look like?'*

Lucy stuck to her guns about wanting to stay with her granny rather than coming on holiday with us, and that's what she did.

Maria was quite happy that Lucy wasn't joining us in the log cabin after all, and the break did us all the power of good. Maria had her moments, as ever, but as Jonathan politely put it, 'a change is as good as a rest'. The weather was great, we had lots of long walks and bike rides around the woodland resort we stayed at, and we even tried our hand at windsurfing on a nearby lake.

Meanwhile, Lucy was delighted to be spending time with her granny. Ivy also had one of her sisters staying with her, Lucy's great-aunt, Marge, who was ten years younger than Ivy, very sprightly and slightly eccentric. When we dropped Lucy off, I could see that she and Marge sparked off each other very well. They shared a love of the outdoors and Marge was very keen on bird watching. She took Lucy on country walks and they also spent a lot of time in Ivy's little garden, peering through binoculars. Lucy helped Marge put up a new bird table for Ivy and Marge helped Lucy start a log, recording which birds they'd seen and teaching her about different breeds. I think the two of them had something else in common: I learned that Marge also had an aggravating streak, like Lucy, and Ivy was given to frequently telling her younger sister to 'Stop that carping!' and 'Wind your neck in!'

Anyhow, the dynamics worked, and as a result Lucy ended up spending nearly four weeks at her grandmother's house, as she didn't want to come straight back when we returned from our holiday. She phoned us regularly to tell us what she was doing and she always sounded cheerful and upbeat. Jonathan and I were becoming quietly optimistic once more.

I heard nothing but good reports about Lucy from Ivy, and she seemed to be on an even keel and behaving really well. We hoped that Wendy and Dean had also had a good summer and would be feeling much more positive and ready to start afresh with Lucy. We'd had no contact with them at all, but Ivy told me she'd spoken to Dean one day. 'Can't understand the man,' she commented to me. 'He was asking all about his "little princess". I told him he's missing out on her growing up. She's growing up fast and you don't get that time back. If you ask me, Wendy and Dean need their heads knocking together. No disrespect to you, Angela, but Lucy should be at home with them and the other kids.'

'Have you said this to Dean?' I ventured.

"Course I have. You know me; I'm not backwards at coming forward. I don't get anything back though. No idea what's going on in that man's head. No wonder my Noreen left him. Like talking to a brick wall. Anyway, I'll put Lucy on the phone. Here she is . . .'

Wendy and Dean didn't turn up at the review meeting held at the end of the summer. This was very disappointing, particularly as they'd promised they would be there and didn't cancel until the very last minute, making it too late to reschedule. We'd had very little contact with Social Services for most of the school holidays. Bella moved on to start a new career back in her native Scotland and Lucy was still waiting to be assigned a new social worker – something we only found out about in the days leading up to the review meeting. Meanwhile Jess had an operation in July, after which she spent the best part of a month on leave, recuperating. She had only recently returned to work and it was good to see her again and to have her support at this meeting. Luckily her absence hadn't been a problem to Jonathan and me because, after the stress of the investigation that never was, everything had run smoothly over the summer. We had the usual emergency numbers to call if need be, but we had no cause to call Social Services and were left to our own devices.

Now, however, arriving at the meeting to discover Wendy and Dean had ducked out at very short notice, I wondered if Social Services had let things slip because of the staffing issues they had. I kicked myself, wishing I'd been more proactive, chasing up Social Services to check on Wendy and Dean or even calling them myself in the run-up to this meeting. I said this to Jonathan quietly while we waited for everyone else to assemble. He told me I mustn't beat myself up, saying that if Wendy and Dean had made their mind up it was unlikely they would have been swayed by any social worker, senior manager or anybody else – and certainly not by us. He was probably right, but it didn't make me feel any better. This was an important meeting. The fact they hadn't bothered to attend didn't bode well at all and I was very worried about what this meant for Lucy's future. The chances of her returning home in time for the new school year in early September – which I had hoped might just be possible – were looking extremely slim, if not impossible. It was already fast approaching the end of August and if Wendy and Dean couldn't even get themselves here, how were things ever going to move forward?

Thankfully, the situation wasn't as bad as I feared. The meeting got started and we learned that Wendy and Dean had told Social Services, in a letter, that though they were still not ready to have Lucy back living with them full time any time soon, they were now prepared to have her for some overnight stays in the future, hopefully building up to weekends and longer stays, as had been the hope right at the start of her placement. Wendy wrote the letter and said they would make a decision by Christmas as to whether Lucy could return home on a permanent basis. The Social Services manager who was chairing the meeting made it clear that Wendy had introduced this Christmas deadline of her own volition and that any decision would ultimately be 'carefully considered by everyone involved in Lucy's care'.

'Does anybody have any questions?'

I said I was concerned about whether Wendy and Dean would stick to the proposed overnight and weekend arrangements when the time came, because we'd tried to go down this road before and it hadn't worked well. I desperately didn't want Lucy to be upset and disappointed all over again. I asked if the social workers could get involved in fixing up the visits, to make things more official, and hopefully more likely that Wendy and Dean would not let Lucy down or try to change plans at the last minute. Jess nodded as I spoke and said she thought this was a very good idea.

'Yes, I agree with that,' said the manager. 'In fact, we already have the first date. I'm told Wendy chose this one as the family is going for fittings that day, for wedding outfits. She would like Lucy to be fitted for her dress.' This sounded very promising; it was the first time we'd heard anything about Lucy being at the wedding. We were told the date for the visit was in the middle of September, after the start of the new school term, and we went on to have a discussion about Lucy's education and how she would stay at St Joseph's until further notice.

'Now she's statemented it will be easy to transfer her back to her old school in due course,' a representative from the LEA commented. I'd never seen this person before, and in fact there were several people in this meeting I'd never met previously, but I thought that was a good sign. Social Services was clearly very motivated to help Lucy return home. They believed her place was with her family, and if she was successfully moved back it would of course also be beneficial to them, as the fostering service was as stretched and underfunded as ever.

Afterwards I chatted to Jess in the car park.

'Good news,' she said, smiling.

'Yes, it's great to have a date in the diary and I'm sure Lucy will be thrilled, but we can't count our chickens, can we?'

'No, not at all. One step at a time, but at least we're going in the right direction.'

I took the opportunity to ask Jess if she ever heard any more about the mix-up with the complaint or the investigation into Wendy.

'I did hear something, just the other day. It seems Wendy had fallen out with the neighbour over the extension work on their house, and she reckoned the call was made spitefully, because the neighbour was jealous.'

'So the whole sorry episode was the work of a malicious neighbour?'

'It seems that way. As far as I know everything was sorted out swiftly and no action was taken. Obviously, the main thing from our point of view is that Wendy never did anything wrong and this doesn't affect Lucy's return home.'

Later, I sat Lucy down and told her the news about her forthcoming visit home, sticking to the one date that was in the diary and being careful not to be drawn into any discussions about what may happen after that. I mentioned the planned dress fitting too.

She didn't react at all.

'So, that's something to look forward to, isn't it?' I prompted.

'Am I a bridesmaid?' she said suspiciously.

'I don't know, sweetheart.'

We had been asked not to resume phone contact between Lucy and her family until after her visit. I imagined this was because of Wendy's original decision that 'cold turkey' was what was required, but I wasn't sure.

'How many days is it I have to wait?'

She started counting on her fingers and then got stuck when she ran out of digits.

'It's just over two weeks,' I said. 'It's back to school first, so the time will fly, I'm sure.'

Lucy nodded. I wasn't sure how she felt because she just stared at me.

'Are you feeling OK?'

'I thought I was going to see Daddy at the end of the school holidays?'

'I know you did, sweetheart. But at least it's not long to wait now.'

'Can I call Granny?'

'Yes, of course.'

The next day Lucy's new social worker, Cedella, was coming to the house to introduce herself, so I told Lucy all about this.

'Will she be my social worker until I go home?'

'I'm not sure but I expect so.'

'Adults don't know anything,' she said, and walked out of the room.

Cedella was a striking young woman who wore a bright yellow and turquoise scarf in her elaborately plaited black hair. Lucy stared at her, and Cedella tried to break the ice by telling Lucy she grew up in Jamaica and loved bright colours.

'Yellow is my favourite. What about you, what do you like?'

'Just colours, or can I say anything?'

'Anything you like!'

Lucy grinned.

'I like horses, and getting muddy. I like blue and purple and green. I like playing football. I don't like school. I'm rubbish at maths and English. I like art. I like making things. I want to be a carpenter when I grow up.'

That last piece of information was news to me; I was impressed by Cedella's way with Lucy.

'Wow! So many interesting things,' she smiled. 'I don't think I've ever met a girl, or a boy, who wants to be a carpenter when they grow up.'

Lucy giggled. She said her daddy called her a tomboy.

'My sister Milly likes dancing and all that girly stuff. He says we're like chalk and cheese.'

I knew Cedella would want to talk to Lucy privately and I left them to it. They chatted for about fifteen minutes before I heard Lucy call me, saying Cedella was leaving. I saw the social worker to the door after she'd said goodbye to Lucy.

'It's been a pleasure to meet you, Angela. I've spoken to Lucy about her visit home and we're all set up. She's keen to please, isn't she? I didn't bring it up but she told me she promises she'll be on her very best behaviour. I hope it goes well.'

I thought it was sad that Lucy felt she had to be on her very best behaviour. I knew she could be awkward at times, but she wasn't that bad. It must have been very tough for her, having to try so hard to please and seeing things unravel despite her best efforts.

It was left for me to call Wendy and make the travel arrangements, and Cedella said that if we had any problems Social Services could provide taxis. She also advised it would be best to stick to the plan and not put Lucy on the phone, 'in case the timing isn't good'. I got the impression Cedella had done her homework on Wendy and I agreed with her. The last thing we wanted was to give Wendy any excuse to change the visit or have any opportunity to criticise or complain ahead of the visit.

From that moment on Lucy was like a child waiting for Christmas, talking to anyone who'd listen about the number of sleeps before her visit and how she was getting a dress for the wedding. She looked through the style and fashion supplements that came with the Sunday papers – something she'd never been interested in before – and speculated excitedly about what type of dress she might have. Lucy normally refused to wear skirts and dresses and even chose to wear trousers for school, though she was the only girl in her class who did so. I'd have been amused about her sudden interest in girls' fashion if it weren't for the nagging doubts I had. Wendy was unpredictable and I didn't trust her enough to believe this dress fitting would go ahead as planned, or even if the wedding itself would pan out the way it was meant to. It seemed a huge leap to go from refusing to see or even speak to Lucy to including her in the wedding plans like this. Still, there was no point in being pessimistic and expecting failure. It was much better to take a leaf out of Lucy's book and look forward with hope and optimism.

I had a call from Cedella to tell me Dean wanted to phone Lucy up before the visit after all.

'What's brought the change of heart?'

'I don't know. I just got a message asking me to let you know. He said he'll call on Wednesday when he's in from work, at six o'clock.'

After that the plan was that I would speak to Wendy during the week of the visit, to make the practical arrangements, as it seemed Dean had said to Cedella that was 'Wendy's department'. I was pleased to hear he'd said that; at least Dean wasn't going to cancel the visit, I thought.

Lucy was very pleased when I told her Daddy was calling, and she sat by the phone expectantly.

'I've missed Daddy so much. I miss Josh and Liam and Milly. And Gemma. And Wendy.' Her voice tailed off. 'When I go home I'll remember to be on best behaviour, I will. I'll remember to call her Mum. Can I tell them all about staying with Granny?'

'I'm sure they'll like to hear about it.'

'No, I won't,' she suddenly decided. 'They might think I'm bragging and I have to be good.'

I prayed that Dean would phone on time and not let Lucy down, but no call came. Lucy hovered by the phone for five minutes, ten minutes, then fifteen. While she waited I had a little chat to her about what she'd said about bragging, trying to explain that there was nothing wrong with passing on her news, and that she should ask her siblings about their holiday. Eventually I suggested she should go in the garden and get some fresh air.

'I'll wait by the phone and call you in as soon as it rings. Don't worry, I won't miss it.'

'Shall I ring him instead?'

'No. It's best to wait. He's obviously not able to talk right now. He might have been held up at work.'

She shrugged, sighed and went outside. Lucy normally kicked a ball, skipped or jumped on the pogo stick – something she'd got very good at over the summer – but I watched from the kitchen window as she sat on the low wall by the rockery, looking dejected and throwing small pebbles into an old plant pot.

She came in after about twenty minutes.

'Look, I need to talk to Wendy in any case,' I said. 'I'll call her shortly and see what's happening, shall I?'

'I suppose. She's probably told him the wrong time, stupid Wendy!'

'Lucy, we don't know what's happened and please don't talk about Wendy like that. Remember what you said to Cedella about being on best behaviour?'

'I know, but I just want to talk to my daddy and I want to see him NOW. It's been aaaaages. I miss him. D'you think he'll have forgotten what I look like?'

'Of course not!'

'Hello Wendy. It's Angela Hart. I was hoping to catch Dean, as Lucy's been waiting for his call.'

'Oh . . . has she? Er, I didn't realise. Right, anyway, how is she?'

I'd obviously caught her off guard and Wendy sounded a bit harassed.

'She's very well. Looking forward to seeing you all. Had a great time with her grandmother and her behaviour has been very good. Thank you for fixing up her visit home, she can't wait.'

I instinctively spoke quickly, for fear Wendy might cut the conversation short before I got everything across that I wanted to.

'Mmm, OK. When are you thinking of bringing Lucy over then?'

I was taken aback and I explained I had been given the date by Social Services.

'It's a week on Saturday. I was told you picked that date, and that you wanted to include Lucy in the dress fitting that day?'

'Oh, yes, I remember. But that's not going to work out now. Hang on a minute.'

I heard Wendy pad away from the phone and return, rustling paper.

'Right. Dean's van will be in the garage a week on Saturday so we can't pick Lucy up or anything, and I'm going to have to change the date of the dress fitting as we won't be able to get to town. Probably the following week is better but I'll have to check. I've got a few things on and Dean needs to take the boys to football. They've got a cup game.'

'Jonathan and I can bring Lucy over a week on Saturday. It's no trouble. She's been counting down the days and I know she'll be terribly disappointed if she has to wait any longer.'

There was a pause.

'How will she get home?'

'We can bring her back too.'

I didn't want to mention the taxi offered by Social Services as I didn't want Lucy to be on her own with a taxi driver. It was a big day, and I wanted her to be in the best possible frame of mind, feeling as calm and happy as possible.

Wendy thought about my offer for a moment.

'Right, but if you bring her over that doesn't solve the problem of how we'll all get to the dress shop. I'll have to rearrange the appointment in any case. Why don't you let me sort that out, and then Lucy can come over whenever I have a new date for the fittings? Seems a shame for her to miss out.'

'Honestly, Wendy, I think at the moment Lucy is more focused on just seeing everyone. It's been a while and she's desperate to see the family. I know she'd prefer to come and not have the dress fitting than not to come at all. If it's any help, we could also bring her another day, when you get the new appointment.'

Wendy reluctantly agreed with my suggestion, but not before she argued that Lucy was 'only a flower girl', so it wasn't essential she went along with Gemma and Milly, who were bridesmaids. I let this go even though my heart sank, but Wendy went on to throw another spanner into the works.

'Oh, damn! I *completely* forgot about the building work.' This sounded forced and I thought to myself, *You'd never make an actress, Wendy.*

'The extension?' I asked breezily, 'How's it coming along?'

'Bloody nightmare, honestly, Angela. Never again. It's still like a building site and it's caused so much grief. I'll be grey by the time it's done, I swear. I've even had one of the neighbours kicking off about it and creating trouble like you wouldn't believe.'

I didn't let on I knew anything about the malicious phone call and Wendy clearly had no idea I'd been accidentally caught up in the complaint to Social Services.

'Anyhow, nothing's finished and the thing is, there's nowhere for Lucy to sleep.'

Wendy explained that Milly and Gemma now shared

the bunk bed in what was Lucy's old room, and that Milly's little bed had been thrown away.

'I can't have Gemma being kicked out of her bed, or Milly either.' Wendy said this very defiantly. 'There's no room for Lucy. She'd have to go on the floor, and I'm not sure she'd fit in the girls' room.'

I felt this was a poor excuse. Milly's little bed used to fit in that room and, besides, I've known kids to top and tail, sleep on sofa cushions, make beds out of piled up duvets or pretend they're camping and curl up in a sleeping bag on the smallest patch of carpet. Lucy was so slight too; I wasn't worried at all about her being able to squeeze in. My only concern was the effect it would have on her to be relegated to the floor in her old bedroom, and to see Gemma and her little sister sharing the bunk bed. This was far from ideal, but if that were the set-up we'd just have to go with it. I knew without asking Lucy that she'd rather put up with this arrangement than not visit at all. In fact, if I knew Lucy, she'd have happily slept in the garden shed with the spiders if it meant she could see her daddy.

I managed to convince Wendy that Lucy could fit in with the girls somehow, and by the end of our call she'd finally run out of excuses, or so it seemed to me, and the visit was back on track. We never heard from Dean and I never got to the bottom of why he said he was calling and then didn't – Wendy had no explanation other than that he 'must have forgotten' or 'got muddled up.'

I was left to pick up the pieces with Lucy, who was miserable and argumentative all night.

'Never mind, you'll see Daddy soon,' I soothed, but this didn't pacify her. Perhaps not surprisingly she said, 'I'm not talking about that any more,' and stormed off, kicking the skirting boards all the way up the stairs.

When I sat down with Jonathan and described my conversation with Wendy I found myself saying, 'It was like pulling teeth. Painful. Awkward. Just *unpleasant*. I've got no idea when Wendy's telling the truth or twisting things to suit herself, and her tone changes like the wind. It's hard to know where you stand.'

'Are you sure they're ready for this visit?' he asked, shaking his head. 'Because after hearing all this, I'm not sure they are.'

'I'm not sure either. But the trouble is, I'm not sure they ever will be. And how can anyone expect things to move on and repair relationships when they are not talking to each other or seeing each other?'

'Quite. And can you imagine the effect it would have on Lucy if it was postponed now?'

At that precise moment there was a loud bang from upstairs as she slammed shut her bedroom door and shouted, 'Shut up Maria, you're a big fat cow!'

Jonathan and I looked at each other and got to our feet.

'No peace for the wicked,' he said wryly.

# 21

## *'You'll have to ask Lucy about that'*

The countdown to the visit was tense, not least because it coincided with Lucy settling into her new school year. Every day of those first two weeks of term was a struggle. Lucy kicked off about anything and everything: the colour of the milk when she poured it on her cereal ('It's stale!'), the 'disgusting' school shoes I'd bought her, which she'd tried on and seemed perfectly happy with in the shop, and even the way I stood in the playground ('It's embarrassing. You're not meant to wait there!') She refused to go to bed on time, got up at six o'clock every day and woke the whole house, had a row with Diane's daughter Clare, calling her 'spoilt and stuck up' and told Jonathan he was 'gay' for working in a flower shop. 'My daddy grows trees and makes whole big gardens and parks,' she said, scowling disparagingly at Jonathan as he prepared a little hand-tied bouquet.

That was one thing that never changed: Lucy continued to idolise her father and she sang his praises at every opportunity.

Lucy began her counselling at the CAMHS centre in our town. After the first session I asked her how it went and she replied, 'Good. But only because it meant I missed school.' Then she started humming loudly and kicking her feet on the back of my car seat.

She still didn't get to speak to her dad or any other member of the family before her visit home. It was radio silence, except when I called Wendy a few days before to make absolutely certain they had remembered the date and were expecting Lucy: I was not leaving anything to chance and I was ready to fight Lucy's corner if I heard any more excuses.

When we arrived at the house and got out of the car we could hear shouting coming from the front room. It sounded like Wendy and Milly, and possibly Gemma, but I wasn't sure as it stopped as soon as we walked up the front path. Lucy looked a little apprehensive when we knocked on the door, and I kept a close eye on her. She brushed down her clothes, as if removing invisible crumbs, then pulled her shoulders back a little. When the door opened and it was Gemma, Lucy smiled bravely and said hello.

'Hi,' Gemma mumbled. Turning, she called to Wendy flatly, 'She's here.'

Wendy appeared and it seemed she was trying her best not to look flummoxed.

'You've made good time. Do you want to come in?'

She was looking at both Jonathan me and hadn't even acknowledged Lucy, who was standing right beside me. I looked down at Lucy and only then did Wendy address her. 'Hi love,' she said. 'Come in.'

Lucy didn't move. Jonathan said we weren't stopping and asked what time we should collect Lucy the next day.

'Twelve sharp,' Wendy said, quick as a flash.

'That's fine. OK Lucy, in you go, sweetheart. Jonathan and I will collect you tomorrow. Have a good time!' I handed over her little overnight bag.

I could hear Milly in the background calling to her daddy and brothers to come downstairs. Lucy then stepped in the house. She didn't turn and say goodbye to us, but that was fine; we didn't mind.

'Bless her,' I said. 'It's a big day and a lot to take in.'

'I know. I just hope she can relax and be herself – or at least be the good Lucy we know and love.'

We drove off with anxious hearts. Wendy was clearly not in the best of moods, Dean didn't even greet his daughter at the door and I had a feeling this could go either way.

It seemed like a very long twenty-four hours, while Lucy was with her family. On the drive to collect her the next morning I felt very nervous, wondering how they'd all got on. When we pulled up I saw the curtains twitch in the living-room window and Wendy opened the front door before we'd even got out of the car. By the time we'd reached the house Lucy was standing behind Wendy on the doorstep, and the rest of the family was packed into the narrow hallway, ready to wave Lucy off. Dean was at the back, with Milly on his shoulders.

'Thanks for picking her up,' Wendy said, nudging Lucy forward.

'Have you had a good time?'

'You'll have to ask Lucy about that.'

I didn't have a good feeling about that comment at all.

Dean shouted, 'Bye love!' down the hallway and all the kids joined in. Lucy handed Jonathan her holdall and then slipped back inside the house, pushing past Gemma and her brothers to give her dad a last cuddle. In the meantime, Wendy handed me a letter and gave me a hard-faced look. 'Please read this,' she said very seriously. 'You need to know this.'

Lucy didn't see the letter or hear what Wendy had said, and when she emerged from the house she said they'd all had the 'best time' and gave everyone big smiles and waves as we headed to the car. The kids all waved back, looking happy and relaxed.

I put the letter in my jacket pocket. I desperately wanted to read it, but at the same time I was afraid of what it said. *It's like a grenade, waiting to go off*, I thought. I'm not usually a dramatic person, but that's truly what went through my mind.

Lucy started chattering. She told us that they went to town because her daddy's van wasn't in the garage after all. They all had fittings for their wedding outfits – I didn't bother querying the fact I thought the appointment had been changed – and Lucy told us the wedding was taking place the following spring. Lucy was a flower girl while Gemma and Milly were bridesmaids, which I already knew from Wendy, while the twins were pageboys. She said she was pleased about being a flower girl because the bridesmaids' dresses were 'too frilly' and she liked her much plainer one. Apparently, Wendy had told Lucy she wasn't to have her hair cut before the wedding as she wanted all the girls to have the same style on the day, with flowing ringlets.

'Do I have to?' she asked.

'Yes, sweetheart. If that's what Wendy wants.'

When a child is on a voluntary care order we're not allowed to have their hair cut without asking permission from the parents, so I felt it best to be clear on this from the start, to avoid any dramas later on.

Lucy sighed and went on describing her stay, giving lots of detail and barely pausing for breath. After the fitting the family visited an indoor adventure play centre. Lucy said they were all given pocket money and she spent all of hers playing on one of those 'claw' machines in the foyer, trying and failing to pick up a prize from the mountain of goodies in the glass case. She wasn't allowed a drink from the cafe, she said, because she'd spent all her money. Wendy and her daddy 'weren't very pleased' about that, but Lucy said she didn't know the money was for a drink too. Gemma met two school friends at the play centre. 'She wouldn't let me join in,' Lucy sulked. 'And I got sent to bed early because I had an argument with Gemma. She was mean – it wasn't fair.'

'You got sent to bed early?'

'Yes,' she said thoughtfully. 'And guess what?'

'What?

She bit her lip and had a look of deep concentration on her face.

'What?'

'You know there was a picture of baby Tia's christening on the wall?'

I remembered it well – the family photograph with Lucy's face obscured, where it looked like she was tagged on the end, like an afterthought.

'Yes, I do remember it, sweetheart.'

'It's not there now. There's a picture of Daddy, Wendy, Gemma, Milly, Josh and Liam. They had it done on holiday, by the pool. Gemma's got my Spice Girls cap on. Can we listen to some music?'

'Of course. What would you like?'

'I don't mind. You choose.'

Jonathan put on a pop mix CD he knew was Lucy's favourite. I found myself feeling very protective of Lucy, to the point where I even hoped the Spice Girls weren't on the CD, in case it reminded Lucy of Gemma wearing her cap on the family holiday, while she wasn't even there. It was as if Wendy had replaced Lucy with her own daughter, and there was no room for the two of them in the new family set-up. I can remember that thought hitting me, and how painful it was to think about. I hoped I was very wrong.

When we got home Lucy went to her room and I retreated to mine. Jonathan stood over my shoulder as I opened Wendy's letter. Her writing was very untidy and littered with spelling mistakes.

Here is a summery of what happened this weekend. Lucy will tell you a different story, no douwt, because she can't seem to tell the truth. But this is it.

As soon as you left she started playing too roughly with Milly, like pushing her around in the garden and kicking balls at her on purpous. I was willing to accept she was over excited about the visit but mind you all the kids were excited. Nobody else was naughty.

She was rude in the wedding shop. It was embarrasing. Showed no interest in her dress and pulled a face when I told her what hairstyle I wanted all the girls to have. She told Gemma she didn't like her dress and made Gemma feel upset. Now Gemma not keen on dress, thanks a lot Lucy for doing your best to sabowtage my wedding!!!

In the play centre I said don't waist all your money on them machines. Dean said the same. She ignored us and then kicked up a stink when we wouldn't give more money for the cafe. She knew the rules. She is not capable of sticking to rules. Either that or she just likes causing trouble.

Lucy met some girls she used to go to school with. She wouldn't let Gemma join in. When I asked her to let Gemma play Lucy got annoyed so I told Gemma to play with Milly for a bit. Lucy then treid to join in with Gemma and Milly but they were on a seesaw for two people at a time. Lucy tried to break them up. This made her father and me angry. We said Lucy would got to bed early for that.

At bedtime Lucy refused to go to bed before the other kids. I told her to sleep on the floor in the girls' room but she refused and wanted to stay up with the other kids and watch a film. I said she'd lost that priviledge and she needed to take her punishment for her bad behavoir at the play zone. She called me a witch and a bitch and a fat cow. I told her to repeat this to her dad but she refused and said I had made it all up.

This morning Dean asked her why she said those nasty things about me. Lucy said I'd tried to hit her, which was another lie. Dean asked why couldn't she get on with me and why is she always causing trouble and making up stories??? She said she doesn't know and she can't help it. She said she tries but can't help herself. It's like a pather-logical problem, if you ask me. She has <u>serious</u> issues.

My conclusion is she needs to carry on having mental health therapy on her own and stay with you, indefi-nitely. She shows you and Jonathan more respect that she shows us. She can behave when she wants to but she CHOOSES to cause trouble between me and Dean. We will have her to visit for family occasions and she can come to the wedding but we CANNOT have her here regularly. This weekend has taught us that it is nor feesi-ble to have Lucy living with us full term. She needs to stay in care. Dean agrees. <u>I cannot take responsibility for Lucy on a full time basis, not now. Not ever.</u>

Jonathan and I stayed silent for a moment before I said, 'I wonder why she shows us more respect?'

'Could it be that we show Lucy more respect than they do?'

'I think it could.'

I felt a lot of bitterness towards Wendy – and Dean, to a lesser extent – but my overriding feeling was one of sorrow for Lucy. She had reluctantly accepted she was staying longer with us than first planned, but how would we explain this to her? How could we tell her she might be in care for a lot longer than she imagined?

'This is terrible news,' Jonathan said. 'Of course she can stay here for as long as it takes, but how long do you suppose that will be?'

'No idea, and that's the problem. That's going to be very tough for Lucy to deal with.'

We went on to talk about the money situation at the play centre.

'I wonder why they didn't give Lucy a set amount of money to spend on what she wanted, and keep back the rest of the money for drinks and snacks?' I said. 'She's only eight. She needs help with managing her pocket money.'

'I know. It's almost like she's being set up to fail.'

I didn't disagree.

I spoke to Jess the next day, who sounded very disappointed and said she'd arrange another meeting and invite Wendy and Dean along, to work out a strategy.

'Things may settle down,' she said. 'Wendy obviously

wrote that note in the heat of the moment. Let's hope this isn't as bad as it seems.'

I told her that of course I wouldn't say anything to Lucy about the future, not until the dust had settled and firm decisions were made.

'That's wise. Let's get a meeting organised as soon as possible. How is Lucy?'

I said she was the same as ever, which was true. She had phoned her granny and chatted happily for ten minutes, telling her all the good things about the visit home, and none of the bad. In the evening she had a strop because she'd left her favourite T-shirt at her daddy's, and then she did her annoying trick with the taps again, setting them so they made a noise and aggravated Maria.

'Then at bedtime her mood improved,' I told Jess. 'She hugged me and told me she loved me, and she said she liked her bedroom in our house, and that she didn't want to be in her old bedroom again anyhow. "Gemma's welcome to it," she said. "I'll have my own room when all the building is done."'

Jess called me a few days later. We'd had more bedwetting and some trouble at school and Lucy had scratched our neighbour's car with her bike and tried to pretend she had no knowledge of it, not realising she had been seen by another neighbour.

'Hi Angela, how are you?'

'I'm fine but I'm afraid Lucy's behaviour has spiralled downwards again since the weekend. I've still said nothing about the letter from Wendy, of course, and she hasn't asked anything about her next visit home. Have you got anywhere with Wendy and Dean?'

'Yes and no. They've refused to attend a meeting, saying there is "no point". The good news is that, on reflection, they are not completely ruling out having Lucy home full time in the future. However, they would like her to stay with you and Jonathan at least until after the wedding next spring – they're talking about six to nine months. Wendy has written a letter stating their wishes, which she's posted to the office today, I believe. They want to be in phone contact with Lucy once a week – on a Wednesday evening – and they will be in touch with you directly to invite her to visit on family occasions and at Christmas. They will also visit her at your house. As Lucy is on a voluntary care order we do of course support all contact. Are you happy with that?'

Happy wasn't the word I'd have chosen, I said, but I told Jess that it was fine, and we'd be very pleased to continue caring for Lucy, as we'd grown very fond of her and enjoyed looking after her.

Jess went on to discuss a few other formalities that she would take care of and asked me if I had any questions.

'No, I don't think so. Thanks for all this.'

'No, thank *you*, Angela. Lucy's situation would be a lot worse if you and Jonathan were not so kind and accommodating.'

'Funny isn't it,' I said to Jonathan later, after relaying my conversation with Jess. 'We've come across so many parents over the years who have fought tooth and nail for increased contact hours, and Wendy and Dean are the opposite – they seem to be doing their best to keep her at arm's length and prolong her stay with us.'

'Funny isn't the word I'd have chosen,' Jonathan said, referencing my words to Jess. I laughed half-heartedly. 'No, more like incredibly sad and frustrating.'

The next day I heard from Cedella, telling me she'd made contact with Lucy's birth mother. Noreen had written back to Social Services to say she was 'very happy' to hear Lucy's news and be back in touch with her daughter, and in her reply she had included a short note for Lucy.

'She would like to see Lucy and I'm going to set up a meeting. It's early days and who knows what will come of it.'

Cedella dropped the note into the shop when Lucy was at school and asked if I wanted her to come back later, to talk to Lucy before or while she read it. I said I was happy to explain things and deal with it, and that I'd be in touch.

'OK and good luck,' Cedella said, knowing how sensitive this could be for Lucy. 'And thank you, Angela. I know you'll handle it well.'

Lucy was in a good mood when she got home from school and I sat her down with a mug of hot chocolate and gently explained how Social Services had written to her mummy, to let her know she was staying with us, and that she had written back and sent Lucy a note. All of this was news to Lucy, as there had been no point in telling her Social Services was attempting to make contact with her mother in case it came to nothing. Lucy didn't say anything and just looked thoughtful.

'Would you like to read it now?'

'Yes please. Can you stay with me?'

'Yes, sweetheart.'

Lucy opened the sealed brown envelope cautiously. It looked recycled. It was one of those with a transparent window on the front and it had been stuck down with a piece of Sellotape. Lucy's name was written in thick black marker pen on the front, and underlined two times.

The note was short and written on a sheet of lined paper ripped neatly from a pad. Lucy studied it and then passed it to me. 'Can you read it out? I can't read her writing.'

'Are you sure?'

'Yes please.'

'OK. Here goes.'

Dear Lucy,

How are you? I think about you lots. I want you to know that. I miss you, my little princess, but Mummy has lots of things to sort out in her life. Sorry I live so far away. I'd like to see you again and hopefully we can see each other soon!!! I heard you are doing well. I'd proud of ya!

Christmas is coming, HO HO HO! I've already started shopping. What do you want? Write and tell me and I will get it for you. I promise this time to keep my promise!

Love and kisses,

Mummy xxx

Lucy frowned and looked like she was concentrating hard, as if trying to remember something.

'What does she mean about promises?' I asked.

She shrugged, gave a brave smile and said, 'I know Mummy would buy me everything in the world if she could.'

'It's nice of her to think about Christmas already, isn't it?' I said. It wasn't even October yet; Lucy and I had recently been talking about a Halloween party she was invited to.

'Yes. I don't know what I want for Christmas.' Lucy put her arms around me. 'I want a cuddle. I want to see Daddy.' She then asked me when we could go cycling in the country park again, what we were having for dinner, how many sleeps until Halloween, what was I going to do with the letter now, and was I going to make her an outfit for Halloween or were we going to buy one?

I answered her questions, telling her that the letter was hers and it was up to her what she wanted to do now.

'Do I have to write back, or will you do it for me? Can you just send her a message when I have decided what I want for Christmas?'

'I think it would be nice if you wrote back yourself, whenever you feel ready. I can help you if you'd like me to.'

'OK. Can I use your nice pen? And shall I tell her to send the present to Daddy's house because I'll be back home for Christmas?'

'You can use my pen, of course. And no, don't put your dad's address.'

'Why not?

I tactfully explained that it wasn't polite to give out another person's address and she accepted this. Lucy thought for a moment before asking, 'Do you know how much money she has to spend?'

'No I don't, Lucy, but I think it would be polite to ask for something that isn't too expensive. It's not about the cost of something, it's the thought that counts.'

I gave her what I hoped was an encouraging smile, but Lucy pulled a disgruntled face.

'I bet she's got loads of money!' She said this in quite an accusatory tone. Then she got to her feet and stomped up the stairs, shouting as she went, 'She must have LOADS because she didn't buy me presents last year! And she doesn't spend any petrol money as she doesn't come to see me.'

## 22

### *'It's lucky I like Angela or I'd be even more annoyed'*

Cedella came round to talk to Lucy about the fact that she was going to be staying with us for a while longer. I was grateful for this; I felt the news was best coming from her social worker, so that Lucy could see this was an official plan and hopefully be more inclined to accept it. I sat quietly in the corner of the living room while Cedella did the talking, so Lucy could ask me questions if she wanted to.

'How much longer?' she scowled.

'Possibly until after the wedding.'

Cedella chose her words carefully and didn't give an exact date because there were several factors that could impact on the length of Lucy's extended placement. Obviously, Wendy and Dean might have a change of heart and want Lucy back sooner, or they might go the other way and delay her return further still. There was also Lucy's birth mother to consider. Now Noreen had been contacted and had expressed a wish to see Lucy again, Social Services would be looking into the feasibility of Lucy living with her mother, even if only temporarily or part time, rather than staying in full-time foster care: it's always preferable for a child to be with one or both parents, if at all possible, or even a close family member.

'Can I still see Daddy?' Lucy asked. That was clearly the main thing on her mind.

'Yes, you can still go for visits and your family can visit you too.'

'OK. So why can't I go home sooner? I don't understand. Wait, the wedding isn't until . . . Easter time. I'll be nine then! I will have been here LOADS longer than everyone said. It's not fair!'

Cedella gently explained that there were still a 'few things' to sort out first.

'You mean the extension? Isn't my bedroom ready?'

'The building work is still going on, and we want to make sure everything – and everyone – is ready for you to move back in, OK?'

'But why's it taking so long? I'm ready NOW. I don't mind about the builders being in. I could help them. I want to go home NOW!'

'I know you do, Lucy, but you're staying here for the time being, with Angela and Jonathan.'

Lucy folded her arms and said huffily, 'I'm not happy about all this waiting. It's lucky I like Angela or I'd be even more annoyed and you know I can get very annoying!'

Lucy eventually replied to her mum's letter, saying she would like a Ninja Turtle cuddly toy or a new riding hat for

Christmas. She didn't ask anything about when they might see each other and only gave one piece of news: 'I like horses and riding horses.' Lucy usually loved using coloured pens and had a habit of adding little drawings or patterned borders to whatever she produced on paper, but the note was very short and plain, written only in black pen and with no pictures. I helped by writing out what she wanted to say so she could copy it but even so it had taken her several weeks to reply.

I knew Lucy struggled with the written word but I thought the way she responded said more about how she felt about her mother than her writing skills; it seemed to me that Lucy was quite indifferent to being back in contact with her mum. Jonathan pointed out that if Noreen left when Lucy was only four it was possible she had very few memories of her mum – or maybe none at all. Perhaps that explained it; even the promise of a Christmas present didn't seem to have particularly excited or motivated her to make an effort with the letter, although from what she'd said before it seemed promises about presents had been broken in the past. Maybe that was why she was in no rush to tell her mum what she wanted this year – perhaps she simply didn't want to be disappointed again?

After finishing copying out the note Lucy hurriedly stuffed it in an envelope. 'What do I write on the front? Mummy or her name? Er, what is all of her name? What's her address? I don't know where she lives. Do you know where she lives? She didn't put her address on her letter. Is Cedella going to post this back, or what? I haven't put my address on here. Should I? Which one? Shall I put Daddy's, in case I'm allowed home sooner? I might be back with Daddy at Christmas . . . Or will I *really* have to wait until after the wedding? It's too long! This is all so ANNOYING!'

Lucy pulled a sulky face and my heart went out to her. It was upsetting to think she didn't even know her mum's full name. I didn't know Noreen's surname either. I wasn't sure if she'd ever been married to Dean or had since remarried, or if she still used her maiden name. I told Lucy I'd give the letter to Cedella to send on and that Social Services had the address, so there was no need to worry. I also said there was no need to put any address of her own on it.

'Just put Mummy on the front. Cedella will put it in another envelope and sort everything else out for you.'

Lucy was already getting to her feet as she scribbled 'Mummy' hastily on the envelope.

'Done! Can I go to Diane's now?'

It was November now, and Lucy hadn't seen her family for almost two months. She still talked regularly and relentlessly about when she was going home, how great her daddy was and how much she missed him. I was bowled over by her resilience and patience. On the whole she was behaving well, keeping out of trouble at school and only occasionally lapsing into the aggravating behaviour we'd seen before. The horses kept her busy, and she'd joined a football team and a swimming club, both of which she thoroughly enjoyed taking part in every week.

She phoned home every Wednesday as agreed, passing

on her news and patiently talking to every member of the family who was put on the phone, although she only really ever wanted to talk to her daddy. Sometimes there were unexplained gaps in the contact, when weeks went by with nobody picking up or returning her calls. She didn't complain. On one occasion she came off the phone and punched the air.

'Are you celebrating something?' Jonathan asked.

'Yes. Daddy and Wendy aren't getting married any more.'

Milly had apparently told her about a 'big row' during which Wendy had threatened to get the builders back to build a wall through the middle of the house, so she and Gemma could live on one side and Dean, the twins and Milly on the other.

'They aren't getting married any more?'

'No. That's good, isn't it? And guess what? They can't build a wall so Wendy and Gemma are going to have to move out, and so I can move back in . . . that's what's going to happen.'

As this had been reported to Lucy by Milly we knew to take it with a pinch of salt; it sounded likely there'd been a row, but the fall-out from it and the implications for Lucy smacked more of wishful thinking on her part than anything else.

'Well,' I said cautiously, 'it sounds like a lot to have happened since you last spoke. I guess we'll have to wait and find out more, from your daddy or from Wendy.'

'I suppose so,' Lucy said slowly. Then her eyes narrowed

and she added suspiciously, 'Milly could be lying, because the builders haven't finished, so why would Wendy have to get them back? They can't have finished, because if they had I'd have moved back in.'

'Like I say, let's wait and see, sweetheart.' It appeared Lucy had convinced herself the building work was the main barrier – or the only barrier – to moving back in, but of course this wasn't true. She was in denial about the other issues, which I found worrying.

The next day Wendy was on the phone first thing, informing us the family wanted to come over on Sunday to take Lucy out for a roast. There was no hint that there was any problem between her and Dean, and in fact she said everyone was 'doing very well, thank you'. Jonathan took the call and told me Wendy sounded a little business-like and bossy, which wasn't unusual, but otherwise seemed perfectly fine.

'She told me that all six of them were planning to come over, if the timing was OK for us and Lucy, and she said she was looking forward to it. She even said the visit was "overdue" and apologised for not fixing something up sooner. What d'you make of that?'

'Who knows? If there was a row with Dean, maybe it was about the fact he hasn't seen his daughter for so long? Perhaps Wendy's had no choice but to finally agree to see Lucy? Maybe that was why she sounded a bit formal, because she's been forced into this and is going through the motions of saying and doing all the right things?'

'It's a very good theory. I mean, it's such a long time for

Dean not to have seen Lucy. Whatever trouble there's been, he loves her to bits. He must miss her.'

I thought back to Lucy's last visit home, when things supposedly went so wrong at the play centre and she ended up accused of telling lies about Wendy threatening to hit her at bedtime. I say 'supposedly' went wrong because we never had got to the bottom of exactly what went on that weekend: as far as we knew Lucy's version of events remained at odds with Wendy's, because the subject was never revisited with Lucy or with us.

'Well, whatever's prompted Wendy to fix up this lunch, hopefully it's a step in the right direction, though I can't say I'm exactly brimming with optimism.'

Jonathan felt the same and said he found it frustrating that we never quite knew where we were with Wendy, feeling compelled to second-guess her like this.

When I told Lucy all the family were coming to take her out her little face lit up and then fell in the space of a few seconds.

'Daddy! Yes! I can't wait. But you mean all of them . . . Wendy and Gemma too?'

'Yes.'

'Do you think Daddy is going to tell me about them moving out? Is that why they're coming? Will this be the last time I see them?'

I explained that Jonathan had spoken to Wendy quite briefly on the phone. 'She said nothing about any trouble or plans for her and Gemma to leave,' I said cautiously, being sure to stick to the facts.

'So I still can't move home yet? It's not fair! I hate Wendy! Milly said they were going. Are they? Why are they even bothering coming to see me?'

'Lucy, let's wait and see. I don't want you to get your hopes up or be disappointed in any way . . .'

Lucy ran out into the garden and began rampaging around. It was a cold, windy day and she had no coat on. I let her run off some of her negative energy for a few minutes then called her in when she started kicking the wall and howling. She ran through the back door leaving a trail of mud across the kitchen floor and telling me she hated me and hated my house. Then she kicked off her shoes and ran up to her bedroom. After ten minutes I went to see if she had calmed down and invited her to come down to the kitchen for a hot drink and a chat. She told me to go away but then appeared sheepishly at the kitchen door about ten minutes later.

'Sorry about the mud,' she said, looking at the steaming mop in my hand and the clean floor. 'Sorry you had to mop up after me, Angela.'

'Thanks for the apology. I can see that what Milly said on the phone has got you a bit wound up, Lucy. How about you clean up your shoes in the utility room while I get you a drink?'

The last time I'd suggested to Lucy that she clean her shoes she'd been in a bad mood and told me it was my job, but I could see she was in a much more receptive mood now and I thought that if she was busy doing something it might be easier for her to talk to me, if she wanted to get things off her chest.

'OK,' she said. 'I need to do my football boots too. Can I still go to training?'

'Yes, sweetheart. I think it will do you good to go to football tonight.' There was a time, earlier on in our fostering careers, when Jonathan and I were taught to 'ground' children and take away privileges like after-school clubs and sporting activities if they misbehaved. Thinking had changed over the years and this approach was largely considered old hat, especially for kids like Lucy who were better behaved when they were occupied. Now it's understood that children in foster care have typically been through some kind of trauma in their lives, and the events that have led to them being placed in care impact on their mental health and general behaviour. I could see that Lucy acted out to vent her frustration at her uncertain family situation, and to stop her socialising and getting exercise at football club as a result would have added to her stress and irritation.

'Thanks,' she whispered. 'I'm sorry I was horrible to you.'

I told her it did make me sad when she said unkind things to me, but that I appreciated her apology. That was the end of the matter as far as I was concerned: Lucy had a big day on Sunday to prepare for, and I wanted her to be in the best possible frame of mind.

The family didn't arrive at the time we'd agreed to take Lucy out for lunch and she got herself into quite a state, asking me every five minutes why they were late, what could have happened, if I knew which way there were driving and so on. I tried not to look concerned and kept repeating the same phrases, 'I'm sure there's a good explanation. I'm sure they'll be here soon.' After about half an hour I tried Wendy's mobile – at Lucy's insistence – but it was switched off. I didn't like to try Dean's phone as I assumed he'd be driving. Lucy said I was 'mean' not to phone her daddy. 'You've got loads of money. You get paid to look after me. I bet you don't want to phone him because it costs too much money!'

I explained to Lucy that it wasn't a good idea to phone someone while they were driving, to which she replied, 'I bet Daddy's run out of petrol. I know you and Jonathan get petrol money paid when you drive me home but my daddy doesn't get any mileage. It's not fair. I bet he's run out of petrol!'

Jonathan and I would not have discussed the fact foster carers receive 'mileage' to cover the cost of driving children around. Lucy's remarks left me wondering who had put this word and idea in her head. Had someone in the family complained about the cost of travelling to see her? It sounded like it to me, but I didn't want to continue this conversation; it was getting us nowhere.

I suggested Lucy did some science topic work on gears and engines that she'd brought home from school and seemed very interested in – anything to keep her occupied – but she told me, 'Nobody does homework on a Sunday. My daddy told me that. It's not allowed!' I didn't argue; now was not the time or the place, even though Lucy had done homework on Sundays before.

Jonathan was replacing some tiles in our bathroom and Lucy asked if she could help. I said I'd prefer her to do something less messy, so she was clean and tidy when the family finally arrived, but when I explained this she became cross and started following me around, clipping the backs of my heels like she used to, invading my personal space and talking non-stop.

'Why can't I? What if they take another hour? What am I supposed to do? I can't play out, because it's raining – look outside. I can't go to Diane's, can I? So what am I supposed to do?'

'What about doing a game on the computer, or building something with the Meccano or Lego? Or maybe you could do some colouring or watch something on TV.'

'It's boring. All that's boring. I want to help Jonathan.'

'How about you help me then? I'm making a cottage pie for tomorrow's dinner.'

'Why would I want to do that? I'm going out for lunch. Why are you making that today? What are you doing that for? Why don't you make it tomorrow?'

In the end Lucy ground me down so much I had a headache. To her delight, Jonathan suddenly called down and asked if she wouldn't mind holding the grouting bucket for him while he was up the ladder, and she was off like a shot. I wished he'd heard me telling her I would prefer her not to help him on this occasion, but it was too late. I told her to be careful not to get messy or dirty.

Inevitably, the family arrived within a few minutes. Lucy ran to the door, a sprinkling of tile dust in her hair and on her clothing and with an old grout-stained rag stuffed in her pocket.

'Daddy!'

'Princess! Hey, look at you! I think you've grown.'

Dean ruffled her hair while Wendy looked on disapprovingly. 'Careful, Dean. What have you done with your hair, Lucy?'

Before she had time to answer, Milly had pushed forward to give her big sister a cuddle, followed by the twins who gave her slightly self-conscious hugs. Gemma managed a thin smile and a half-hearted wave as she said, 'Hi.'

I welcomed everybody in and quickly explained about Lucy helping Jonathan in the bathroom. Wendy did not look pleased. I felt like telling her that if they hadn't been late Lucy would have been immaculately presented, but I held my tongue. Dean muttered something about the traffic being bad and I said it wasn't a problem; at least they were here now.

'Why don't you quickly go up and get cleaned up again?' I said to Lucy. I smiled at Wendy and made a comment about Lucy being such a willing helper, but she didn't react.

Milly asked if she could go upstairs with Lucy and the sisters ran off together. Wendy and Dean refused my offer of a cup of tea, saying they wouldn't stop, which was understandable as they were running so late. The boys accepted a drink of orange squash each and Jonathan popped down to say hello. He told them he'd never met a young girl who was so interested in helping with jobs around the home. Dean nodded and proudly shared a story about Lucy helping him rebuild a little wall when she was seven. I wanted to tell them about how Lucy helped my mum with her garden but the vibe I was getting from Wendy put me off. She had a disapproving, judgemental look on her face, though I didn't know if that was because she was still cross about Lucy being dusty and with the rag in her pocket when they arrived, or because she had difficulty listening to any kind of praise for Lucy.

Dean, thankfully, made up for Wendy's coolness. He was in a friendly, chatty mood and he thanked us both for continuing to look after his daughter.

'I appreciate it, mate,' Dean said, shaking Jonathan's hand. 'I know when you took her in you didn't expect to have her this long, but we're working on it. I can't thank you enough.'

Lucy and Milly reappeared in no time at all. Lucy looked lovely. She'd washed her hands, brushed her hair and had decided to change into a new pair of jeans and her prettiest sweatshirt, though the clothes she'd had on could easily have been dusted down.

Wendy immediately got to her feet. 'We were going to have a roast but I think it'll have to be a quick pizza now. We'll have her back by three.'

The boys cheered at the mention of pizza while I glanced at the clock and felt a wave of sadness: it was already one thirty.

'Three is fine, but please don't rush. If you take longer it's not a problem, we're not going anywhere.'

'Thanks,' Dean said. 'That's good to know, isn't it Wendy?'

'Three o'clock is plenty of time.'

The family returned at ten to three. Lucy was in a great mood, telling me all about the pizza she'd had, the ice cream with chocolate sauce on top and the game she'd played on an arcade machine at the pizza restaurant. Dean brought her to the door while the rest of the family stayed in his van. He said they'd all had a 'good catch up' and that he hoped they'd do it again soon.

'See you soon, princess,' he said, kissing her on the forehead. 'Great to see you!'

'When am I coming home?'

'Not that question again! What have I told you? As soon as I can fix it, OK?'

He ruffled her hair as he had done when he first arrived.

'OK Daddy. I don't want to live with Mummy. I want to live with you. I miss you.'

Dean caught my eye. 'Oh, yes. I know all about the letters and all that with Noreen. Thanks for helping Lucy write back to her mum. I'm ever so grateful for all you've done for her.'

'We love having her here, Dean. She's a smashing girl. I'll miss her when she's gone. I wish you all the best. Good luck.'

He smiled and gave me a nod. He was a gentle soul, but I really wished he'd stand up to Wendy more and fight a bit harder to have his daughter home, where she belonged.

# 23

### *'I don't want to make you sad'*

Cedella called round the next day after school. The visit was unplanned and to my dismay she told me Wendy had contacted Social Services complaining that she felt it was 'unreasonable' for Lucy to be 'expected to do building work' in our house. Exasperated, I explained all about what happened on Sunday before the family arrived.

'I assume you need to talk to Lucy? She can tell you herself how much she enjoys helping out with DIY and things like that. If the truth be told, she nagged me to let her help with the tiling but in the event all she did was hold the grouting bucket for a couple of minutes while Jonathan was up the ladder. We certainly wouldn't ask her to do any kind of work that we felt was inappropriate or dangerous.'

Cedella nodded and thanked me for filling her in. 'But I do need to speak to Lucy, of course. Wendy's made the call and it's my duty to look into it. Also, I'm afraid Lucy told her dad that Jonathan treats her badly sometimes, and she said that you don't care.'

I sighed and Cedella said sweetly, 'Angela, I'm just doing my job here. I'm afraid I have to do this . . .' I could tell she wasn't enjoying it one bit. She looked at me with genuine sympathy and I didn't think she believed for one moment that Jonathan or I had done anything wrong, but her tact and sensitivity didn't stop this feeling like another blow. *I could really do without this,* I thought; the upset caused by the malicious allegations from Wendy's neighbour was still very fresh in my mind.

I fetched Lucy and left her and Cedella to talk privately. When they were finished Lucy called me to come up from the kitchen and I sat beside her on the sofa in the living room, facing Cedella who was in one of the armchairs.

Lucy looked ashamed of herself and couldn't look me in the eye.

'I'm really sorry, Angela,' she said, examining her knees and hands.

'What are you sorry for, Lucy? I'm not sure I understand what has happened.'

She looked at the floor.

Cedella spoke now, explaining that they'd had a good chat and it seemed that Lucy had 'got muddled up' when she said Jonathan treated her badly and that I didn't care. She encouraged Lucy to talk to me.

'Er, that's right,' she said quietly, continuing to study her fingers. 'That happened to someone else – that boy who's staying with Diane. It was when he was in another foster home. I forgot, I got muddled up. The foster carers he had were horrible, but you're not like that.'

Lucy looked sideways at me now.

'I'm really sorry Angela. I said it because . . . I said it because Wendy was cross about me being dusty when they came to collect me. I said you and Jonathan made me do the tiling. I said you didn't care and he didn't treat me nicely. I'm sorry. I don't know why . . .'

'I see. Well thank you for telling the truth now. I appreciate that, though it would be helpful if you could try to remember how important it is to tell the truth *all* the time. Then we wouldn't get into situations like this, would we?'

'I know. I don't want to make you sad, Angela. I don't want you to have a pain in your heart. I'm sorry.'

Lucy shuffled along the sofa and gave me a little hug. Cedella then had a brief chat with her, reiterating the importance of telling the truth, before wrapping up the visit and reassuring me that no action would be taken, and that she'd explain the 'misunderstanding' to Wendy. I saw Cedella out and told her I understood she had to report back to Wendy but was concerned it would reinforce her view of Lucy as a troublemaker, just when progress was being made.

'Leave it with me. I'll handle it, Angela. I do understand.' She gave me a big smile and I felt reassured; I could tell Cedella knew where I was coming from.

Later, an optimistic thought struck me, which no doubt shows how much I wanted Lucy to be reunited with her family. *Maybe Wendy cares more about Lucy than I think, because raising this complaint with Social Services could have derailed the placement. Why would Wendy risk that if she wanted Lucy to stay in our care for as long as possible?*

I shared my thought with Jonathan. He mulled this over for a moment but then said he didn't think my positive take on the situation rang true.

'Unfortunately,' he said, 'I'm afraid Wendy could simply be one of those people who doesn't like the fact one of her dependants is in foster care and for that reason alone is happy to share criticism of us.'

'Even though she doesn't want to care for Lucy herself?'

'Exactly. I hate to talk about somebody like this, but I think that might describe Wendy. Maybe she doesn't like the fact we're happy looking after Lucy and we cope well with her 'behaviours'. I hope I'm wrong; I'd love it if this was all about Wendy making moves towards taking Lucy back, but I'm just not feeling that. I think she wants Lucy in care as long as possible, with us or with another carer. In fact, as cynical as this may sound, if Lucy's placement with us broke down then it would give weight to Wendy's argument about how difficult she is to look after. This is all about her, not us and not Lucy. I think she's pretty ruthless and is putting herself first.'

I had to agree that this sounded very plausible. I'd been clutching at straws, trying to find any hint of silver lining I could in amongst the clouds that continued to hang over Lucy's future happiness. Maybe it simply didn't exist?

A few days later Lucy and I were driving to school when she suddenly started to talk about what she'd told her dad and

Wendy when they went out for pizza. I don't know what prompted it, although sometimes children find it easier to open up when they are strapped in the back of the car and don't have to give you eye contact.

'You know the other day . . . well, I did get muddled up, like I said, but it was accidentally on purpose.'

'You got muddled up, accidentally on purpose?'

'Yes.'

'OK. Thanks for telling me this, Lucy, but I'm not sure I understand what you mean.'

There was a pause and I waited for her to fill the silence.

'Well,' she said slowly. '*I* thought if *Daddy* thought I wasn't happy with you and Jonathan, then he would get me home faster.'

'I see.'

There was another pause, a longer one this time, and again I waited for her to carry on.

'I didn't want to get you into trouble or anything. I do like you, I like you a lot. I think you're kind and nice. I like Jonathan too. Sorry.'

'We like you a lot too, Lucy. As I've told you before, you're a lovely girl. Thanks for being truthful with me now.'

'I'm not a liar!' she said, suddenly sounding agitated. 'I didn't lie on purpose. It was an accident, not on purpose. Wendy asked me about the tiling and other jobs I do and . . . I really don't want to make you sad. I just want to go home . . .' Her tone softened towards the end and she fell silent again.

I thanked her again for being honest and said I understood how much she wanted to go home. 'I know you miss Daddy, sweetheart, and I can see what you've tried to do. But saying things that aren't true isn't going to get you home any faster, is it? In fact, if you're not being honest – "accidentally on purpose" or not – that's something that needs sorting out. And that could mean it takes even longer for you to be ready to go home.'

It was a lot for a little girl to take in but I think Lucy understood the main point, that meddling of any kind was only ever going to lead to trouble. Privately, I wondered if Wendy had stirred things up to prompt Lucy's unfounded complaints and criticisms. The trip to the pizza place had gone well and when Dean had brought Lucy back he certainly didn't appear to have an issue with us, so what had caused Wendy to call Social Services after the event? In the absence of any bad behaviour from Lucy that would have given her grounds for complaint, had Wendy deliberately gone digging for trouble on the day? Then waited until they got home to share her grievances with Dean? I really would not have put it past her.

That evening my mother babysat for Lucy and Maria while Jonathan and I went out for a meal with friends. We left the three of them happily playing a game of Cluedo and as we set off I told Jonathan about Lucy's 'confession'.

'Poor Lucy,' he said. 'Creating trouble with us so she can go home, when being involved in trouble of any kind makes it *less* likely she'll go home any time soon.'

'That's about the size of it,' I frowned. 'It all seems so unnecessary.'

While I was getting ready to go out I'd been thinking back over Lucy's past. From what we knew it seemed that she'd successfully 'got rid' of her first stepmother, Val, by reporting her nasty ways to her daddy. But who knew how true Lucy's alarming version of events was? Pins in the bed, salt in her tea and dog muck in her hair . . . These were serious allegations, but had Lucy been telling the truth? To our knowledge no official action was ever taken, by Social Services or anyone else. Perhaps Lucy had made the whole thing up, or had she at least embellished the facts? Either way, she got what she wanted because her daddy appeared to have believed what she said and he and Val split up.

As I dried my hair I considered whether Lucy had tried to make history repeat itself. Had she invented or exaggerated Wendy's faults and caused trouble deliberately, so her dad would get rid of her and Gemma? Wendy had shown us her hard side, but was she really as unpleasant and cold-hearted as we'd come to think?

I shared all of this with Jonathan as he drove us to the restaurant. We often talk things through when we're alone in the car and there's no chance of being overheard or interrupted, particularly by the children. I think we're both quite good at trying to see a situation from all sides; it helps us make sense of tricky problems and it's also a good way to unload, when your head's full of worries and theories and you're looking for answers and solutions.

'So are you saying that maybe Wendy isn't as bad as we

think she might be? That Lucy has wound her up, told lies and caused trouble to get rid of her like she did with Val?'

'Basically, yes. It's only a theory but it's possible. Maybe Val wasn't that bad either, and now Dean's had time to reflect – and now there are issues between Lucy and Wendy – he isn't sure if Lucy was truthful about everything Val supposedly did wrong? Perhaps he now takes things Lucy says with a pinch of salt, and that's why he's reluctant to take her side and stand up to Wendy?

'Wow,' Jonathan said. 'I present the first prize for amateur psychology to Mrs Angela Hart!'

I laughed. 'Well what's your theory, clever-clogs?'

He thought for a moment. 'What I think is this: Mrs White did it, in the library with the lead piping.'

I rolled my eyes and laughed, an image of Lucy smiling as she played Cluedo with my mum and Maria flashing into my mind.

'But seriously,' he went on. 'I think the truth probably lies somewhere in the middle. Wendy and Lucy are both capable of being manipulative and I think they each feel threatened by the other. We've talked about feeling stuck in the middle and having to be diplomatic, but the real piggy in the middle is Dean. I think he has the power to sort this out, by making it clear to both Lucy and Wendy that they need to show more tolerance and kindness to each other if the family is ever going to gel. I'm afraid he doesn't see this, or he doesn't want to see this. He's a very gentle character who doesn't like conflict, so his natural tendency is to back off and sweep things under the carpet rather than confront problems head-on. This leaves the way for Wendy to rule the roost, which is precisely what she wants. She's a naturally controlling person, and Dean's subservience gives her even more power, which puts Lucy's nose out of joint and fuels the whole vicious circle of resentment and bitterness.'

'Wow! Some excellent observations. Second prize to Mr Jonathan Hart!'

'I'd say joint first prize, wouldn't you?'

'Maybe. I'll have to think about it – it's certainly food for thought. Talking of food, let's go in. I'm starving.'

We'd been in the car park, finishing off our conversation, for about ten minutes. Unbeknown to us our friends were already in the restaurant and had seen us arrive.

'What's going on?' they laughed. 'This is a rare night out without kids, and you two are sitting in the car park! Come on, our table's ready.'

Jonathan and I looked at each other and smiled; foster carers do have nights out and time 'off duty' but, just like any parent, we haven't felt 'without kids' for a very long time and we wouldn't have it any other way.

# 24

### *'We can't have Christmas ruined'*

The next time Lucy would see her family was at Christmas. She was invited to stay for one night shortly after the schools broke up, returning to us a couple of days before Christmas Eve. Lucy didn't question why she couldn't spend Christmas Day with the family; the more time that passed the less she challenged the restrictions placed on her contact with the family, although that didn't stop her talking about her daddy frequently, or regularly checking with Cedella and me if there was any news on when she was going home.

Unfortunately, unprompted by Lucy or anybody else, Wendy took it upon herself to explain to me exactly why Lucy wasn't welcome on Christmas Day.

'Dean's been very busy at work and he's been to the doctor because he's stressed and not sleeping well,' she told me on the phone. 'We can't have any trouble. He's been told to take it easy and I've got to take care of him. I've told Lucy we can't have her here because it will cause complications and upset her dad.'

'Complications? Upset her dad?' My heart sank and I thought, *Surely Dean will be upset not to see his daughter on Christmas Day? What on earth was the point in saying that to Lucy?*

When Lucy spoke to Wendy, before passing the phone to me, I'd been pottering around the kitchen and I heard her talking to every member of her family. Wendy was the last person she spoke to, and Lucy had done what she always did when she talked to her stepmother: she sounded uncomfortable and couldn't wait to finish the conversation. This was nothing unusual, but now I knew what Wendy had been saying I wished I'd intervened and asked Lucy if everything was OK. It seemed unnecessarily cruel to spell things out for Lucy like this, and as Wendy carried on repeating to me what she'd told Lucy I felt my blood rising.

'Yes, Angela, let me explain. By complications I mean that I know you and Jonathan will buy her some presents and if she were here on Christmas Day she'd have to bring them with her. Then the other kids would be asking me why Lucy had more than them. It would cause no end of trouble and Dean can do without the upset. I have to look after him.'

I kept my voice even and told Wendy, tactfully, that Jonathan and I wouldn't mind if Lucy opened our presents to her at our house afterwards, if that would mean she could spend Christmas with her family.

'You're very kind, but you know how Lucy is. She'd only be bragging to the others that she was going to have more when she got back to yours. I can just see it all. No, I've made my mind up. Dean has been so stressed and we can't have Christmas ruined.'

I didn't argue; Wendy clearly wasn't moving on this. I found the whole conversation particularly upsetting as Lucy had heard nothing back from her birth mother. Social Services had posted off Lucy's note, in which she'd asked for the Ninja Turtles cuddly toy she longed for or a riding hat, but her mum hadn't responded. We'd recently heard from Jess that Social Services had decided it wasn't possible for Lucy to live with her mother again, on any basis. We weren't given a reason, but Jess told us she was still looking into arranging some contact sessions for Lucy and her mum, though it was 'proving difficult to tie Noreen down.' Lucy was shielded from all of this as she had been all along: she would quite rightly only be told if and when a meeting with her mother was definitely going ahead.

As Christmas approached Lucy did ask what was happening about her present from her mummy, because she wanted to ask Father Christmas for a new riding hat and the cuddly toy if her mum wasn't getting either gift for her. I told her to keep waiting, because sometimes Christmas presents arrived just in time and they might be on their way. Privately, I had my doubts after hearing what Jess had to say, and when time started to run out I decided Father Christmas needed tipping off after all, and I helped Lucy write a note to the North Pole.

Lucy was excited when she broke up from school for the Christmas holidays and her overnight stay with the family went well. The extension was finally finished and she got to share a bedroom just with Milly, which she was pleased about. Her relationship with Gemma wasn't brilliant. The girls seemed to tolerate each other nowadays, but I thought that was fair enough, and as much as we could hope for. It must have been so hard for Lucy to see Gemma fitting into the family while she was still on the outside. Also, I thought back to the best friends I'd had at primary school. At that young age they were never best friends for long and I couldn't imagine what it would have been like if one of those girls subsequently moved in with my family. I'd have hated it.

Wendy and Dean sent Lucy home with a big bag of presents and made a point of telling us that all the kids were getting the same.

'She's been a little angel,' Dean told me. 'What have you been feeding her?'

I smiled politely, thinking rather smugly to myself, *Healthy portions of respect and kindness, it seems to be working well.* 'She's been behaving very well with us too. We're really pleased with how she's getting on.'

Even Wendy had a kind word to say, praising Lucy for being helpful in the kitchen. 'You've got her well trained, Angela,' she said. I took it in good spirit, though in hindsight I wondered if she was having a little dig, criticising me for encouraging Lucy to pitch in with cooking and tidying up, as I always did.

No parcel arrived from Noreen. On Christmas Day Lucy was bowled over when she opened her sack from Santa and found she had a brand-new riding hat and the exact Ninja Turtle cuddly toy she wanted.

'Do you think he told Mummy he'd sort everything out for her, to save her the trouble?'

'I don't know how Father Christmas works his magic,' I smiled.

She phoned home and had a brief chat with everyone and we enjoyed a fantastic dinner and played board games for hours with my mum and Maria. Lucy seemed very happy, and at bedtime she said she'd had the 'best Christmas ever.'

When Lucy's birthday came round, in the new year, similar arrangements were made. The family had her over on the weekend before her birthday but it was left to us to organise a treat on the day itself. Once again Wendy created a drama about presents, telling me exactly what she was spending on Lucy and checking what we were buying. She also told me what Lucy was allowed to tell her siblings and Gemma about her birthday, to avoid any jealousy. Again it all seemed unnecessary to me but I let it go.

The main thing was that another overnight visit home had gone well. We had no reports of lying, irritating behaviour or any disputes about what Lucy had and hadn't said and done. Wendy was in a good mood when we arrived for the pick-up and Lucy said she enjoyed herself and loved being with everyone. She was particularly thrilled that her brothers and Milly had given up their clubs and sports on the Sunday so everyone could go out for a birthday lunch together.

Lucy's granny had given her a calendar for Christmas, showing pictures of different birds for each month and season. She loved it, putting it in pride of place next to her bed and carefully adding important dates, including that of the forthcoming wedding in April. When I was changing her bed one day I noticed some scribbles at the bottom of the chart: Lucy had worked out the number of days until the wedding and was keeping a tally. She was going to see her family on a couple of occasions before the wedding, to finalise her dress fitting and to attend a twenty-first party for one of her cousins. Those dates were marked clearly, and she wrote in all the relevant boxes: 'Seeing Daddy!!!'

Not long after her birthday Lucy told me, 'There's only eight weeks until I go home after the wedding! What is eight times . . . how many days in a week?'

I asked her to count from Monday to Sunday and, using her fingers, she arrived at the number seven. Then I encouraged her to recite the seven times table but she got stuck after seven times five and asked me to carry on.

'Seven sixes are forty-two, seven sevens are forty-nine and seven eights are fifty-six,' I said, making a note to dig out some times table flash cards I had in one of the games cupboards.

'So I'm going home in fifty-six days!' she declared. 'Why didn't you just say that?'

Cedella and I had both talked to Lucy about the fact we didn't yet have an exact date for her return home. We told her there were still quite a few details to sort out and she mustn't pin her hopes on any one particular date. I had to gently remind her of this, as I had done several times already, and she gave me the reply she always did. 'I know, but I'm going home after the wedding, so it's all fixed.'

I'd heard from Social Services that Wendy had made it clear she wasn't going to any meetings concerning Lucy until after her big day. I knew it could take weeks to gather all the relevant parties together and, even if Wendy and Dean were ready to have Lucy back, it wouldn't happen overnight. There would be red tape to wade through and she would need to be enrolled back in a local school, for one thing. I explained to Lucy that there was going to be a big meeting after the wedding and only then would we know more.

'OK,' she said. 'But I'm behaving myself, aren't I?'

'You're been behaving very well, Lucy. I'm really pleased.'

The final dress fitting and the family twenty-first soon came and went, and both events ran relatively smoothly. Lucy said she hated the way Wendy wanted her to have her hair for the wedding because it was 'too girly and flowery' but she told us, 'I was good and didn't make a fuss. Daddy said I was a good girl. Daddy said it's more trouble than it's worth to argue with Wendy.' Jonathan and I shared a look but tried not to let Lucy see how readily we could identify with Dean's observation.

I was very pleased that Lucy's visits home were going

well but the more time passed, the more it became apparent that simply avoiding arguments with Wendy wasn't enough: the way I saw it, you had to dance to her tune, every time.

'Basically,' I said to Jonathan. 'Everything has to be done Wendy's way. Things are fine if she gets her way – like with Lucy's hair for the wedding. But not disagreeing with Wendy isn't enough. It's her way or the highway. It's not a healthy way for a family to operate, is it?'

Jonathan said he could see my point but said we should probably make allowances for the time being, because of the wedding.

'It's Wendy's big day, after all,' he said. 'Hopefully after the wedding things will calm down.'

As usual he was trying to look for something positive to say. Wedding planning is fraught and frenetic at the best of times – I remember my own like it was yesterday, even though it was way back in the seventies. I said it was no wonder Dean had been suffering from stress and that I hoped Jonathan was right about things calming down. 'Yes, fingers crossed that Wendy will settle down and be less overbearing once she and Dean have tied the knot,' I commented.

Jonathan gave me a cheeky look and burst out laughing. 'What?'

'Oh nothing, it's just that in my personal experience, I'm not sure women become less overbearing once they get married!'

We laughed. In retrospect, we probably shouldn't have.

We were asked to collect Lucy straight from the evening do after the wedding. She wasn't staying the night at the family home because Wendy and Dean were going away on honeymoon for a few days and Wendy's mother – a person we'd heard no mention of before – was looking after the children. When we arrived at the community centre where the party was being held Wendy swept over and greeted us like long-lost friends. It was clear she'd had a few drinks, which was no surprise on her wedding day, and she gushed about how brilliant a day she'd had, how pretty all the girls looked and how thankful she was to us for collecting Lucy. Dean hugged Lucy tight as he said goodbye and called her 'my beautiful little princess'.

'See you when we get back, all right?'

'Yes! See you when you get back! Happy honeymoon! I love you Daddy!'

'I love you too Lucy-lu! See you soon!'

Lucy was full of pop and crisps and was bouncing about all over the place. On the way home she said, 'See, what did I tell you? I'm going home. Daddy told me. Wendy told me. I'm going home!'

'Wendy told you?'

'Yes, well, I mean Wendy was there when Daddy said it and she let him say it. So that's it. It's HAPP-EN-ING!'

## *Epilogue*

Lucy lived with us for a further seven years, until she was sixteen years old. Unfortunately, once Wendy was Dean's wife, she didn't calm down or soften one bit. In fact she seemed to use her new married status to wield even more power over the family, becoming increasingly bossy, controlling and manipulative. She took charge of all dealings with Social Services and refused to come to the review meeting that was arranged shortly after the wedding, stating bluntly, 'My husband and I need time to adjust to the new family dynamic. It is far too soon to risk having Lucy back.' Dean didn't get involved at all, and as time went on he appeared to shrink further away. On one memorable occasion Wendy told him to be quiet on his own doorstep, when he hadn't managed to spit a single word out and was actually just clearing his throat.

We began to notice that whenever Lucy, Wendy and Dean were together, Wendy positioned herself in between

Lucy and her dad, and she never once let Dean come to our house on his own: it was the whole family, or nobody at all.

Lucy kept her hopes up, always. When she found out she wasn't going home soon after the wedding she took it remarkably well. There was no howling or tantrums; in fact she promised me she would 'try even harder to be good'. Then she bravely set her sights on the next month, then the next. The calendar, however, ended up in the bin long before the year was out.

When Lucy was still living with us at Christmas, and on her next birthday, when she turned ten, she continued to talk positively about 'when I go home', saying, 'I miss Daddy. I love Daddy! How long will it be now? It's AGES! I want to go home.'

Occasionally I'd overhear Lucy telling other people, like my mum or Barbara in the shop, that she'd be going home by a certain point in time. My chest would tighten every time; it was a heart-wrenching situation. Jonathan and I had to constantly walk a tightrope, trying to be honest with Lucy while at the same time protecting her feelings. We always tried to defect her questions and manage her expectations as best we could, but it wasn't easy. We were constantly attempting to dress up the ongoing rejection as something the family was still working towards sorting out. The very last thing we wanted was for Lucy to be crushed by so much disappointment, but the fact was we had no idea if 'promises' Wendy and Dean made about what might happen in three months or six months or nine months would ever come to fruition. In some ways we were in the same boat as Lucy, always wondering if Social Services were going to call and tell us Lucy was moving out next week or staying for another year. We accepted this, however, telling our support social worker we would always have room for her in our house, however long she might stay.

All things considered, Lucy's self-esteem was good. She was doing well with her various sports and rubbed along OK with Maria most of the time, although they were never close. She had plenty of friends in the neighbourhood and at school and was often invited to their houses or out for trips. Lucy still loved spending time with her granny whenever she could too, and she enjoyed staying with her during the school holidays as she had done before.

Visits home became fewer and further between. Lucy had learned the hard way that she had to be on nothing but her very best behaviour or else, and she was always very careful to try to please Wendy and avoid any trouble. Wendy rarely had a complaint but she never had a good word to say about Lucy either – or anything at all, for that matter. At best, it was as if she begrudgingly tolerated Lucy; at worst, I got the impression she tried to ignore her. Jonathan and I would often hear about the dancing medals Milly won, the footballing triumphs of the twins or a success Gemma had at school, but whenever I asked Lucy if she'd told the family about her latest swimming gala or football trophy she'd always say no. 'Nobody asked me and I don't want to be accused of bragging,' she said more than once. The peace was kept, but at what price? It seemed that

Lucy was expected to edit her life when she was with her family, for fear of rocking the boat. Wendy had won, I guess. Everything was on her terms, and she was so dominant and controlling that she didn't even have to say anything: just the threat of upsetting Wendy was enough to keep Lucy in line.

Lucy's behaviour took a turn for the worse when she was at secondary school. She hated it and was in the bottom set for everything. Puberty was a battle. She was very moody, ate a lot of junk food, was covered in spots and her weight yo-yoed, which made her miserable. When exam classes were decided she was told she wouldn't be doing any GCSEs and was offered some other less challenging courses she wasn't interested in. She gave up swimming and football and stopped horse riding for a while, though she later picked it up again, and when she turned fourteen she began helping Diane teach younger children, which she thoroughly enjoyed and was very good at. She also took on several other jobs. Ever the willing worker, Lucy did odd jobs for local farmers and builders, or painters and decorators who Jonathan and I knew. She was in her element when she was outdoors, getting her hands dirty, although she developed a habit of not coming home on time, forgetting to let us know where she was and telling lies to both her employers and teachers about why she was late, or tired. It was always the fault of the third party, or she'd claim her watch wasn't working, her bike had a flat tyre or I hadn't told her I was cooking her dinner that night – though I had a hot meal on the table every night without fail. Lucy also went through a phase of refusing to get changed and would walk around in dirty clothes, scattering mud or bits of paint or plaster everywhere. When I complained, her stock reply was to shrug and challenge, 'What are you going to do – call the cops?'

At fifteen Lucy was caught stealing money from other pupils. She went through their bags and blazers during PE and at break times, and she got away with it for a long time. Before she was found out we had letters from the school about the thefts, warning all parents and carers of the problem, advising us to limit cash brought into school and asking us to talk to our children and encourage anyone with information to come forward. Lucy could have won a BAFTA for her performance: we never suspected the culprit was right under our nose. She hadn't attended therapy for years; the one-to-one sessions she had at CAMHS petered out, I think when it became apparent the original aim of them – to help prepare Lucy to live in harmony with her family again – had gradually slipped off the agenda. She had another short course of sessions after the stealing episode and had to apologise to a lot of other children and save up her pocket money and wages to pay back what she'd taken. The value of what she took wasn't high; Lucy said she did it 'just because I could' and not because she coveted money, and she spent it all on chips, sweets and fizzy drinks. The school handled the situation well, but afterwards Lucy hated being there even more. She couldn't wait to leave and made no effort with her final exams.

Wendy and Dean never wanted anything to do with Lucy's problems. They knew what went on through Social Services but made it clear they were 'happy for Angela and Jonathan to deal with it as they see fit'. Lucy still loved going home for visits and she still talked on the phone with every member of the family most weeks, but conversations were always limited to what was happening to everybody else.

After falling out with her mum, Gemma left home at sixteen and went to live with her boyfriend's family. At the same time Lucy was offered the chance of a summer job, working at some stables on the other side of the country. She jumped at the chance. Lucy was sixteen now too, and about to leave school. We spoke to Social Services and were told that if she took up the position her placement with us would have to officially come to an end, as she'd be away for at least three months and out of our care. When we explained this to her she announced, 'It's OK. I'll just go home afterwards.'

It transpired that Lucy had spoken to Wendy and Dean about this possibility already. They had told her they would be happy to have her back once she'd left school, as long as she paid keep. Lucy was confident she'd pick up work locally after her summer job ended and she agreed to pay them a certain sum each week. Incidentally, we found out later that Gemma had fallen out with Wendy over money, preferring to stay with her boyfriend than pay Wendy the cut of her hairdressing salary she asked for each week.

Jonathan and I were very concerned about how the

arrangement would work out once Lucy finally moved back home – if she ever did. She'd pined for years to do this and now her childhood was almost over. It smacked of too little too late, and I didn't like the fact she could only return if she paid her way. Lucy wouldn't be earning much, however hard she worked. Of course, we didn't interfere. Lucy was very happy with the turn of events and her attitude was, 'I told you all along I was going home!' We didn't want to burst her bubble and kept our worries to ourselves. As for her seemingly blasé reaction to leaving us after all these years, we understood Lucy didn't mean to hurt our feelings. Deep down she cared a great deal about us; we knew that and that's what mattered. She was young and making her way in the world, and we had to put our feelings second.

Lucy had a fabulous summer and gained valuable work experience. Unfortunately, just as we feared, things started to unravel not long after Lucy finally moved back in with her family. She rowed with Wendy from the word go and within a few months she asked if she could move back in with us. After checking with Social Services we welcomed her, of course, despite the fact we were no longer her foster carers. We set about helping her find a place in supported lodgings nearby, which are provided by Social Services to help children leaving care to live semi-independently. Lucy moved into her own flat when she was seventeen, and for her birthday we bought her a course of driving lessons. I sat with her every night for weeks on end to help her through the driving theory test, which she found very difficult. Happily, she passed both the theory and the practical test first time and from that moment on began working even harder than before, doing whatever manual work she could find so she could buy her first car – a red Polo that was constantly breaking down! Lucy loved having her head under the bonnet as much as she loved driving and eventually she took a mechanic's apprenticeship and did day release at our local college.

Today, Lucy is 30 years old. She runs her own MOT business with her partner Michael and they are expecting their first child next year. They have settled in a town many miles from us but we still see Lucy at least once a year. The last time was at a reunion party we held at home just a few months ago, and she always calls in to see us if she's in the area or passing through. She also phones us every week, without fail. She is still in regular contact with her family too, but she is not close with any of them and, from what she tells me, she has no expectations any more. She never did see her birth mother again, despite several years of broken promises made to Social Services, when Noreen agreed to supervised contact sessions then backed out and made excuses at the last minute. Lucy took it all in her stride, just as she eventually learned to do with the rest of the family.

'That's the best way,' she said to me, when we had a quiet moment together at the reunion party. 'I've learned that from Michael. He made me see that you can't change people and you just have to get on and do the best you can. All I can do is be myself. I accept that Wendy won't ever change, or my dad, or anybody else. I don't know why they're the way they are, but that's how it is. I'm doing OK despite them. It's their loss.'

I was the first person Lucy called to share the news of her pregnancy. I was thrilled to bits for her and Michael, and I told her I felt very honoured to be the first to know.

'You deserve it. You and Jonathan are diamonds, and I'm going to be taking all my parenting tips from you when this little one comes along.'

It was a heart-warming compliment and brought a tear to my eye. I can't wait to see Lucy in action. I'm sure she'll be a wonderful mother and I can't put into words how happy I am that she will finally have a family of her own – one to which she belongs, unconditionally.

## The Girl With Two Lives

A Shocking Childhood. A Foster Carer Who Understood.
A Young Girl's Life Forever Changed

*As I stepped back into the kitchen, Danielle looked very proud as she held her notepad up for me to see.*

*'Finished!' she declared cheerfully. I was surprised to see that the surname Danielle had printed wasn't the one I'd seen on her paperwork from Social Services, and so I asked her casually if she used two different names, which often happens when children come from broken homes.*

*'Yes,' she said. 'But this is the surname I'm going to use from now on, because it's the name of my forever family.'*

Danielle has been excluded from school and her former foster family can no longer cope. She arrives as an emergency placement at the home of foster carer Angela Hart, who soon suspects that there is more to the young girl's disruptive behaviour than meets the eye. Can Angela's specialist training unlock the horrors of Danielle's past and help her start a brave new life?

*Available now in paperback and ebook.*

# The Girl and the Ghosts

The true story of a haunted little girl and the foster carer
who rescued her from the past

'So, is it a girl or a boy, and how old?'
Jonathan asked as soon as we were alone
in the shop.

My husband knew from the animated
look on my face, and the way I was itching
to talk to him, that our social worker had
been asking us to look after another child.

I filled Jonathan in as quickly as I could
and he gave a thin, sad smile.

'Bruises?' he said. 'And a moody temperament? Poor little
girl. Of course we can manage a few days.'

I gave Jonathan a kiss on the cheek. 'I knew you'd say that.
It's exactly what I thought.'

We were well aware that the few days could run into weeks
or even longer, but we didn't need to discuss this. We'd looked
after dozens of children who had arrived like Maria, emotionally or physically damaged, or both. We'd do whatever it took to
make her feel loved and cared for while she was in our home.

Seven-year-old Maria holds lots of secrets. Why won't she tell
how she got the bruises on her body? Why does she run and
hide? And why does she so want to please her sinister stepfather?

It takes years for devoted foster carer Angela Hart to uncover
the truth as she helps Maria leave the ghosts of her past behind.

*Available now in paperback and ebook.*

# The Girl Who Just Wanted to be Loved

A damaged little girl and a foster carer
who wouldn't give up

*The first time we ever saw Keeley was in a Pizza Hut. She was having lunch with her social worker.*

*'Unfortunately Keeley's current placement is breaking down,' our support social worker, Sandy, had explained. 'We'd like to move her as soon as possible.'*

*We'd looked after more than thirty youngsters over the years, yet I never failed to feel a surge of excitement at the prospect of caring for another one.*

*Sandy began by explaining that Keeley was eight years old and had stayed with four sets of carers and been in full-time care with two different families.*

*'Why have the placements not worked out?' I asked.*

*'Both foster carers tell similar stories. Keeley's bad behaviour got worse instead of better as time went on. That's why we're keen for you to take her on, Angela. I'm sure you'll do a brilliant job.'*

Eight-year-old Keeley looks like the sweetest little girl you could wish to meet, but demons from the past make her behaviour far from angelic. She takes foster carer Angela on a rocky and very demanding emotional ride as she fights daily battles against her deep-rooted psychological problems. Can the love and specialist care Angela and husband Jonathan provide help Keeley triumph against the odds?

*Available now in paperback and ebook.*

# Terrified

The heartbreaking true story of a girl nobody loved
and the woman who saved her

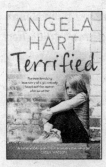

*Vicky stared through the windscreen, her eyeballs glazed like marbles. She was sitting completely rigid in her seat, frozen with fear.*

*I took a deep breath and then asked Vicky as gently as possible, if she was alright.*

*'I'm here, right beside you Vicky. Can you hear me? I'm here and I can help you.'*

*She still didn't respond in any way at all. Her normally rosy cheeks had turned ivory white and the expression of terror on her face was like nothing I'd seen before: I had never seen a child look so scared in all my life.*

*'Take a deep breath, love. That's what I've just done. Just breathe and try to calm yourself down. You're with me, Angela, and you're safe.'*

Vicky seemed all self-assurance and swagger when she came to live with Angela and Jonathan as a temporary foster placement. As Vicky's mask of bravado began to slip, she was overtaken with episodes of complete terror. Will the trust and love Angela and her husband Jonathan provide enable Vicky to finally overcome her shocking past?

*Available now in paperback and ebook.*

# The Girl with No Bedroom Door

**A true short story**

Fourteen-year-old Louise has been sleeping rough after running away from her previous foster home. Unloved and unwashed, she arrives at foster carer Angela Hart's door stripped of all self-esteem. Can Angela's love and care help Louise blossom into a confident and happy young woman?

*Available now in ebook*

extracts reading groups

competitions books new

discounts extracts extracts

competitions events discounts

books

new extracts reading groups

events books

new books extracts

new titles reading groups

interviews

events extracts

discounts

new books events

events new

**www.panmacmillan.com**

discounts extracts discounts

extracts events reading groups

competitions books extracts new